ARGENTINE, MEXICAN, AND GUATEMALAN PHOTOGRAPHY

ARGENTINE, MEXICAN, AND GUATEMALAN PHOTOGRAPHY
Feminist, Queer, and Post-Masculinist Perspectives

◆ ◆ ◆

David William Foster

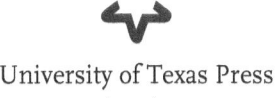

University of Texas Press
Austin

First edition, 2014
First paperback edition, 2015

Requests for permission to reproduce material from this work should be sent to:
    Permissions
    University of Texas Press
    P.O. Box 7819
    Austin, TX 78713-7819
    http://utpress.utexas.edu/index.php/rp-form

♾ The paper used in this book meets the minimum requirements of
ANSI/NISO Z39.48-1992 (R1997) (Permanence of Paper).

Library of Congress Cataloging-in-Publication Data

Foster, David William.
    Argentine, Mexican, and Guatemalan photography : feminist, queer, and
post-masculinist perspectives / David William Foster. — First edition.
       pages   cm
       Includes bibliographical references and index.
       ISBN 978-0-292-75793-6 (cloth : alk. paper)
1. Photography—Latin America. 2. Photography, Artistic. 3. Portrait photography—Latin
America. 4. Gender identity—Latin America. 5. Gender identity in art. I. Title.
       TR27.5.F64 2014
       770.98—dc23
                                                                                    2013043127

ISBN 978-1-4773-0980-3 (paperback)

CONTENTS

◆ ◆ ◆

– ◆ –

PREFACE

◆ ◆ ◆

One of the important cultural responses to the return to institutional democracy in Argentina in 1983 is a resurgence of urban photography. A blend of art photography and photography for purposes of social documentary, the production of a solid group of professional photographers has provided a new interpretive gaze at Buenos Aires, one of the major urban centers of the Latin American continent.

Photography, like all cultural production, is a translation. It is certainly a "translative interpretation" of the sociohistorical reality with which it concerns itself. But it also bears a "translative relationship" to other forms of cultural production, into whose constellation it intervenes. I would argue that this is particularly the case when major sociohistorical events are involved, such as the Argentine so-called Dirty War against subversion, a project of the neofascist military dictatorship, and the return to constitutional democracy. It is quite impossible to view any block of cultural production as not involving some degree of translative relationship to such wrenching events that dominate the consciousness of an entire society.

In the case of photography, there is certainly the visual intertextuality with film, including video (both narrative and documentary, and in both big-screen and television formats), graphic art (cartooning, for example), and painting. But photographs often relate or imply or constitute the framework for narrative, and the translative relationship with verbal narratives is difficult to ignore, which explains why a photograph (or other visual image) may often serve to illustrate the cover of a novel or, to take another prominent form of narrative, a historical or socioanthropological treatise.

In sum, an analysis of contemporary urban photography, one that would take into account women's roles and issues, while concerned with the specific semiotics of photography, necessarily insists that the photographs only "make sense" if they can be viewed as part of the dense process of relationships that characterizes a heightened moment of sociopolitical consciousness in contemporary Argentina.

Argentina has always been a country of photographers, and there is a long tradition of commercial, journalistic, documentary, and art photography, with the sort of international recognition such a production merits. In the 1990s Sara Facio, certainly the dean of Argentine photography and a strong exemplar of women's (if not always self-avowedly feminist) cultural production in Latin America, whose publishing operation La Azotea publishes many of the newer practitioners, began to curate a permanent collection of Argentine photography at the Museo Nacional de Bellas Artes.

Yet, while the work of the majority of the current Argentine photographers is available, if not always in published book form, at one site or another on the Internet, there is little in the way of interpretive academic studies. I included a chapter on Facio—the work she has done on her own, as well as her famous collaborations with Alicia D'Amico—in my book *Buenos Aires: Perspectives on the City and Cultural Production* (1998), and it stands as the only in-depth critical examination of her work, despite extensive brief notes, catalog presentations, and blurbs in overviews of photography.

In mid-1999, the International Center of Photography in New York held an exhibit of eleven Argentine photographers, *Myths, Dreams, and Realities in Contemporary Argentine Photography*, curated by Anne Wilkes Tucker. Although I had never worked critically with photography as a scholar, I had, because of family connections, a long exposure to professional photography. Since I was struck by the eloquence of this exhibit (rather limited in the number of photographers involved, as the ICP was still in its small upper–East Side quarters), it occurred to me that this work could be integrated into my work on other forms of cultural production in Argentina in the context of the neofascist military tyranny (1966–1973, 1976–1983) and the period of redemocratization in the late 1980s.

That work had concerned itself with a significant amount of graphic material, in the form of a study, *Contemporary Argentine Filmmaking*
(1992), which looked at films that had been produced since the return to
constitutional democracy in 1983; many of these films examined issues
from the period of the military dictatorship. Moreover, I had also worked
on another genre of nonprint culture, the Argentine theater, which in
1981 had mounted the first large-scale refutation of censorship and the
culture of neofascism. But I had focused predominantly on print culture,
whether what is conventionally understood as literature (mostly the novel
and short fiction) or, to calque a word from Argentine Spanish, "contesta-
torial" journalism (periodical writing that analyzed from a critical point of
view sociopolitical events, such as the writing on the Malvinas [Falkland
Islands] invasion or on the Dirty War of repression during the early years
of the neofascist dictatorship following the military coup of 1976). I had
also, along the way, published a book on Latin American graphic humor
(material with a certain amount of sociopolitical commentary), but it was
not of the level of focused analysis that underlay the work on Argentine
cultural production of the military period and the subsequent return to
constitutionality. All of this work—on film, theater, and graphic humor—
included an extensive incorporation of gender and feminist perspectives.

Photography, like film, is a very public form of cultural representation,
which allows it to be displayed in many sorts of spaces in conjunction
with many sorts of other productions (e.g., photography as an adjunct of
sociological analysis, as in the case of the Jelin-D'Amico collaboration on
poverty in Buenos Aires, or D'Amico and Facio's photographs illustrating
Julio Cortázar's text on the city of Buenos Aires). But the public nature of
photography also means that it is easily censored, and one can, therefore,
speak of a hiatus of critical photography in Argentina: concomitantly, one
can refer to the way in which this hiatus is filled by the celebratory photography of someone like Pedro Luis Raota, who functioned as something
like the official (and, of course, undeniably masculinist) photographer of
the dictatorship.

The studies brought together in this volume are an integral part of the
research that resulted in the publication of my *Urban Photography in Argentina* (2007), in the sense that they were written during the same period
but represent lateral moves toward specifically identified gender issues
from that project, which focused exclusively on important photographers
to emerge in Argentina in the context of the return to institutional democracy in late 1983.[1] Additionally, Mexican social history, although it has
been significantly different than Argentina's experience with twentieth-

century military governments, provides a rich photographic record of gender-marked work from early decades in the century, whether in the case of native-born Dolores Bravo Álvarez or foreign-born Tina Modotti.

There is much work to be done on founding and historical figures of photography in Latin America, particularly as regards gender issues and especially where close analysis—rather than anecdotal reports and general overviews—is concerned. Photography is an extremely appealing form of cultural production, and the work of many important Latin American photographers circulates widely, especially on the Internet. But what is lacking is detailed scrutiny of major texts in terms of ideology and semiosis.

This collection of essays is only one possible intervention in the complex and extensive history of gender-marked photography in Latin America, limited as it is to the work included in this volume and juxtaposed as it is to accompanying feminist poetic texts. Rather, it is an attention to the role of photography in the continuing development of culture in Argentina following the military dictatorship, the project of redemocratization, the imposition of a neoliberal economic policy, the collapse of that policy in the context of corruption and high but officially ignored social costs, and the abiding political instability of democratic institutions. It would be foolhardy to believe that, with fully democratic elections in 1983 in Argentina and the transition from dictatorship to constitutionality, Argentina's problems were solved: indeed, they were only beginning, not because democracy created problems, but rather because it allowed for the attempts at a full public debate over where Argentina was in its national history and in what ways problems could be addressed. In chronicling the conflicts between those who believed that a new day had come for the country and those who believed that it was business as usual, between those who believed that institutional ineptness essentially perpetuated authoritarian structures and those who believed that such structures could be adequately deconstructed, between those who subscribed to Argentina's alleged potential to be a First World country and those who believed that such triumphalism only perpetuated a hypocrisy that covered over the undeniable misery that failed institutional practices encouraged, and between those who felt it was more important to project an international image of a vibrant society restored and those who sensed the imperative to recognize the many social subjects being ignored by such projections, there has been a lot of critical work for cultural production to take on in post-1983 Argentina.

In the case of Mexico, what has been at issue has been a slow but steady evolution away from the masculinist-dominated post–1910 Revolution ideology that defined gender along rigid heteronormative or heterosexist lines that made it difficult for women or other social subjects uncomfortable with that ideology to intervene in national culture. However, by the 1960s, women were doing so, and visible queer cultural production did not lag far behind. Although gender equity in cultural production may still be problematical in Mexico,[2] there is no question that women and a gender-marked cultural discourse are quite prominent there now.

Overall, the work I have undertaken on principal post-1983 photographers represents the way in which critical cultural production has been taken on by the current generation of photographers, in the same way in which my earlier studies charted examples of such production in the realm of filmmaking and print literature.[3]

The thirteen essays brought together in this volume are grounded in four interlocking areas of my research over the years.[4] The first involves urban cultural production. While much photography focuses on rural settings and the physical landscape, photography is essentially an urban genre, in that city-based journalism has been one of the dominant forums for photography and one of the principal sources of income for its practitioners. New York may be the most photographed city in the world, in terms of both the camera-based record of its physical presence and the day-to-day events of the city, but there is not a single major metropolitan area of the world that has not been extensively photographed. In Latin America, this has meant that the metropolitan triangle of Buenos Aires, Mexico City, and São Paulo has, not surprisingly, been the extensive subject of photography. Indeed, it is impossible to conceive of governmental, commercial and financial, and tourist industry publications unaccompanied by photographic images, whether done in a purely documentary vein or with artistic aspirations. To be sure, there is much that is repetitious about these images, but I cannot forget how the Argentine photographer Sara Facio admonished me when I said that I refused to photograph the Caminito in Buenos Aires, one of the most repeated images of a city not exactly rife with tourist destinations: "But it will be *your* photograph of Caminito," she sternly said.

Of course, when I speak of urban cultural production I do not mean only images of the city, whether tourist monuments or whatever. I mean also human lives in the metropolis, not only on the immediately recognizable level of the street and other public spaces, but also in terms of experiences that relate to how the city impacts human lives: the particular institutions of the city, the particular rituals of city life, and the particular

forms of human anguish and suffering—or human joy and revelation—
that are the result of an urban dynamic.

The second, but dominant, line of research interest featured in these
essays is the feminist matrix and that of gendered cultural production. I
do not know if it is reasonable to argue that photography provides special opportunities for women competing in a universe of cultural production dominated by men, but I do wish to foreground here how immigrant women like Grete Stern and Annemarie Heinrich in Argentina
and Brazilian immigrants Hildegard Rosenthal and Madalena Schwartz
are founding figures whose work goes back to the early professionaliza-
tion of photography in Latin America in the first decades of the twentieth century.[5] I have elsewhere devoted extensive attention to feminist
photography in Latin America. Adriana Lestido, Gabriela Liffschitz, and
Gabriela Messina are three of the nine photographers examined in my
Urban Photography in Argentina. The Mexican Graciela Iturbide's *Juchitán
de las mujeres* has intersected with my attention to queer studies and queer
cultural production in Latin America, as has Paz Errázuriz's *El infarto del
alma* (with texts by Diamela Eltit), and I have examined the portraiture
of Madalena Schwartz in my attention to Jewish artists in Latin America
(Foster, "Madalena Schwartz"). The first photography that I analyzed in
detail was that of Sara Facio (which included her joint work with Alicia
D'Amico) in my monograph *Buenos Aires: Perspectives on the City and
Cultural Production.*

The third research area is that of Jewish cultural production, even if its
representation here is complicated very much by the partial or not immediately evident relationship between these artists and Jewish society. Grete
Stern was the paradigm of the Jewish refugee in Latin America, having
arrived in Buenos Aires with the first signs of anti-Semitism in Hitler's
Germany. While Hildegard Rosenthal was not a Jew, her emigration to
Brazil, also in the 1930s, was the consequence of having had the temerity
to marry a Jew. If she was, therefore, a "vile Jew" for purposes of the Final
Solution, she was also an "honorary Jew" among the Jewish artistic community in São Paulo, and it was the Lithuanian-Jewish artist Lasar Segall
who encouraged her brief but enormously productive stint as a woman
photographer who, with camera in tow, roamed through the mostly emphatically masculinist spaces of the burgeoning financial and industrial
capital of Latin America. In the case of Annemarie Heinrich, she had no
biographic connection with Jewishness, although it is interesting to note
that, in the sometimes heated ethnic cauldron of Buenos Aires, Heinrich
was, because of her "pure" German origins, accused on more than one

occasion of being anti-Semitic and pro-Nazi. This, to be sure, did not keep her from interacting with Jewish artists and from having Jews as clients in the extensive work in portraiture and fashion photography that was her principal source of income. Argentine Silvina Frydlewsky and Mexican Pedro Meyer also have Jewish origins.

Finally, these essays are grounded in my interest in attempting to understand the ideological principles of cultural production and the relationships between what are recognized as examples of cultural work and the sociopolitical and historical contexts in which they were produced and that, therefore, are part of their meaning in the overarching text of Latin American society. Yet my view of ideologically grounded cultural studies bears with it the imperative to attempt to understand the structures of meaning that function within a text. Certainly, the identification and assessment of those structures are equally a matter of ideology—why does one discuss such-and-such features of a text and not others?—such that the contextual outside of the text and its structural inside are inseparable and are, in fact, part of a seamless system of meaning. Although I long ago renounced any privileged identity for the "work of art" (the identification and promotion of which are also an ideological gesture) and also long ago understood that the work of art of any text does not enjoy a phenomenological independence but only exists in relation to its embeddedness in messy historical processes, I do remain committed to the proposition that texts must be examined in detail. The enormous human effort invested in their creation and interacting with them demands, from the viewpoint of both one more circumstantial spectator and a professional cultural scholar, an equal expenditure of interpretational work. More than anything else, my goal has been to demonstrate not only the imperative to take Latin American photography seriously in the academy, but also to model seriously ways to talk about photographic texts that invest them with the same degree of importance we routinely attribute to more canonical forms of cultural production.

The following are the photographers whose work is examined here:

Grete Stern and Annemarie Heinrich are, simply put, two figures who established photographic standards in Argentina and whose work ranged across a wide array of gender-marked themes. Stern's famous psychoanalytic collages of women's dreams and Heinrich's glossy portraits of women (mostly related to fashion and advertising) are significantly different photographic idioms, but both placed images of women before the Argentine public at crucial moments of social development.[6]

Perhaps the earliest photographic images we now have of Latin American women are those of prostitutes in the found collection Ava Vargas brings together in the photobook *La casa de citas en el barrio galante* (1991), images that are particularly fascinating for how women's bodies, the modernist elegance of the high-class brothel, and the hostile Mexican landscape intersect.

Silvina Frydlewsky's photography deals with a different hostile landscape, that of the mean streets of Buenos Aires during the economic crisis that began in late 2001 and generated the *cartonero* (paper picker) movement that included many women and single-mother families. Against the backdrop of the exponential modernity of Buenos Aires, these women and their families must survive, literally, on the garbage they gather.

Daniela Rossell's now legendary—and still rather notorious—dossier *Ricas y famosas*, on the wives and daughters of the great male power brokers of Mexico, was roundly denounced when it came out in 2002 for what, by implication, it excluded: the destitute and forgotten women of Mexican society. Even though some critics have assured us that the look on the face of these women is that of the spiritually impoverished, such commentary does little to ameliorate a certain measure of revulsion these images might engender even when they fascinate. I have placed them here in dialogue with Frydlewsky's marginal Argentine women and Meyer's nonprivileged Mexican subjects.

The photography of Mexican Pedro Meyer moves the agenda toward a gender-marking that deconstructs masculinity, especially the highly ideologized masculinity of postrevolutionary Mexico. Meyer, unlike Frydlewsky, does not engage in documentary photography, but rather finds in complex constructed collages, like those of Grete Stern, the means to question themes of male-dominated Mexican society.

Argentine Marcos Zimmermann engages in something like an anti-urban focus in his documentary images of rural Argentine men's naked bodies. There is, with only one or two exceptions, nothing resembling the beefcake pinup here. These are the scarred and often wasted bodies of men who work hard to survive in natural settings that can never be idealized or romanticized. By portraying these men unclothed, he reduces them to a struggling core of masculine identity that belies the Latin lover mystique of the glossy and well-fed men of Buenos Aires that is part of that city's self-image.[7] In this sense, his male images parallel Frydlewsky's female ones, which subvert the sophisticated image of privileged-class women Buenos Aires also customarily entertains.

Perhaps the most famous gender-marked photography in all of Latin America is Graciela Iturbide's work on the women of Juchitán, Oaxaca. Or, as she prefers to frame it, Juchitán of the women. It is debatable whether the lives of these women, and, therefore, the lives of their men, can be called feminist, especially with the metropolitan resonances of the term. But, under the gaze of Iturbide's camera, they are most certainly queer, not only in the assertive power they project, which transgresses the traditional hegemonic imperative of female docility in Mexico, but also in their homosociality, which, although it may not segue into homoeroticism, is one of the bases of their power. And Iturbide would have us understand that the nonconventional gender identity of the women of Juchitán gives way to the nonconventional gender identity of the men of Juchitán.

Iturbide's images of an indigenous sexuality beyond—or behind— the heterosexuality of modernity are complemented by Alessandra Sanguinetti's Arcadian play romance between two country girls. Because of its grounding in a rural setting that is tangential to the modernity of Buenos Aires, it is implicitly a commentary on the heterosexual story of romance imposed on the Argentine heartland by the metropolis. Shot in high-density color more typical of cosmopolitan advertising, the adventures, so to speak, of Guille and Belinda discovering each other's bodies and their erotic engagement take place in a context in which heterosexuality may be closely guarded as part of the need to adhere to the values of the metropolis through a commitment to a traditionalism that is prized by that metropolis, while at the same time it may be relaxed or contravened as the two young women play out their attraction to each other in terms of an Arcadian setting that enhances their homoerotics, as in a concluding image in which a pool of water of the sort that abounds in the Pampas is a vessel for their shared romantic reverie.

I examined Marcos López's highly complex constructivist photography in the chapter devoted to him in *Urban Photography in Argentina*. But I was left, so to speak, with a residue of perception about his photography in which the central interest regarding construction by the photographer is that, as feminism and queer studies famously assert, gender identity and gender behavior are socially constructed. Of particular interest was the way in which López played with constructing and deconstructing male gender identity in his work, and in this sense, his photography relates directly to that of the Mexican Pedro Meyer. But where Meyer questions conventional Mexican masculinity, López is more interested in teasing out the homosociality that segues into the homoeroticism of Argentina's male-privileged society.

Stefan Ruiz brings us back to Mexico and the world of Mexican soap operas. He does not photograph the action of soap operas, but rather concentrates on the fictional characters of major series captured in the context—the semantic network—of the sets in which they work. He too is aware of how much sexuality and gender identity are socially constructed, and his photographs always make certain that the spectator understands that a constructed set is involved and, therefore, a constructed identity. Mexican soap operas enforce heterosexism and continue the sexual ideology of postrevolutionary society. There may be some fissures in the façade of heterosexism, and I attempt to identify some of them that can be perceived in his work, but the dominant frame of Ruiz's images reproduces, at least in an initial instance, that heterosexism of the Mexican soap opera.

Helen Zout's forensic-like photography is very much devoted to an inquiry into the violence of human rights violations during the 1976–1983 neofascist military regime in Argentina. Gendered violence was integral to the process of that regime: in addition to the persecution of Jews, it specifically involved women and gays. Zout's photobook *Desapariciones* (2009) focuses principally, although not exclusively, on women and their direct and indirect experience of state-sponsored terror.

Finally, state-sponsored terror is also at issue in the work of the Guatemalan Daniel Hernández-Salazar, where his gender-marked exposed male bodies are a major site of government-sponsored terror in Guatemala for several decades at the end of the twentieth century. Hernández-Salazar also shows women ranged against the masculinist armed forces, with their male-enforced violence for purposes of repressive social control. Hernández-Salazar provides something like a supplement here, in the sense that the other essays all deal with Mexican and Argentine photographers. However, I wish his presence to be taken as a sign of the work remaining to be done regarding the important photographic record elsewhere in Latin America.

An observation is in order here regarding the order of these essays. Although it might appear chronological in beginning with Grete Stern and Annemarie Heinrich, whose work goes back to the 1930s, this is only because I wished to begin with two strong feminine/feminist voices who chart the origins of a photography in Argentina that transcends the presumed masculine origins of Latin American photography. It is also true that the study closes with the late twentieth-century/early twenty-first-century human rights work of Daniel Hernández-Salazar, but what comes in between is a grouping of essays that do not represent a historical trajectory. A historical trajectory would, perhaps, not be the most advantageous one for a scholarly treatise that does not announce itself as dedicated to the history of photography in Latin America. And since nowhere near all of the major photographers of the past one hundred years are included, a convenient historical grouping by the main era of their work would hardly be revealing about the artists included here.

I did consider the possibility of grouping the photographers by the three gender categories of feminist, masculinist, and queer, but that idea quickly broke down, and not only because these three categories, rather than being three separate legs of a stool, are really like a three-dimensional Möbius strip. I identify queer elements in some of Heinrich's feminist work and queer elements in Hernández-Salazar's images of a crisis of masculinity occasioned by state-sponsored terrorism. Meyer's photography deals with both feminine and masculine subjects who are gender-marked, while homosocialism (perhaps segueing into queerness) is present in Marcos López's male subjects. Sanguinetti's female subjects are juxtaposed to the strongly masculinist world of Argentine provincial life, but they interact in what is a lesbian (or, at least, a protolesbian) love story. And Stefan Ruiz's subjects perhaps fit none of the three categories neatly, because they are enacting a heterosexist fantasy that is virtually caricatured by the cultural products in which they appear. Finally, where does one put the work of Ava Vargas's anonymous photographer? We might want to suppose it is a masculinist view of the brothel, of female sexuality, and of even the homoerotic relationship between women, but such a view cannot be sustained with any certainty, and it is not impossible to envision one of the prostitutes herself as the photographing agent or, perhaps more likely, the madam herself. It is only by convention that we assume these images to have been made of these women by a man for other men. In the end, then, it is my hope that a good measure of synergy will occur across the boundaries of the various essays so that a more verisimilar social image will emerge in which complex ranges of gender identities and gender enactments will be on display photographically, and not just a simple gender binary of male and female photographers, male and female subjects.

◆ ◆ ◆

As always, I dedicate this volume to my students, who are my best colleagues. My assistants Francisco Arrellano Serratos, Solymar Torres-García, Charles St-Georges, Daniel Holcombe, Ileana Baeza, and Kyle Black have all made important contributions to the execution of this volume. Amanda Mollindo assumed the responsibility of putting the images in proper form. Patricia Hopkins has been an exceptional first reader. I remain grateful to the programs of Arizona State University, which generously supports my research in numerous ways. Finally, a special note of gratitude to the photographers who have graciously allowed me to reproduce their work here.

ARGENTINE, MEXICAN, AND GUATEMALAN PHOTOGRAPHY

DREAMING IN FEMININE
Grete Stern's Photomontages and
the Parody of Psychoanalysis

♦ ♦ ♦

*Las mujeres hicieron la fotografía en la Argentina. Somos suficientes;
yo incluida.*

—Sara Facio, "La fotografía. Género: femenino"

I would like to propose that the motivating semiotic principle behind Grete Stern's photomontages is the need to create a language for women's dreams; this language may be, in the first place, sympathetic toward repressed and oppressed women, and in the second place, critical of the psychoanalytic project with regard to women's experiences.

Stern's *Sueños* was published at a time when there was still a considerable amount of interest in the Freudian concept of dreams,[1] and Stern, who was born in Germany in 1904 and worked in Argentina from 1936 until the late 1990s (she died in Germany in late 1999), was undoubtedly quite familiar with psychoanalysis, both as it had been promulgated by Freud in Europe and as it put down deep roots in Argentina (Vezzetti; Plotkin; see Bécquer Casaballe for an overview of Stern's career; other published volumes of Stern's work are cited in my Works Cited list). Moreover, Stern was, like Freud, Jewish (her mother committed suicide in 1935 because of growing anti-Semitism), and she would have had the Jewish artist/intellectual's interest of her day in sociocultural analysis (and in photography as an important form of Jewish cultural production). The introductory note to the published collection of the *Sueños* describes their origin: "Grete Stern publicó en la revista *Idilio* [entre 1948 y 1950] cerca de 150 fotomontajes de la serie dedicada a los sueños. De esa obra sólo existen, en la actualidad, 45 negativos fotográficos—de éstos se conserva un único ejemplar—que la autor entregaba a la redacción de la revista" (59).[2]

Idilio was a woman's magazine typical of the sort published in the mid-twentieth century, which mixed images of traditional roles for women with images of bourgeois modernity, although, from the perspective of today, it would still be called essentially a masculinist version of women's lives, with the sort of coverage of women's lives provided in the postwar United States by the *Ladies Home Journal*. Stern's photomontages appear in a section of the magazine called "El psicoanálisis le ayudará" (Psycho-analysis will help you), a formulation that represented the popularization of psychoanalysis during the Peronista prosperity of the period beyond the highly professionalized and elitist confines of clinical practice and research undertakings. Apparently, the practice was for women to submit to the magazine the text of the dreams, and Stern would create a photo-montage to accompany their publication.[3] The fact that over two-thirds of the originals have disappeared and that the magazine is virtually impossible to locate indicates the ephemeral nature of the enterprise, and one wonders to what degree Stern saw it as centrally related to her oeuvre as a photographer.

Yet there has been exceptional interest in this dimension of Stern's work, and one could easily maintain that, were it not for the *Sueños*, Stern would be counted as just another of the legion of photographers who have done fine work in Argentina since the emergence of professional photog-raphy as early as the middle of the nineteenth century. One is reminded of the contemporary work of the French émigrée in Buenos Aires Gisèle (Gisela) Freund, who is best remembered in Argentina as one of the most important photographers of Eva Perón, a body of legendary images (they are prominently featured in Alicia Dujovne Ortiz's biography *Eva Perón*) that has overwhelmed any other work Freund may have.

Stern, however, was an exceptional artist and renowned portraitist, and her work is very much in the same vein as that of subsequent women pho-tographers like Alicia D'Amico and Sara Facio (the director of La Azotea Editorial Fotográfica) and, among younger photographers, Adriana Les-tido and Gabriela Liffschitz (Lestido is a Guggenheim fellow, and her project, *Madres e hijas*, was published by Facio; see the various studies by Foster). There are several hundred web pages on the Internet with Stern's photography, and the most frequently visited ones that I have consulted all included prominently the *Sueños*. I think it is clear that the importance now accorded the *Sueños* has very much to do with the feminist analysis of culture, both in the way in which Stern's work can be seen to intervene in cultural production (male-dominated photography in this case) from a (proto)feminist perspective, and the way in which Stern's photographs lend themselves to a feminist reading as part of a feminist survey of cultural productions regarding women's lives. Certainly, Stern's work enjoys intertextual relationships with other feminist work of the same period, and one recalls the psychoanalytic dimensions of the Catalan/Mexican Remedios Varo's surrealist paintings in general and, specifically, the anticipation of the feminist critique of classic psychoanalysis in her 1960 *Mujer saliendo del psicoanalista* (Varo 71 [Woman leaving the psychiatrist's]).[4]

There is an entire gamut of undoubtedly classical psychoanalytic motifs in Stern's *Sueños*, intertwined with widely recognized motifs of the particular traumas of women's lives. Indeed, in the latter sense, Stern's photomontages are something like an inventory of topoi of women's lives as regards their repression and oppression by masculinism. Moreover, these works figure a bourgeois patriarchy, such that the control of women through the principles of decency and propriety is particularly evident. Although none of this work alludes recognizably to a questioning of heterosexism or even to female erotic imagination—perhaps this is part of the hundred lost images; perhaps letters from women of this sort were not forwarded to Stern for illustration—it is not preposterous to propose that such dimensions are as much a part of the silent text of women's lives as what is overtly portrayed belongs to what is allowed by the circumstances of the production and publication (and archival survival) that made the *Sueños* possible.[5]

A survey of what is included in *Sueños* reveals the following details. In terms of circumstances of women's lives (and I repeat, this is a universe of women whose clothing, grooming, and body language adhere to middle-class respectability—which perhaps only makes the images all that more eloquent), we see women engaged in paradigmatically female/feminine activities such as cleaning house (a singular activity of the domestic sphere), staring dreamily off into space (the evocation of women's purportedly superior emotional sensitivity, or, conversely, their inability to focus on the practical and pragmatic), displaying their availability as sexualized bodies (thereby fulfilling the injunction to seduce men into procreative activity), performing for the cultural edification of an audience (women as accomplished decorative beings), and engaging in maternal care (the paradigmatic role of women as the key figures in patriarchal reproduction). In all of these images, women are properly and discreetly dressed in ways that confirm their middle-class stature.

Since Stern did photography among the rural and suburban populations of Argentina, these photographs cannot be alleged to reveal any class bias. Rather, they capture the social identity of the women who were the presumed typical readers of *Idilio*, those who would be in a position to submit to the editors texts describing their dreams. It is in only some of the photomontages that the subjects are engaged in characteristically womanly activities. In the majority they are seen only in terms of confronting threatening situations: dreams as the site of the representation of conflict and its attempted resolution, even if only absurdly. What is important to underscore here is the fact that in no cases are women seen engaged in activities that would be considered unfeminine by the strict bourgeois standards of Argentina of the day (only in a handful of cases are women directly eroticized, but always in the context of their submission to a male prerogative, as in No. 16, *Sirena del mar* [Sea siren]).

Indeed, *Idilio* may have received texts that would have been considered sexually transgressive by the standards of the day, and may or may not have chosen to publish some of them (unfortunately, a complete run of *Idilio* from the period is not available for this study). Additionally, *Idilio* may or may not have chosen to forward them to Stern for illustration, and she may or may not have chosen to undertake that illustration. The point is that the surviving dossier of illustrations includes none that can be called sexually transgressive. What is significant about this point is the fact that one of Freud's great contributions was the specification of what the highly charged sexual fantasies and dreams of women contained—that is, eroticization of the female body, an eroticization that displayed alarming deviations from bourgeois decency and heterosexual parameters and, moreover, identified the potential for women to engage in what was coming to be identified as sexual perversion.

By the early 1950s, Peronista Argentina had reaffirmed a commitment to a regularizing sexual hygiene, and this was a period of open persecution of public sexuality, especially anything that could be perceived as deviant (Sebreli, "Historia secreta" 313ff.). Hence, it is not surprising to find that Stern's photomontages reflect women in psychologically distressing situations, but never in any that manifest any sort of compromise with imposed female sexual boundaries: no prostitution, no female sexual activism, no polymorphous perversity, and, certainly, no lesbianism. Thus, in the main one could assert that these images represent the dreams of the real-life women who chose to submit them in a textual form to *Idilio*. Yet, at the same time, Stern represents dreams in her photomontages only insofar as they maintain women strictly within the confines of patriarchal heteronormativity, leaving one to speculate on the queer representations that must naturally occur in an uncircumscribed world of female human experience, whether represented by these women in their letters or by Stern in her montages.

What is the nature of the threats to which these women claim to be exposed, as they perceive them in the fantasies of their dream experiences? If one holds in mind that the narrative perspective of these photomontages is that of women telling their own story, the compromising situations in which they find themselves are those that are imposed upon them by the world in which they live. Thus, it is not surprising to find that the vast majority of them emphasize women directly or by implication exposed to the power of men—and in some cases, a society as a whole—that are controlling, threatening, and violent. A partial thematic inventory would be as follows:

1. Woman's body at the disposal of the hands of men: this is the aforementioned Sueño No. 16, *Sirena del mar* (*Sueños* 74; Sea siren), where a set of hands of a man emerges from the water as though about to massage the metonymic buttocks of a woman on the shore (no other part of the woman is seen but her buttocks). One of Stern's most amusing photomontages, Sueño No. 1, *Artículos domésticos para el hogar* (*Sueños* 61 [Domestic appliances]), involves a man's hand holding the base of a lamp; the lamp's pedestal is the body of a languid woman, who holds up the lamp shade with her upraised arms.

2. A demurely posed woman is overwhelmed by the reptilian presence of a debonair (macho) man: if his suave masculinity is confirmed by the perfect manipulation of the cigarette in his hand, his menace is represented by the open maw of a tortoise head that replaces his human one (image No. 28, *Amor sin ilusión* [*Sueños* 89 (Love with no illusions)]).

3. Woman as an artifice of man—Eve as derived from Adam, woman as defined by the male patriarchy—is represented by the figure of a woman emerging from a broad paintbrush manipulated by a male hand. Her hair replaces the bristles of the paintbrush (Sueño No. 31, *Made in England* [*Sueños* 93]).

4. There are several images of women enclosed in the manner of the woman in the gilded cage: in one image, it is a literal cage; in another, it is a corked glass vessel. In the former case, the woman displays the conventional happy face women are supposed to display to the world, while in the latter, an enigmatic glance is partially hidden by a demure fan.

5

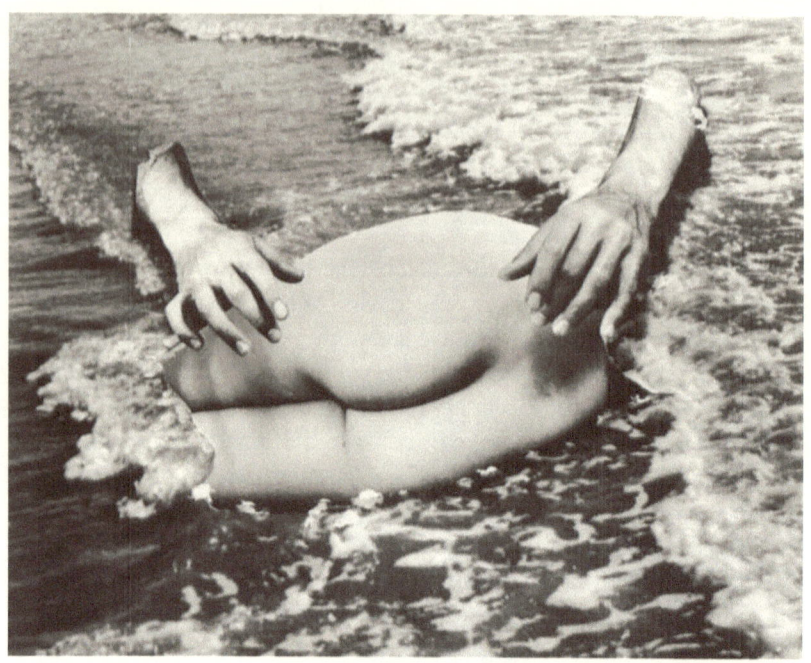

Figure 1.1. Grete Stern,
Sirena del mar (Sea siren).

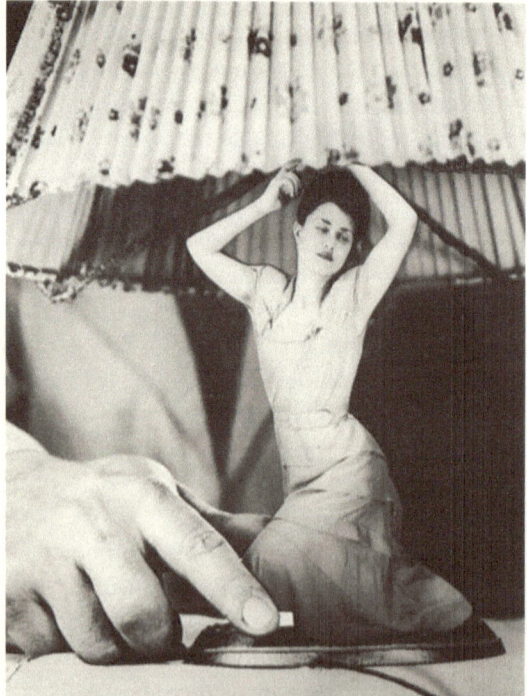

Figure 1.2. Grete Stern,
*Artículos domésticos
para el hogar*
(Domestic appliances).

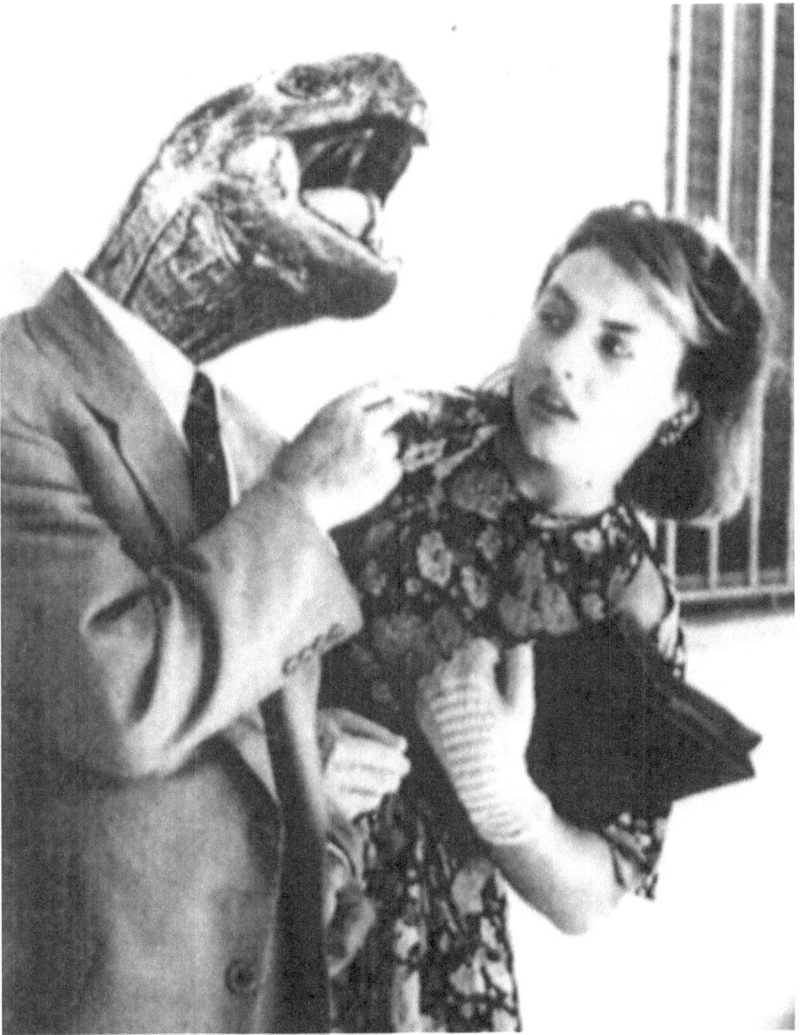

Figure 1.3. Grete Stern, *Amor sin ilusión* (Love with no illusions).

Not only does such confinement emphasize the harem-like circum-spection of women, but it underscores their ideal femininity. What is in-teresting is that, from a patriarchal point of view, such reservation protects women from the dangers of the world (including their loss by the master), while from a feminist point of view—which may emerge here in an un-conscious fashion—such reservation is a form of entrapment and incar-ceration. In another image, a woman is in a glass-walled room: she looks frightened as a lion lunges toward one side of the glass paneling; in the

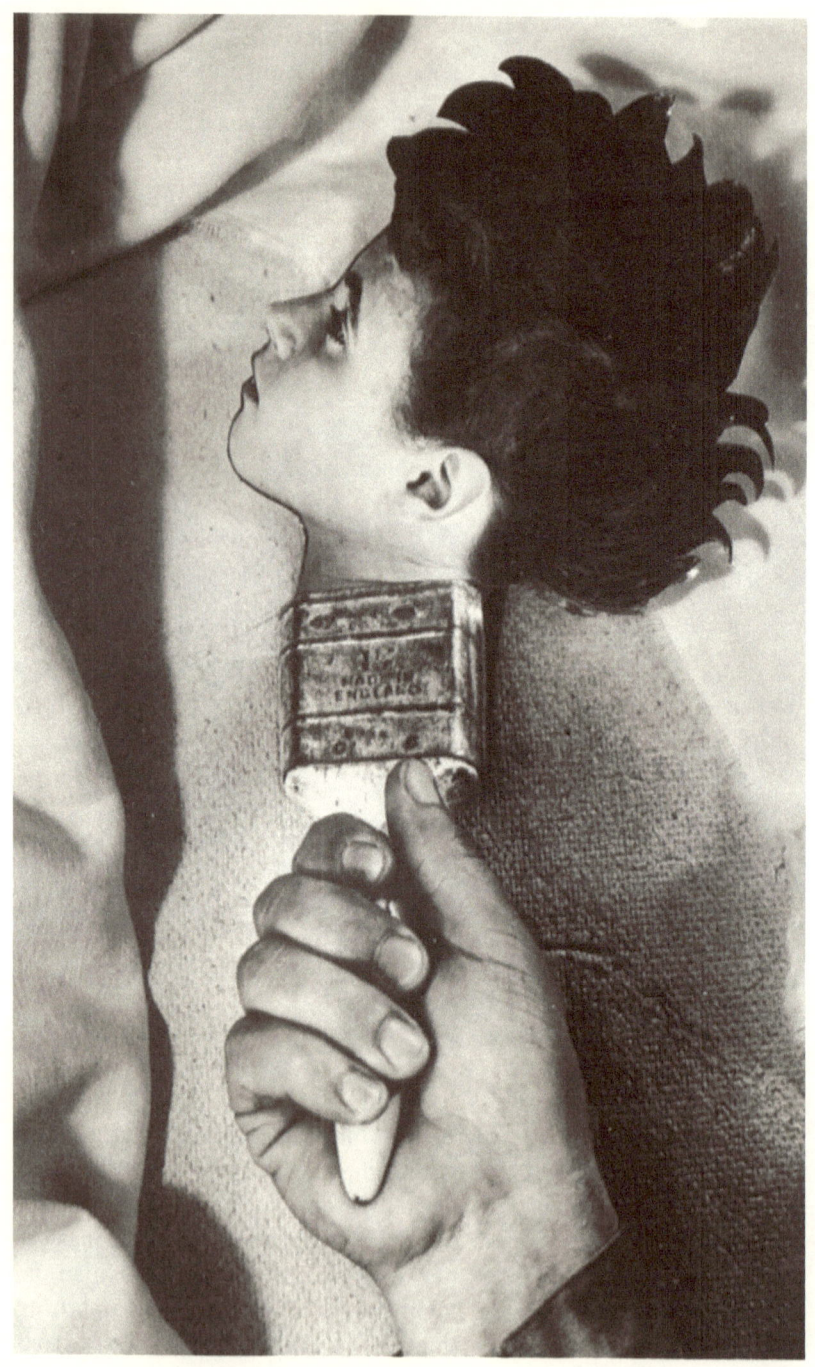

Figure 1.4. Grete Stern, *Made in England*.

corner formed by the panels, there is a prominent padlock, but this does not diminish the woman's fright (Sueño No. 12, no title [*Sueños* 117]).

5. There are several images of women in public spaces that are threatening to them: if a woman does emerge from her sphere of protection, she is exposed to the very threats that the masculinized agent claims to be protecting her from. In one image, a woman appears to be trapped in the foyer of a vaulted-ceiling gallery such as the imposing Edificio Barolo, the Edificio Güemes, or the pre-remodeled Galerías del Pacífico; caught between two enormous lines of twine, she recoils from an advancing string of numbers, 1, 0, 4, 8 (Sueño No. 23, *La acusada* [*Sueños* 99 (The accused woman)]). In another image, a woman flees down a street, escaping from a group of people staring and pointing at her, as though admonishing her for her shortcomings; there are also miscellaneous pieces of furniture around her, as though she were fleeing from her proper domestic realm.

Few of the images depict actual violence against women, but in one, a woman wearing slacks (as opposed to the women in the remaining images, who predominantly wear classically feminine skirts) finds herself on a beach on which huge spikes arise from the sand, and one of them has embedded itself in her foot, as though a punishment for entering a dangerous and solitary public space (Sueño No. 39, no title [*Sueños* 145]).

6. Of particular interest are the dreams in which maternal images are represented as threatening: woman is deranged by what is her most fundamental calling as a human being and social agent. In one image, a woman covers her face in horror (we see her eyes through the open fingers of her palms) as a baby advances toward her down what looks like a dead-end alley; the baby's arms are raised in the sort of supplicating gesture that calls for the support of an adult (Sueño No. 24, *Sorpresa* [*Sueños* 83 (Surprise)]). In another, a woman contemplates with what we can call loving maternalism a large, partially broken egg from which the newborn must have emerged—yet the egg is empty and no newborn is to be seen (Sueño No. 33, no title [*Sueños* 135]). Finally, in a less threatening but enigmatic image, a woman holds up a calla lily from whose inner folds, along with the phallic stamen, a beautiful blond baby boy emerges. Since the background of the image is a dreary rural Pampas setting, it is as though the child is somehow too beautiful to be real (Sueño No. 11, *Niño flor* [*Sueños* 115 (Flower child)]).

Unquestionably, these thematic groups could be tabulated against a registry of the commonplaces of recurring fears, nightmares, and terror-filled deliria of women who live in conformance with patriarchal normalcy and who yet sense, in reality or in a paranoid fashion, the destructive

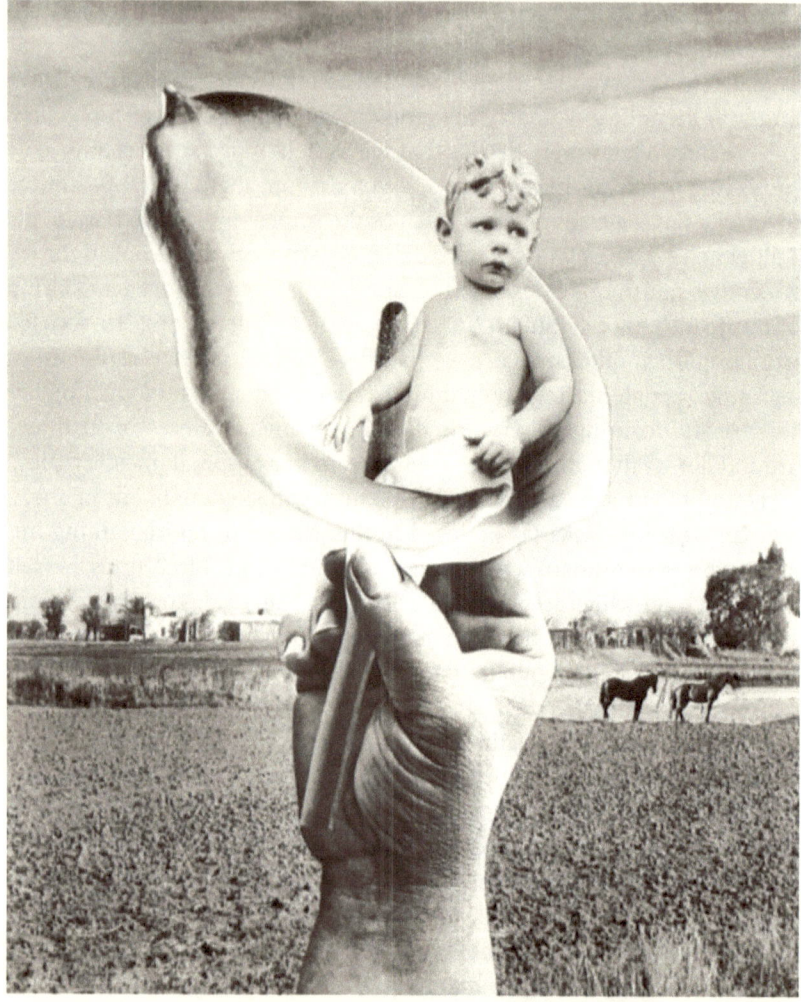

Figure 1.5. Grete Stern, *Niño flor* (Flower child).

forces directed against and from within that normalcy. On the one hand, any constructed normalcy is meant to constitute a bulwark against the destructive forces from without (in another image, a woman, shrunken in size, hammers with her fists against a closed door, clamoring to get inside the walls of protection [Sueño No. 40, no title (*Sueños* 147)]), while at the same time that bulwark functions to enclose within itself its own tyrannical threat.

To summarize, I have been characterizing up to this point how Stern's photomontages exemplify complex texts. If in the first place they are based on (presumably) naïve attempts of real-life women to formulate verbally in a conscious state, ex post facto, preverbal dreams they have experienced (and one cannot exclude the possibility of men writing as women, or of women pretending to have dreamed what they relay), Stern's photomontages are a pictorial re-creation of those verbal texts underlain by preverbal dreams. Not only are they a third-level semiotization, but they present the question of how one woman reinterprets the interpretations of an array of anonymous women (assuming they are all real-life women; moreover, the texts in *Idilio* may have been signed, but Stern's images are not identified with texts by specific authors).

Additionally, Stern's interpretations are conscious works of art, in which she enjoys considerable latitude in producing a text with multiple layers of intentional meaning, which one can assume to be lacking in the unconscious preverbal dreams and in their verbal write-ups by the magazine's readers. This allows Stern both to directly engage with the topic of the dream as described textually and to introduce strategies for a reflexive interpretation of what she is representing. That is, there is a level of irony in her photomontages, at which there is not simply the attempt to provide unmediated re-representations of the written texts, but to introduce a commentary on them.

I would suggest that this commentary, while it may concomitantly constitute a critical stance on the workings of psychoanalysis/the analysis of dreams, is fundamentally feminist. This is so because the photomontages in their majority transmit an overall understanding of the repression and oppression of women in a patriarchally dominated society. It is true that the sense of repression and oppression begins in the original dreams on which the photomontages are based. However, Stern's texts make explicit a criticism of women's lives. In order to understand how this functions, I would like to examine in detail a couple of the several dozen of the photomontages.[6]

En el andén is identified as Sueño No. 2 (*Sueños* 105 [On the train platform]); when it was published in the *Idilio* series, it was titled *Los sueños de los trenes* (Train dreams). It is possible to approach these texts in terms of their thematic elements on a level beyond the characterizations I have already provided, which would be with reference to the canonical interpretation by psychoanalysis of recurring motifs in dreams—in this case, a subset of women's dreams—especially as to how these symbols have sexual overtones. More on this in a moment.

However, my principal interest here is in the rhetorical organization of the photomontage and the semiotic processes involved, leaving a precise psychoanalytic interpretation to someone more qualified in this area than I am. Since all of these images are dominated by the figure of women, it is reasonable to begin with the placement of women in them. Although the vast majority of the *Sueños* involve well-dressed women—dressed as middle-class women in Argentina might have been in public places in the 1950s—the woman in *En el andén* is particularly well dressed, to the point of wearing a hat with a trailing veil. It would seem that she is dressed in the particular way in which women of comfortable means would dress for train or air travel in the period, as can be determined by looking back to the advertisements of the early 1950s, especially in journals like *Idilio*.

Moreover, also in contrast to the women in the other *Sueños*, this woman is not terrified or horrified by what she is experiencing. While she does have one hand demurely raised, palm outward, as though to ward off an unpleasantness, and her other hand is, though clenched, nevertheless turned back in a genteel fashion, her facial expression is more neutral than anything else; if anything, it is inquisitive. What she sees is a train rushing toward her. But in place of the locomotive, there is the same sort of open-jawed tortoise head described above for photo No. 28, *Amor sin ilusión*. In the image at hand, the tortoise's head is turned somewhat to the side, as though in an attack position.

If both trains and reptiles (or reptile heads, in the case of tortoises)

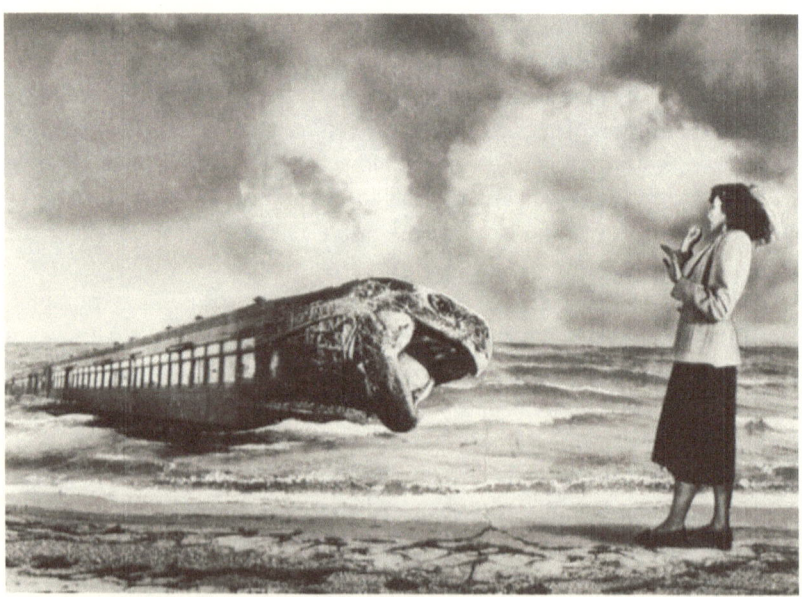

Figure 1.6. Grete Stern, *En el andén* (On the train platform).

probably can be read as phallic symbols by standard Freudian dream interpretation, their conjunction here is something like a doubling of that meaning, and in compositional terms, there is a direct line from the tortoise's snout to the genital area of the woman. Thus, what the photomontage images in general is sexual aggression toward woman—or, perhaps more generally, the overall threat of physical violence to which many women in society may feel exposed. Where sexual aggression is specifically sensed is by reference to montage No. 28, since the man in whose presence the woman in that image is cringing has the same sort of reptilian head as the train in Sueño No. 2.

Since Stern's goal is to capture dreamlike states in her photomontages, she studiously eschews anything that provides for an overly "natural" setting to the circumstances depicted. As a consequence, the rushing train appears here as emerging out of a large body of water, and the station platform is actually the edge of the water, more parched earth than sandy beach; the sky beyond the sea is filled with what looks like stormy clouds. It is a moot point as to how many of these details correspond to the verbal text of one woman's dream. What is important is the way in which there is, on the one hand, what we can call the realistic detail of the woman's presence (in other images, this presence is not always strictly "realistic" or "natural"), juxtaposed, on the other, to the fantastic or surreal—even bizarre—conjunction of the train (realistic in what of it is depicted) and the reptilian head (realistic in what of it is depicted). There is an equally disturbing conjunction between the unusual and even desolate appearance of the water's edge and the gently roiling waves of the body of water. A final detail: the sea is often taken—not just in Freudian interpretations, but beyond—as maternal in nature, and the threatening train emerges from this abstractly maternal realm to menace a specific characterized woman. This fact is confirmed by the way in which her body casts a shadow— that is, it intervenes naturally in the landscape—while the train does not: it is the startling Other, perhaps even the terrifyingly unknown, that menaces the woman.

While the vast bulk of Stern's photomontages feature women in situations of psychological discomfort and physical aggression, some of them are focused on less immediately menacing, but no less sexist, facts of women's lives. This is the case with Sueño No. 6, which is untitled in the *Sueños* collection, but which was published in *Idilio* with the title *Un sueño de frutas* (A dream of fruits). In it, we see a miniature woman walking over a shelved row of books; she is placing freshly picked strawberries, complete with leaves and blossoms, on top of one of them. Not all of the book titles are discernible, but those that are are eloquent. They are apparently all by men, and some of their titles signal clearly a masculinist ideology. The book the woman is adorning with the bunches of strawberries is T. E. Lawrence's *Los siete pilares de la sabiduría* (*The Seven Pillars of Wisdom*), notable for the homoeroticization of the noble male art of soldiering. The woman is bending over Lawrence of Arabia's book to add another bunch of strawberries, and she balances herself with one foot on Lin Yutang's *La importancia de vivir* (*The Importance of Living*) and the other on Walter de la Mare's *Memorias de una enana* (*Memories of a Female Dwarf*).

The fact that the woman is dwarfed by the row of books makes the in-

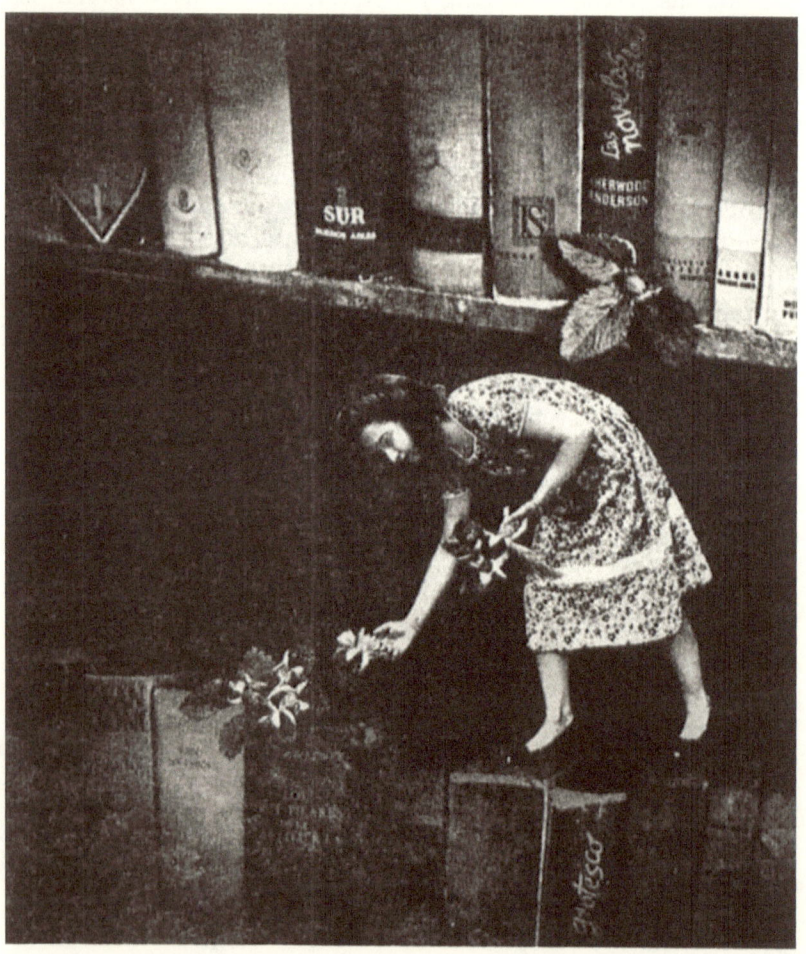

Figure 1.7. Grete Stern, *Un sueño de frutas* (A dream of fruits).

clusion of de la Mare's novel especially hilarious. Indeed, it is at this point where one can most question the degree to which Stern's photomontages are not merely illustrations of the preverbal texts written by naïve women, but an ironic commentary on the psychoanalytic validity of the staging of dreams: psychoanalysis is grimly serious in its determination to seek out the deeply embedded meanings of dreams, which are understood to be, themselves, deeply embedded narratives of the human psyche, and there is no room for irony, and much less parody, in their manipulation and interpretation.

Moreover, it is understood that dreams may appear to be absurd or ludicrous when compared to an allegedly normal waking reality. The process of interpretation in which the grimly serious analysis of dreams engages could never contemplate the possibility that dreams might manifest a play of humorous irony or parody, since such a play would destabilize the semantic anchor dreams must have to be interpretable. Certainly, someone may have dreamed being a woman belittled by books, and one of those books might just happened to have been *Memorias de una enana*. But unless one is willing to invest in such a high degree of unlikelihood, Stern's image must be viewed as playing with the legitimacy of dreams as conveying a recoverable embedded meaning of a psychoanalytically serious nature.

Stern's interpretation of the process of interpreting dreams can only be viewed, in this photomontage, as rather sardonic with regard to the reputed allegorical literalness of dream sequences. Indeed, the book that is shelved between the two on which the woman stands is Sherwood Anderson's *Las novelas de lo grotesco* (Stories of the grotesque; published as "The Book of the Grotesque" in *Winesburg, Ohio*), surely a meaningful choice as regards the texture of the dreams Stern illustrates. My point here would be the way in which Stern sees these women as caught in a narrative universe in which they do dream—or think they dream—dreams that are allegorical representations of their diminished (i.e., midget-like) presence in a world dominated by men, one in which they are menaced, persecuted, subject to mental and physical violence, and imprisoned in a web of social convention, mystification, and exploitation.

Yet it would be disingenuous to view psychoanalysis, which is one of the master narratives/narratives of the master of the late nineteenth century, not merely as a system for decodifying the tropes of women's oppression, but rather, as one segment of contemporary feminism has quite vociferously maintained, as one of the very tools of the repression and oppression of women.[7] Women who buy into the discourse of psychoanalysis are buying into a hegemonic narrative of their problem as hysterical—and, therefore, marginal, inferior, and damaged—human beings (Clara Cordia speaks of "la dependencia de la mujer en el psicoanálisis" [the dependency of woman on psychoanalysis; 284 ff.]). From this point of view, the women writing narratives and sending them in to *Idilio* are not beginning the process of their restoration to full mental health via the science of psychoanalysis, but rather are endorsing the very discourse that subjects them to a marginalizing scrutiny by an implacable masculine gaze.

As I have already noted, the title of the *Idilio* series was "El psicoanálisis le ayudará": Stern, in her essay on the photomontages, does not evoke the title of the series in any ironic way, but it is telling that she notes that the academic who was in charge of the series, Gino Germani (who, it is also significant to note, wrote under a pseudonym, Richard Rest), often instructed her as to how to handle certain of the details of her images (51)—that is, the male interpreter was insistent on ensuring that the female interpreter got things right.[8] Nevertheless, as Priamo has noted, "En ninguna de las exhibiciones de sus fotomontajes Grete utilizó los títulos que Germani les había dado en *Idilio*" (Grete used in none of her exhibitions of her photomontages the titles Germani had given them in *Idilio*; 32), which was certainly one way of asserting her creative distance from his specifically psychoanalytic project.

It would be perhaps too much to have hoped Stern would have included one of Freud's books among those the woman of her photomontage is stepping over, but yet the presence of the books that are there is telling enough, between the masculinity of the titles on the one hand (John Dos Passos's *El gran dinero* [*The Big Money*] is another one) and the grotesqueries of Sherwood Anderson and Walter de la Mare on the other (Sueño No. 6, no title [*Sueños* 111]). Moreover, we see the midget woman trapped between two rows of books: she is bending over to place the strawberries on the Lawrence book, but if she stood up, she would bump her head on the row of books above her. However, this is not just another row of books. Rather, they are the same books she is treading on: this row of books is cut off midway by the bottom border of the image, but the remainder of their body and the shelf on which they sit is reproduced as the row above the woman's figure, and it is as though she is not only trapped by books and the sexist narratives they contain, but specific books that repeat themselves in a circular, imprisoning way.

Grete Stern's *Sueños*, thus, points in two directions. On the one hand, the collection constitutes a major Argentine entry in a bibliography of cultural production based on Freudian psychoanalysis, a production that has had considerable vitality in that country. On the other, however, to the extent that Stern was not a psychoanalyst—and her other photography appears not to reveal any specific commitment to that narrative—her work is only indirectly related to the purportedly serious psychoanalytic purpose, even if rather mediated by the popular culture venue of a woman's magazine, of giving voice to women's dreams. It is in the process of converting verbal narratives taken seriously into creative works of photographic art that a space is created for an occasional ironic and perhaps even feminist stance toward the rigorous claims for the legitimacy of the psychoanalytic project.

ANNEMARIE HEINRICH
Photography, Women's Bodies,
and Semiotic Excess

♦ ♦ ♦

With the death of Annemarie Heinrich in Buenos Aires in late 2005 (she was born in Germany in 1912 and came to Argentina with her parents in 1926), Latin America lost one of the master artists of twentieth-century photography. Heinrich's death signaled also the disappearance of a role played by an important subset of women, often immigrant women, and often women of Jewish origin, in Latin American photography, especially in Argentina and Brazil. The four photographers I have in mind are the German-born Grete Stern (1904–1999), Gisèle Freund (1912–2000), and Annemarie Heinrich, and the German-Swiss Hildegard Rosenthal (1913–1990). Rosenthal worked briefly but intensively in Brazil, while all three of the former made their careers in Buenos Aires; Heinrich died in Buenos Aires, while Stern returned at the end of her life to Germany, and Freund left Argentina at the end of the Peronista period in the mid-1950s, subsequently publishing outside Argentina many of the officially sanctioned photographs she took of Evita (Freund, *Intinéraires* 76–79).[1]

I do not want to exaggerate any privileged cultural importance of the

German—and Jewish—connection of these women (at least for Stern, Freund, and Rosenthal), but they constitute an important facet of the history of photography in Argentina. All have been widely recognized (except for Rosenthal, who has only very recently garnered appropriate recognition); all of them played an important role in the photographing of women by women and in bringing a feminine/feminist gaze to their overall photographic scrutiny of society; and none of them has received anything corresponding to an adequate level of critical analysis.

Stern is unquestionably the most internationally known of the group, to judge by the number of Internet hits her name generates. She is most renowned for her photomontages, the *Sueños*, which were composed beginning in 1948 in collaboration with the sociologist-turned-armchair-psychoanalyst Gino Germani. Women were encouraged to write in their dreams to the popular weekly *Idilio* (one may want to assume that many came in an almost illiterate Spanish). Germani would generate an off-the-cuff interpretation of the dreams submitted, and Stern would provide the illustrative material in the form of her montages. It appears that Germani gave Stern rather precise instructions as to how to provide the graphic interpretations, but Stern claims that she had a great time playing with the material, and, as I have argued in chapter 1, one can read a parodic intent into the montages. It is a parodic intent that at once mocks the psychoanalytic process, at least in its popular woman's-magazine format—after all, the series was breezily titled "El psicoanálisis le ayudará" in what must have been an early version of the self-help genre in Argentina—and the virtually unconsciously self-caricaturizing commentaries Germani provided. If there is a juxtaposition between his smugly serious pronouncements and Stern's delightfully playful images, it is also important to point out the gap between his thoroughly academic Spanish and the casual register of the language in which his newsstand clients write.

Freund, by contrast, never had much of a public face, and it is often pointed out that she appealed more to an artistic, bohemian crowd. However, her most famous images are those of Evita Perón, as she served virtually as the official court photographer of the First Lady. Alicia Dujovne Ortiz, in her marvelously feminist biography of Evita, describes how Heinrich was lucky enough to save her photographic files by turning over at the demand of one of Juan Domingo Perón's security agents all of her negatives of Evita (except one she held back)[2] after La Señora's death (Dujovne Ortiz 220).[3] Freund's images of the First Lady being done up for official events, the details of her wardrobe, and the fashion-plate splendor of virtually all of her public appearances hardly gibed with the veneration accorded populist saints. Moreover, the number of Dior dresses Evita could fit in her closets was not one of the miracles that counted for the Vatican, whose support for canonical sainthood Perón intended to seek. Thus, Freund's images became a sort of secret record of Eva Duarte de Perón's brief splendor, although many of them subsequently went on to become part of the standard visual repertoire of her public life.[4] Heinrich, on the other hand, saw her photographs of Evita, which had a much greater range than did Freund's more official images, published in magazines like *Life* and *Paris Match* without her permission, apparently sold by Perón's agent, who had demanded their forfeiture.[5] Dujovne Ortiz includes a dossier of photographs by Heinrich, Freund, and others in her biography in Spanish, and they also appear in the English translation (unfortunately, in both editions without proper attribution).

By contrast to Stern's photomontages (although she did do much formal portraiture, I stress these compositions as her most original work) and Freund's candid takes on La Señora (Freund also did much formal portraiture), Heinrich's work is the most studiedly commercial of the three (see Travnik, "Un cuerpo," for a detailed overview of her career). Heinrich was essentially a fashion photographer, and her principal intersection with the life of the then Eva Duarte was to photograph her for advertisements and cover-girl shots (Sarlo has examined this work in an exceptionally lucid way). But of course, Eva Duarte was only one of her clients. While Heinrich also did some interesting art photography, my principal interest here will be the gendered nature of her photography: how she photographed women, how specific gendered markers can be remarked on in her photographs, and how these markers may even reveal a certain preoccupation with female sensuality, perhaps even a privileged and female-female charged communication between photographer and subject. Certainly, all fashion photography, including advertising and its derivatives (since the girlie pinup shot in a magazine is also an advertisement for the general nature of the forum in which it appears), is sexual in nature, in that it calculatedly appeals to known, recognized, accepted markers of sexual identity, sexuality, and eroticism (for an overview of research on advertising and the female body, see Duffy).

Yet there is a major difference between such photography as it appeals to conventional parameters and a photography that pushes the edges of those parameters through the inclusion of details that are something like a semiotic surplus to be read in nonnaturalized ways.[6] When this happens, the photography becomes outrageous, scandalous, or even for some obscene. I am not arguing that there is anything as notorious about Heinrich's photography, but only use outrageousness as an outside example, so to speak, of the sort of semiotic excess that might be identified, especially when one ranges over a large body of work.

Certainly, semiotic excess is a feature of the sort of publicity and fashion photography that Heinrich in part made a living from. One only need spend a short amount of time perusing the pages of a prominent glossy fashion publication like *Vogue* (in any of its international editions) to understand how the subject, whether a particular individual or a particular item of fashion, is encrusted in multiple layers, within multiple parameters, of meaning. It would be safe to say, however, that the proliferation of signs that one could call the semiotic excess of such photography is meant to reinforce the primary focus of the photograph, which is to sell fashion and the accoutrements associated with it. While the photographer may be allowed a certain amount of license in the introduction of only tenuously, if not outrageously, related material, there can be little doubt as to what the photograph is all about, and the viewer need engage in little work in identifying—or, alternatively, ignoring—signs that are extraneous to the unmistakable centrality of the commercial object interest, which will routinely be firmly anchored to the manufacturer's logo that appears somewhere prominent in the spread. Indeed, the presence of this logo, by making irrelevant anything else but the product being sold, is what allows for the considerable license in the marshaling of excessive signs on the part of the photographer. Even if the viewer cannot easily sort them out in relation to the principal focus of the spread, it does not matter: they are there as so much visual noise in the frame in which the viewer can or cannot find meaning as may be the case, as long as the image tied to the brand name is unmistakable.

Where publicity and fashion photography become interesting as art is when one can begin to organize interpretively the multiplicity of signs such that they work off each other in patterns of reduplication, eloquent redundancy, complementarity, intensive reinforcement, and the like. Excess here, therefore, does not mean jumbled and irrelevant clutter, but rather a systematic organization of the field of meaning to produce an artistic product of meaningful density.

Let me attempt now to indicate what I am talking about with regard to Heinrich's photographs.

An excellent example with which to begin is Heinrich's image, dated 1950, of the actress Ana María Lynch as La Quintrala. La Quintrala, whose legal name was Doña Catalina de los Ríos y Lisperguer, was a seventeenth-century Chilean noblewoman who killed her lover as part of a scheme to seduce a priest. Hugo del Carril's film about her apparently was released in 1955, and I can find no information as to the discrepancy in dates between Heinrich's image and the release of *La Quintrala*.[7] It is interesting that in Manrupe and Portela's entry in their encyclopedia of Argentine films, both their synopsis and the reviews from the period of *La Quintrala*'s release underscore the lavish visual nature of Carril's production,

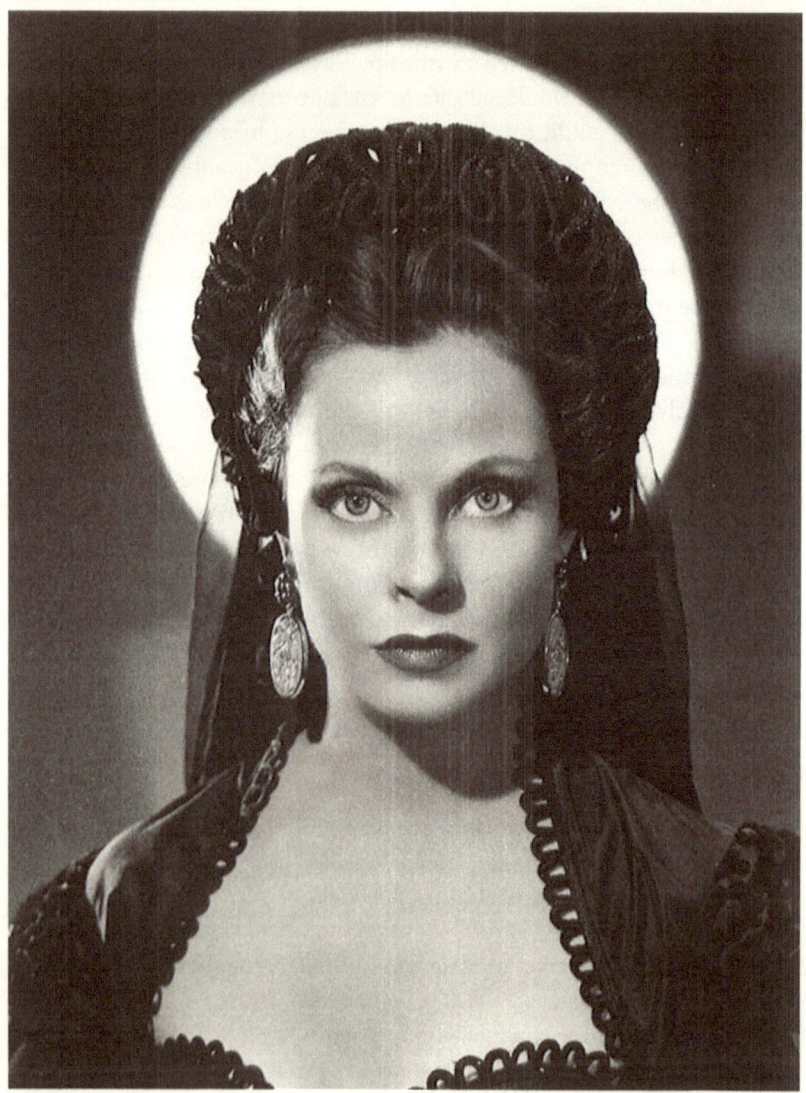

Figure 2.1. Annemarie Heinrich, *Ana María Lynch*. *La Quintrala*. Used with permission of Estudios Heinrich Sanguinetti.

the way in which images dominate, and even the way in which the film is like a piece of exquisite jewelry (493). All of these, indeed, are features in general of Heinrich's meticulously composed studio portraits.

The portrait of Lynch is, in fact, rather outrageous in its compositional details and imagistic rhetoric. In the first place, Lynch is dressed totally in black. A deep décolletage is accentuated by scalloped piping that runs down her chest from her neck to loop around the cups of the dress that support her breasts. The shoulders of her black satin or silk dress are accentuated with some design made of fur. The hat she wears is made of swirling black cords and is accentuated by a filmy black veil that cascades down over the back of her shoulders. This abundance of textured material, starting with the simple material of the basic dress and the veil but complicated by the fringe work, the swirling cords of her hat, and the mottled fur of her shoulders, might cause one to think of the textured body of an animal or insect, and given La Quintrala's story, the motif of the black widow spider suggests itself. The complex pattern of black tones sets off the pale silkiness of Lynch's upper breasts and her facial features, which are impeccably made up in the style of the day (that is, the 1950s, not the seventeenth century). Full and perfectly sculpted lips and bold and coldly staring eyes accentuated by high eyebrows and fulsome eyelashes convey the intractably seductive imperative of the protagonist of Carril's film, while heavy and elaborate earrings signify her commanding social and economic power.

Heinrich was a master of lighting, making full use of technical properties that were only beginning to be fully exploited in photography and filmmaking in the early mid-century, indicating the marvelous visual continuity between Heinrich's photograph and Manrupe and Portela's description of Carril's film. But what makes the former strikingly outrageous is the way in which Heinrich has added an intense backlight to La Quintrala's head. Quite different from the photographer's complex use of different sources of light to create dramatic shadows in her portraits (the one of Baronesa von Bernhardt, dated 1967, on the same page of the Ediciones Larivière collection is a splendid example), an effect that becomes densely layered when she makes use of multiple exposures as well, the added light in the image of Lynch as La Quintrala has the effect of creating a Madonna-like halo around her head. The conventional Catholic iconography of the halo that frames the heads of Jesus, the Virgin Mary, and the saints is meant to highlight the plenitudinous presence in their soul of the Holy Ghost (or Holy Spirit, one of the three persons of the Holy Trinity). Therefore, the attribution of such a sign to La Quintrala is semiotically quite jarring, even more so in that her central capital sin was to undertake the seduction of a priest invested with Holy Orders and, as a consequence of her machinations, bring about his execution by public hanging. Although in Carril's film, La Quintrala does not go without receiving her due punishment for what she has wrought, she is hardly redeemed and much less sanctified in the process.

Heinrich's image exhibits a stark interplay between the black of La Quintrala's dress, which bespeaks both the deaths she occasions and her embodiment of the symbolism of the black widow, and the intense white brilliance of the backlighting. Moreover, her bold—indeed, brazen—stare into the camera is far removed from the lowered-eye demureness of typical images of the Virgin and female (indeed, also most male) saints. It is as though Heinrich were defying the conventions of Catholic iconography, and doing so precisely in an era in which the strong-arm government of Juan Domingo Perón was strongly supported by institutional Catholicism in Argentina.[8] However, seen today, this image cannot help but also evoke the conflicting images of Eva Perón, images that Heinrich herself was quite instrumental in distributing. Evita, both during her life and subsequently, was portrayed both as saint and sinner (see Taylor's careful analysis of these conflicting images), and Perón was touchy enough about the nasty rumors concerning his wife and political partner that he demanded the surrender of all prints of Mario Soffici's as yet unreleased 1945 film starring Eva Duarte, *La pródiga* (The loose woman), in which she portrays a reformed woman of ill repute. The film was only released, thanks to one carefully sequestered copy, forty years later (Manrupe and Portela 478). Although Evita was never accused of the sort of crimes associated with La Quintrala, she might as well have been, given the dreadful nature of the reputation attributed to her by the opposition or even those opposed to her within Peronism. By contrast, the myths of Saint Evita are accompanied by the icons of the purity of her soul, and the trope of a cheap holy card that serves to illustrate the cover of Tomás Eloy Martínez's 1995 novel on the twenty-year necrophilic wanderings of Evita's body between her death and her final interment in the Recoleta cemetery in Buenos Aires (under several meters of cement so that it cannot likely be purloined again) evokes those myths. Martínez's novel is appropriately titled *Santa Evita*.

I do not know if Heinrich had any intent to parody images of Evita Perón or the hyperfemininity associated with fashion, movie, and celebrity shots. After all, the Lynch portrait is dated 1950, and it is only with Evita's death in 1952 that full "canonization" of her person begins.[9] Yet there is little in the way of religious photography in Argentina and little interest, beyond the fervent commitment to Saint Evita, in religious iconography, and certainly not among members of the artistic and literary community. This explains Heinrich's evident enthusiasm for transgressively inscribing La Quintrala within a wholly unsuitable Catholic hagiographic iconography and how, as a European, she must have taken a rather bemused stance toward the trappings of Evita's sanctification both during and after the latter's life. Dujovne Ortiz's account of Gisèle Freund's abrupt departure from Argentina with her negatives of La Señora after her death, negatives that Perón wished to destroy because he was set to create the totally religious image of Evita suitable to his regime, indicates, along with the fate of the Soffici film, the extent to which there was no room in Argentina in the 1950s for independent images of the new national patroness, "siempre viva en el alma de su pueblo" (alive forever in the hearts of her people). It is in such a context, one in which one feminine icon dominates all possible inscriptions of women, that Heinrich's photograph of Ana María Lynch representing La Quintrala can also be understood (for a brilliant study of the iconography of Eva Duarte/Eva Perón/Evita, see Sarlo). It is an image of semiotic excess, typical of Heinrich's portraits, I would argue, in that, in this case, the language of the lighting contributes to opening up dimensions of meaning that go far beyond the basic story of La Quintrala.

Heinrich photographed most of the major Argentine actresses of the so-called Golden Age of Argentine cinema of the 1940s and 1950s, but she also did work for the French-based *Vogue*, which had at that time become the international standard for fashion photography. I have not been able to discover who Irene Luc was, but Heinrich photographed her for *Vogue* in 1940. Luc was virtually a Joan Crawford look-alike and possessed the same sort of intense, almost harsh visage that Crawford used to such advantage as a *belle dame sans merci* throughout her career. Indeed, Heinrich's image of Luc is virtually a riff on one of the famous publicity shots of Joan Crawford (who, moreover, was also of French origin; her birth name was Lucille Fay LeSueur), which features her with her chin haughtily upraised and her full head of hair surrounded by a black hat, as though it were the reverse image of the sort of halo associated with the Virgin Mary and used by Heinrich in her photograph of Ana María Lynch.[10] Luc, too, is crowned by a magnificent head of hair and topped off with a full-fledged lily-pad hat. Luc's, however, is apparently made of different shades of woven straw and is not uniformly black, but rather, in this black-and-white photo, different shades of gray. Luc's outfit, however, is starkly black (again, at least in the black-and-white photograph). Her chin is also raised in a haughty fashion, but as the consequence of resting it on her gloved fist. It is difficult to tell if the glove Luc is wearing is wrist- or elbow-length, as it blends in with her dress. Equally, it is difficult to tell if the two visible diamond brooches on her arm are part of the dress or part of her gloves (her other gloved hand can be seen along the edge of the table or other article of furniture against which the model is leaning). She is also, as one might expect, appointed with spectacular pearl and diamond earrings.

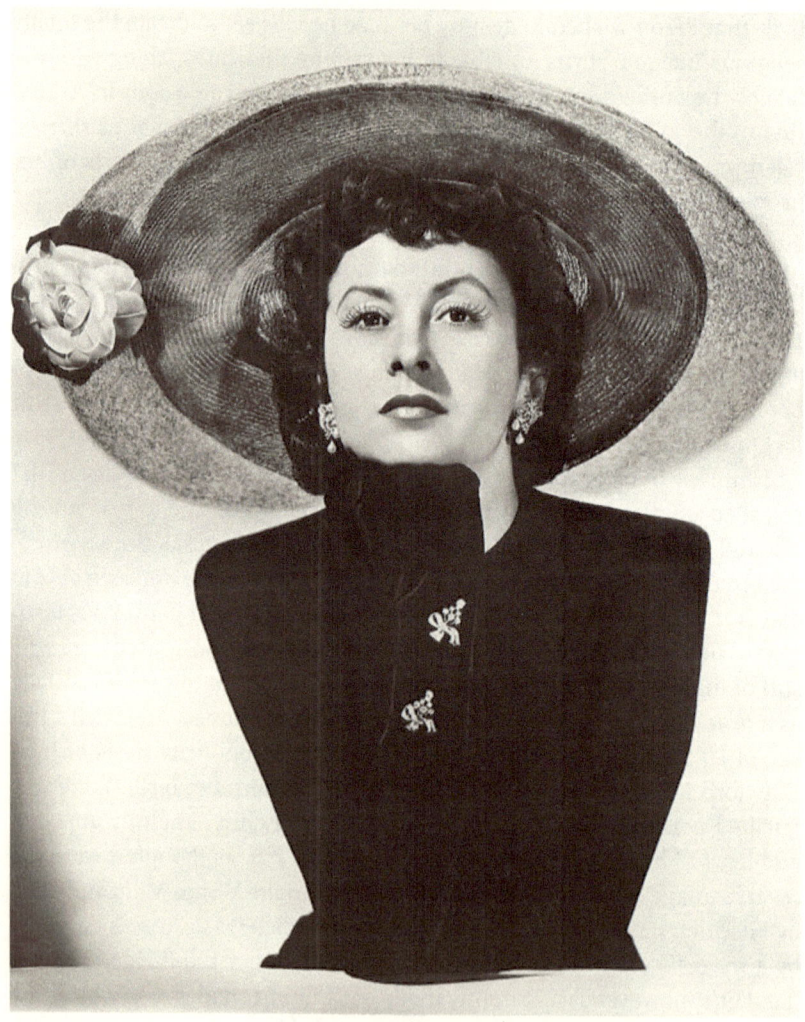

Figure 2.2. Annemarie Heinrich, *Irene Luc*. Used with permission of Estudios Heinrich Sanguinetti.

There are two details of this image that are particularly indicative of the semiotic excess that characterizes Heinrich's fashion and publicity photography. The first complements the use of black as the basic color of the model's dress, and that is the angular severity of her shoulders. The cloth of her dress literally flares out in both directions from her body, which displays the sort of pronounced inverted triangle associated with the athletic male body of the period.[11] The arm on which Luc rests her chin almost, but not quite, bisects the geometric shape of her upper body and points to the perfect symmetry of her stunningly gorgeous, if Crawford-harsh, face.

The geometric symmetry of Luc's image is, however, "disturbed" by the second excessive element, which is a huge fabric flower that decorates the right-hand edge of the immense lily-pad hat. Almost half as large as the model's face, the flower is pronounced enough to just by a hair fit into the frame of the picture without bleeding off in the left-hand margin. If the model's body is perfectly symmetrical, the photograph is initially so, such that her body is precisely centered in the frame, as is her immense hat. However, the fabric flower pushes the image, so to speak, to the right, such that there is minimally more space between her body and the edge of the photograph on the left than on the right. In this way, if the flower disrupts the symmetry of the model's body, it also disrupts the symmetry of the photographic composition and risks distracting the gaze of the observer from Luc's striking beauty and the lush composition of her image to the contemplation of what is, after all, not much of a notable fashion detail, at least not in comparison with dress, gloves, hat, earrings, and brooches.

Such a flower, one will recall, carries a significant meaning of female sexuality, especially when the flower is a rose or a stylized version of it (Conner et al. 286–287); the Spanish philosopher Cirlot, however, speaks of the rose as also a symbol of completeness and perfection, which certainly would apply particularly well here (263). Although fully dressed, Heinrich's model is intensely erotic, since it is her original fashion that is intended to highlight the sexuality of the model/wearer—and, conversely, it is the sexuality of the model/wearer that is meant to sell the fashion as effectively symbolic of that sexuality and of sexuality in general (the fact that it is only feminine sexuality being used as the commercial lure here is immaterial and only reflects the sexist imbalance of advertising during the period, as Heinrich never did male fashion photography; moreover, *Vogue* has historically, in all of its national versions, concentrated on female haute couture). The sinful, "daring" black of her dress and the troped halo (that is, as nonvirginal) of her hat foreground the woman's sexuality, which is only reinforced more categorically by the explicit reference of the rose, whose whiteness (although the artificial petals are black) only ironizes the relationship to the actual anatomical referent of its symbolism (in color photography, deep red would, of course, be the most explicit symbol of a fully engaged female sexuality). Fashion is transparent in its use of sex and sexuality (although certainly more the latter than the former in 1940, if the former is understood to mean sexual acts and their correlates) to sell itself, and fashion is transparent in its iconic, symbolic, and semiotic grounding in sex and sexuality.[12] There is the tendency to believe that black-and-white photography is more sober, less emotional or sensual, than color photography, but the sort of image Heinrich creates with Luc as the model is paradigmatic of the sexualized language of *Vogue*, where, in this case, the haughty pose of the woman is matched by sexual agency signaled by the adornment added or in excess of her lush costume.

If semantic excess is present in the Luc photograph, where I would stress that it does not merely serve to display feminine sexuality, but to overdetermine the sort of complex sexuality of the figure of the *belle dame sans merci*, it is virtually spun out of control in the 1946 photograph of the actress Zully Moreno, one of the major stars of the Argentine Golden Age of filmmaking, whose work is an anthology of titles that refer to woman as a sexualized agent (a standard, albeit now rather sexist, treatment of the topos of the *belle dame* is to be found in Praz 187–286). Almost iconic is *Amor prohibido* (1958), Tolstoy's *Anna Karenina* rewritten in the hands of director Luis César Amadori as mediocre Argentine melodrama. When Heinrich's portrait is done in 1946, Moreno is playing in Mario Soffici's quite sophisticated *Celos* (Jealousy) and Francisco Múgica's less interesting *Cristina* (see Manrupe and Portela 26, 103, and 138–139, respectively).

Moreno under Heinrich's camera comes off almost as one of the models in Grete Stern's whimsical photomontages. Staring off sultrily into space, Moreno's gorgeous, statuesque face is framed by the full, flowing blonde locks characteristic of one prominent hairstyle of the time. Like most of the stars and models of the period, she has a full and painted mouth, and eyes made large by dramatic lashes and brows, and one would expect her body to be portrayed in equilibrious tandem with her head. But instead, what Heinrich provides is Moreno's bust: her head and her equally gorgeous shoulders. Enveloped in a radiant glow captured fully by skin and locks—another superb use of lighting by the photographer—Moreno's bust is not seen placed on the flat surface of a shelf or a pedestal such as one associates with the display of busts, but rather the lighting gives the impression that it is submerged in a lake of light. The ethereal

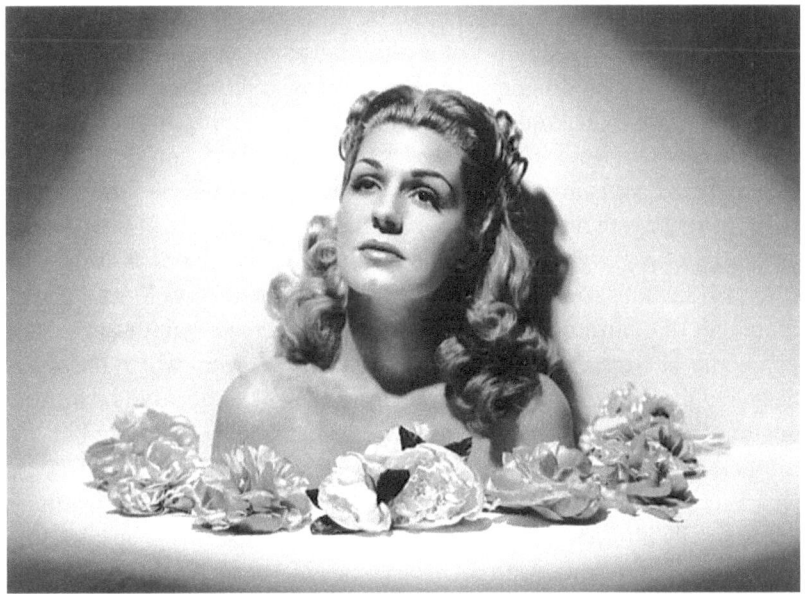

Figure 2.3. Annemarie Heinrich, *Zully Moreno*. Used with permission of
Estudios Heinrich Sanguinetti.

quality of the substance that encases Moreno's body below her shoulders,
which means essentially below the bottom edge of the frame, is unde-
terminable because of what is the excessive touch of the photograph.
If there is one strategic flower to symbolize female sexuality in the Luc
photo, the one devoted a few years later to Moreno contains no fewer
than seven such fully opened blossoms arranged in a semicircle around
Moreno's shoulders.

Whereas the features of Moreno's head and shoulders reveal the sort of
anatomical symmetry considered integral to female allure in the aesthetic
language of the time, the flowers are almost chaotic in their difference and
in the exuberant profusion of their petals. All are white or near white (a
few have dark leaves), but there is nothing symmetrical in their distribution around Moreno's shoulders; some have a few fallen petals, indicating
their fullness and the beginning of their decay. One of Moreno's minor
films of the period is Amadori's 1951 *Pecado* (Sin; Manrupe and Portela
do not register this production), and the flowers bring to mind the trope
of the Seven Deadly Sins. If the dominant role of women in Golden Age
filmmaking is that of an Eve-like real or alleged sinner and sexual agent
in the downfall of Man, the representation of Moreno festooned with not
one but a full contingent of seven open flowers is unquestionably one of

Heinrich's most excessive photographic displays. Of course, the Seven Deadly Sins do not refer only to sex, although as with the things forbidden in the Ten Commandments many do, directly and indirectly. But in the dominant patriarchal and hegemonic narrative, sinning for women, the daughters of Eve, leads insistently back to sex, and the observer will, therefore, perceive no contradiction in the sexual symbol of one flower being reduplicated in the number seven (see fellow Argentine Ana María Shua's anthology of writing in Spanish about women as daughters of Eve).

It is difficult to know if Heinrich's image of Moreno, like Stern's photomontages that purportedly were interpreting the male-oriented armchair psychiatry of Germani that they accompanied (but from which they have detached themselves to enjoy fame on their own), is meant to be humorous or even parodic. Certainly, the repeated strikingly stunning but, for the period, quite conventional images of female models and actresses, which like pornography become very quickly tiresome, demand treatment substantially different from the hackwork that one recovers by spending only a small bit of time with archival copies of *Vogue, Antena, Radiolandia*, and the like from the period. One way to be original is consciously to move toward the parodic and to make use of elements of kitsch for purposes of foregrounded originality. Such use involves a highly proficient technological display, and Heinrich never backs away from her position on the cutting edge of photographic perfectionism. Yet such a display may enhance the foregrounded texture of a consciously deployed strategy of kitsch, as in the case of the contemporary compositions of the Argentine Marcos López (see the chapter on his work in my *Urban Photography*).

Perhaps there was nothing consciously kitschy about Heinrich's early (1938) publicity shot of the then run-of-the-mill aspiring actress and model Eva Duarte. Taken almost a decade before Eva Duarte fully emerged as La Señora de Perón with her Cleopatra-like grand tour of Europe on behalf of her husband's government in 1947, the much-heralded Rainbow Tour, or as Evita with her subsequent politico-charitable works, Heinrich's image is that of an ingénue starlet. The ingénue Duarte appears in the photograph as though hoping that Heinrich's technical mastery can help make her as much of a megastar as other women the photographer had tended to. Sarlo describes the photographic images of Eva Duarte from the early years of her career in Buenos Aires and underscores the exceptional interest Heinrich seems to have taken in photographing her well: "La falta de interés [hasta por los fotógrafos que trabajaban para el amante protector de Eva Duarte, Emilio Kartulowicz, dueño de la revista *Sintonía* que sacó varias imágenes de Eva Duarte] contrasta con las fotografías magníficas que, por esos mismos meses [mediados de 1939] tomó Annemarie Heinrich. El descuido, entonces, no puede ser explicado solamente por la insignficancia de la modelo sino por la mediocridad del fotógrafo" (43).[13] Sarlo goes on to describe the famous Heinrich photo of Eva Duarte in a bathing suit and maintaining a cheesecake pose that Heinrich took in 1938, although it was not published until 1940 on the cover of the magazine *Guión* and in the context of the Concurso Stampa, which featured women who would go on to become recognized stars: Zully Moreno was among the twelve contestants (43).

However, Sarlo does not mention the single Heinrich photograph of

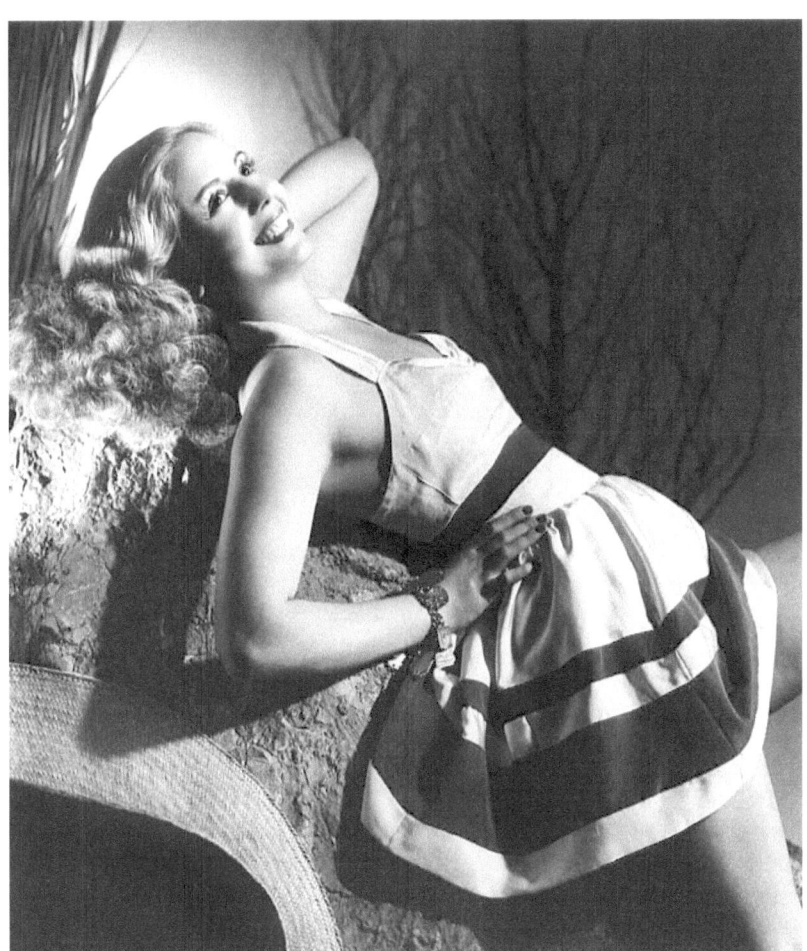

Figure 2.4. Annemarie Heinrich, *Eva Duarte*. Used with permission of Estudios Heinrich Sanguinetti.

Evita that appears in the Heinrich dossier, *Un cuerpo, una luz, un reflejo* (A body, a light, a reflection), on whose collected images this essay is based. Dated 1938, this single image of Evita is also of the cheesecake variety. Rather than a swimsuit, Duarte is wearing a summer sun dress, consisting of a flared skirt and a halter top that allows for maximum exposure of the arms, shoulders, and upper chest. Evita's shapely arms and legs are amply displayed (the arms much more than the legs), and the tightness of the top reveals how underdeveloped her breasts were (Sarlo cites Heinrich as having stated that she enhanced Evita's bodice in the swimsuit photo [43]). Since the secondary sexual characteristics of the breasts are certainly not a basis of excess here, the viewer must turn to other features of the photograph in the attempt to grasp Heinrich's unusually careful attention to her subject's portrayal—that is, unusual vis-à-vis the hackwork of most of the other early Evita photographers.

In this case, it is the subject's hair that comes off as the most singular detail of the photograph (see Weitz for an extensive discussion of sexist and feminist, erotic and reappropriated, versions of women's hair). Throughout her relatively brief public career as a mediocre actress and model and then as the stunning First Lady, many different hairdos were associated with Evita. Most were highly stylized, but this one is the essence of the carefree summer look, in accordance with her dress. Full and flowing golden hair captures the only emphasized lighting in the frame. Indeed, much of the frame is shadowy, both in terms of the way the lighting makes the model's arms cast a shadow and the way the background setting—two groups of dried branches—is only barely visible. What is, however, most notable is the way she leans back over a large boulder in a pose of submission and suggestive self-offering. She smiles radiantly and fully in apparent happiness, and her pose is one of physical abandon of the sort that contrasts strikingly with the portraits of careful and often severe self-control that characterize her person as La Señora.

In the lower left-hand corner of the frame, one can make out part of a large, round straw hat that appears to be one of the signature icons of Heinrich's photography, and it is placed there as though the woman being photographed has just removed it and placed it on the ground beside her in order to give herself over to the carefree abandon the mock summer setting presumably invites her to transmit. The fact that the details of that setting are patently staged, and that the rays under which she stretches her youthful body belong not to the sun but to powerful studio lights, underscores the way in which, even after allowing for Heinrich's careful and conscientious work, a fan-magazine or advertising-layout shot is hardly the setting for interesting visual art. What I would identify as the semiotic excess of this shot, then, lies not so much in any exuberant details of Evita's bodily display, although this must have been one of the early photos that Perón's propaganda apparatus could not have wanted preserved, much less after Evita's death, with the attempts to canonize her. Rather, what is excessive is the texture of the image for such a slightly (at that time) interesting object. Using Heinrich's talents to photograph what hack photographers understood to be nothing more, well, than a hackneyed subject was tantamount to using the Sinfónica de Buenos Aires to record a toothpaste jingle. In this sense, the contrast between Heinrich's publicity shots of what was, in the end, a meager talent, shots that would be of little interest today if it were not for the subsequent emergence of Evita as La Señora Eva Duarte de Perón, and Freund's record of the Peronista sumptuousness could not be more vivid. It is little wonder that *Un cuerpo* does not include any further example of Heinrich's work with Evita, which, even if she lost control of the negatives (as Sarlo and Dujovne Ortiz relate), is recoverable from published sources both within Argentina and abroad. Heinrich would, a decade later, produce one of the most canonical images of Eva Perón, by then a woman in complete command of her public face.

It is, therefore, a visual pleasure to turn again to Heinrich's work with subjects that more clearly deserve—at least, at that time—the sort of exquisitely wrought gaze she organizes in her best work. Around the same time Heinrich was beginning to work with Evita, she did a magnificent portrait of the dancer Mecha Quintana and her students (1939), and it is with a discussion of this image that I will conclude this study. It is apparently impossible to speak of any motif of lesbianism in Heinrich's work, although the case of her nude portrait of Tilda Thamar is well known. Taken in 1949, but displayed in the showcase of Heinrich's studio in downtown Buenos Aires in 1991, this image led to the photographer's being unsuccessfully denounced for producing pornography. Heinrich photographed many women in the nude, and often with a full display of the pubic area (one particularly stunning example is the 1940 *Desnudo XIX* (*Un cuerpo* 88; Nude XIX). Although one suspects that by the early 1990s it was the suspicion of lesbianism or something equally "evil" in the eye of the beholder, and not nudity as such, that led to the accusation of pornography. Perhaps it was the public display of the portrait, but one might also entertain the idea that it was the customary overdetermination of the image that provoked the outrage in a way in which a less layered and more representationally transparent image might not have.[14]

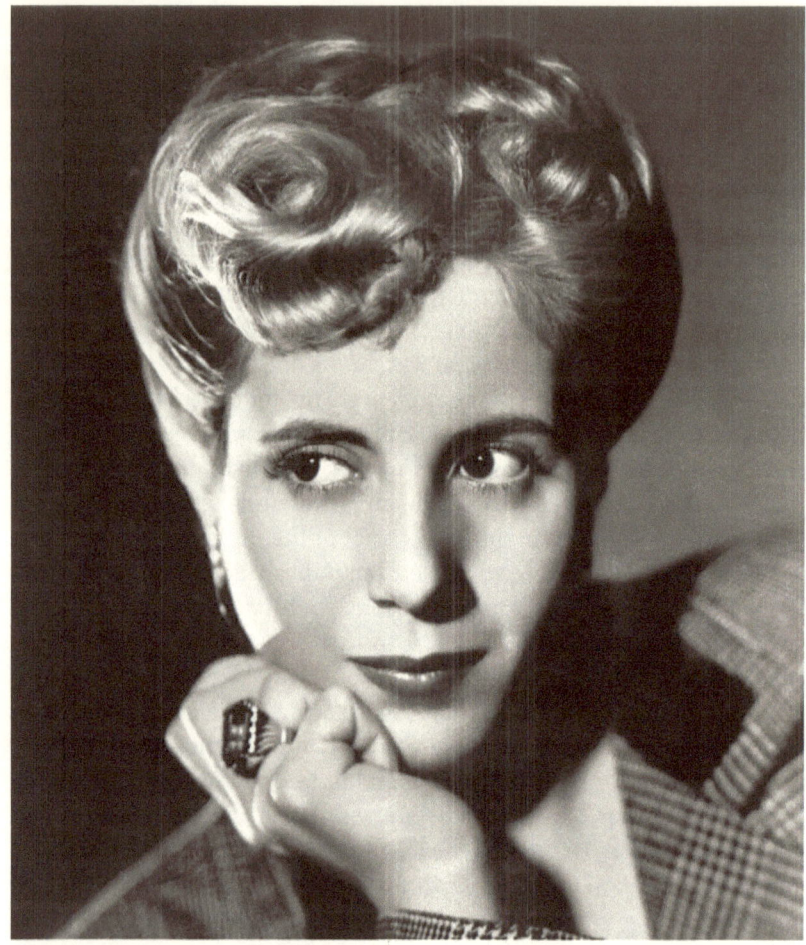

Figure 2.5. Annemarie Heinrich, *Eva Perón*. Used with permission of Estudios Heinrich Sanguinetti.

Quintana is centered in the frame of the photograph in a languid but very posed position. Although most portraits of dancers tend to focus on the body as a whole, with arms and legs in particularly iconic dance positions, Heinrich's image of Quintana, by contrast, captures her at rest, dressed in what appears to be formal wear rather than the conventional outfit of the dancer. Quintana's body, in turn, is, shall we say, festooned by the heads (with or without partial torsos and a few hands captured in the image) of her students, all women. Interestingly enough, seven students are included, echoing the number of roses of the Zully Moreno photograph, as though Quintana's students were, in some way, the flowers of her terpsichorean garden. All eight women are languidly staring off into space as though lost in reverie, with their eyes closed, downcast, dazed, or startled.

However, what is most compelling about this image of a totally feminine world determined by the women's interactions on the basis of the dance mistress Mecha Quintana is the explicit physical intimacy of their corporal disposition. They are, in a word, all snuggled around the mag-

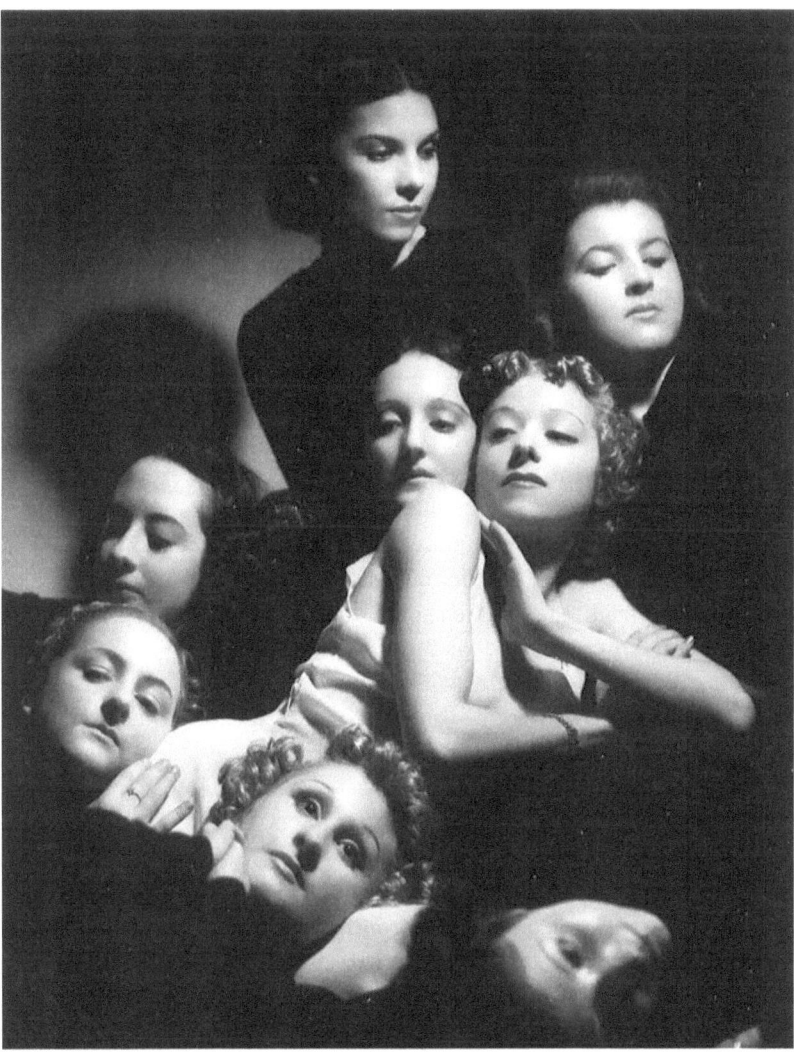

Figure 2.6. Annemarie Heinrich, *Mecha Quintana y alumnas* (Mecha Quintana and her students). Used with permission of Estudios Heinrich Sanguinetti.

nificent female body presented by Quintana: one has her head in the woman's lap; another rests her head on Quintana's hip and her hand on her upper thigh; a third has her face resting against Quintana, her chin apparently on her shoulder back; a fourth (she fades off into the lower right-hand corner, a bit out of focus) rests her head against Quintana's right thigh, while Quintana partially rests her crossed arms on this woman's abdomen; another (the shadows of the photo make it impossible to be sure) rests her elbow on the small of Quintana's back; and finally, a sixth woman hovers over Quintana's head, as though on the verge of resting her cheek on the woman's brilliant hair, but as though refraining from doing so in order not to disturb its carefully arranged curls. Only one of the seven women, who dominates the center of the upper third of the photograph, appears not to be communing directly with Quintana's body.

This is a very suggestive image, which some viewers might choose to read in a sexual or erotic way. This might be stretching a point, since, while Heinrich did many images of female nudes, some quite audacious in their display of the mature female pubis, none of her work puts on display anything that might be called a play of sexuality. Many of her subjects are quite physically alluring, and made even more so by the lushness of her photography, the highly unique experiments with lighting, and the multilayered nature of the poses. The bulk of such images are devoted to women, usually the most famous Argentine and international entertainment stars or the top-of-the-line fashion models, so it is reasonable for their sensuality to be very much in evidence because of the very nature of the exploitation of the feminine body by the entertainment trades and fashion modeling. However, some images are of men: men from the world of entertainment, such as the famous actor Alfredo Alcón (the fascination of his physical beauty will be enhanced for some by knowing that he is reputed to be gay; the photo of Alcón, taken in 1961, may be found in Heinrich, *El espectáculo* [The spectacle] 59). And a few men posed in something like pseudoclassical fantasies. Yet nothing that I can find comes close to the manifestly homoerotic, except for what one might attribute to Quintana's physical intimacy in this photograph with her students, which is something like a feminine version of what is found historically in all-male Socratic relationships (see in the same vein the photograph of Heinrich and her four female assistants [Heinrich, *El espectáculo* 65]).

Yet the suggestion of an all-female universe anchored in the person of Mecha Quintana is highly intriguing, a universe of shared confidence, much like that of Heinrich and her predominantly female portraiture, in which only women are invited to participate. This is not the place to detail the Adrienne Rich lesbian continuum (which, for Rich, is not grounded necessarily on genital sexuality) or the propositions of an advantageous female separatism (which ranges from convents to all-women colonies, passing through sororities, all-girls schools, solidarities, Boston marriages, and gynoecia). Women may strategically tighten the ranks among themselves as a form of defense against the all-male homosociality that continues to prevail in most human societies. And that homosociality may erroneously, flippantly, and in a sexist manner dismiss such formations with condemnation of them as "lesbian," without ever having to come to terms with the complex meanings of such an epithet. Suffice it to emphasize that Heinrich is, with her manifest interest in female subjects, doing nothing more nor less than capturing (or, in reality, posing) an instance of female homosocial formations.

With her photography establishing its reputation in Argentina at a time in which the profession was (as it continues to be) dominated by men—and by men who would prefer to see women and their bodies in transparently sexist ways—Heinrich's devotion as a woman to seeing other women with her camera provides for a particularly significant realm of cultural production (see the encomium of Heinrich's search for beauty by Sara Facio ["La búsqueda"], the deaconess of Argentine photography; see Evans for some general guiding comments on feminist photography). The fact that Heinrich approaches her subjects with an almost expressionistic lens and engages in various forms of emphasis and overdetermination that I have been calling here the "semiotic excess" of her images is what provides the particularly distinctive way Heinrich foregrounds her female bodies and the contexts in which she situates them. Like Stern with her photomontages, perhaps on occasion Heinrich may be understood to be suggesting a parody of the conventional or clichéd forms of the masculine/masculinist gaze. What is for certain is that there is nothing conventional about the particular gaze she constructs.

WOMAN, PROSTITUTION, AND MODERNITY IN FIN-DE-SIÈCLE MEXICO

◆ ◆ ◆

*At the center, both the false and the true one, of houses of assignation
and zones of tolerance are the prostitutes, as much indispensable as they
are belittled, human beings at the disposal of pleasure and scandal in
the abstract, which is also persecution as a real fact.*

—Carlos Monsiváis, Introduction to Ava Vargas,
La casa de citas (my translation)

The phenomenon of the whore and female prostitutes during the
early years of the twentieth century in Mexico intersects with two
features central to the project of modernity: the systematic organization of business and the generalized exploitation of women. Prostitution and the generalized exploitation of women stretch back to times
immemorial, but there can be little doubt that the social outburst of modernity could hardly exclude, as in everything, these two universal phenomena. If prostitution depended on the overdetermined eroticization
of the female body, the culture of modernity—modernism, in a word—
provided the cultural practices to stimulate this excess valorization. If it
is undeniable that modernity included a mythification of woman, in the
interests of producing a specific patriarchal social model, that involved en-
shrining icons of sacred matrimony and sacrosanct maternity, the simple
truth is that what is more fascinating are the women who, in Dijkstra's apt
phrase, were "idols of perversity."[1]

As a consequence, no matter how much one might, today, construct
a defense of prostitution as body-based employment like any other and

assert that female—and male—prostitutes are engaged in "sex work," it would be difficult to find in the imaginary of the early twentieth century any other interpretation of prostitution than as the perversion of the divine role of woman and a dire assault on the integrity of the family. It matters little that the masterminds of the hegemonic imaginary, which included high functionaries of the state, leaders of the Church, and magnates of industry and commerce, were the principal clients of the whorehouses, which, after all, were organized to satisfy the needs of these very men. Although there existed alongside the organized system of prostitution forms of prostitution that serviced the needs of lowlife clients, whether in the zones of tolerance or in outlying streets, prostitution that served the interests of the ruling class had all of the characteristics of the most refined elegance of the mansions of sin, which were not very different from the *petits palaces* of the great families. Although, as the saying of the famous paradigmatic grand New York madam Polly Adler went, "A house is not a home."

The images collected by Ava Vargas in 1991 in the dossier *La casa de citas en el barrio galante* (House of assignation in the red-light district) date, in her estimation, from sometime between 1900 and 1920 (Vargas xv).[2] These are photos that were taken in stereoscopic format and thus to be viewed in the corresponding apparatus that was customarily to be found in the homes of the well-to-do as part of the material trove of culture, along with the piano, the violin, and the phonograph. That is to say, we are to understand that the photos whose discovery Vargas describes (she came upon them thanks to the filmmaker and antiquarian Raúl Kamffer, who found them in 1975 in one of his "prowls" among markets and fairs in search of forgotten material) were part of some artistic project in which women were posed and photographed, so to speak, for posterity. It is reasonable that such types of images would have circulated in a clandestine market that allowed "refined" gentlemen (including undoubtedly other women with a taste for feminine nudes) to treasure in their hearts recollections of their transit through the world of brothels or, absent such experiences, the dream of having done so.

These images are parallel to the so-called French postcards that fulfilled the same function of erotic entertainment, and such stereoscopic photos constituted a cultural production industry that came out of the new technologies of the period that included, in this case, photography. If it is true that photography, from the earliest time of its origins, served to immortalize the mighty and to record majestically in time sober bourgeois families, while at the same time being the basis for the postcard that was exchanged as part of the ritual of formal visits and contained the image of the person visiting, it is important to remember that photography also lent itself from the time of its invention to giving a new image-based dimension to anecdotal accounts of sexual practices: pornography now had another extremely potent vehicle for its divulgation. In the realm of feminine prostitution as much as in that of homoerotic pursuits, two exemplars of high modernity, photography served to provide a priceless aide-mémoire (see Waugh; Mavor; Köhler).

When one opens Vargas's dossier, it is hardly possible to be surprised at the array of naked or seminaked women. We can, today, hardly expect to discover corporal novelties, largely because the widespread publication of images of women's bodies from time immemorial has achieved such ubiquity that one hardly pays attention anymore, since there is so little new to see. Aside from contortionist erotic poses of the body or unheard of manipulative practices, women's bodies, although always a source of delight, no longer surprise. Only the grotesque stance of a Joel-Peter Witkin could be capable of providing surprising images of the female body. It goes without saying that the plastic optics of photography allows us a constantly renewed gaze at all material phenomena, and, hence, the possibilities for framing are innumerable. By the same token, although no one any longer is astonished at the photographic exploitation of the feminine body in the contemporary world, there is a certain frisson that derives from the realization that our most respectable great-grandfathers had the same interests and that, more than likely, one of the women portrayed here might just possibly be one's own great-grandmother . . .

But such mitigating circumstances aside, the greatest enchantment and astonishment that arise from the photographs in the Vargas dossier do not have to do with the bodies of the women as such, but with their setting in the interior and exterior spaces of the turn-of-the-century Mexico of a hundred years ago.[3] There is a really remarkable disconnect in these images we have the privilege of seeing all together (by contrast with the original spectators, who certainly must have seen them in small installments owing to the nature of their commercial or semicommercial distribution). Such a disconnect has to do with one of the most formidable characteristics of Latin American modernism: the attempt to meld cultural motifs of a profoundly classical origin (with certain derivations to be found in Western Europe) with the harsh landscape realities of Latin America that had little to do with the origins of such motifs. If it is true that literature could transcend such contradictions by placing its texts outside of Latin America or simply ignoring its geophysical parameters, the

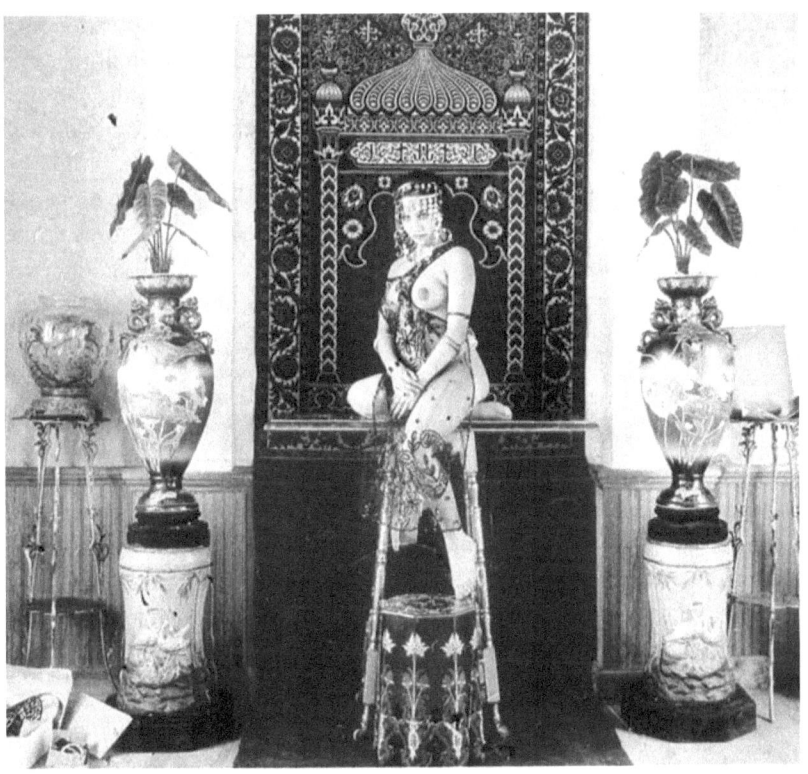

Figure 3.1. A prostitute as part of formal room décor.

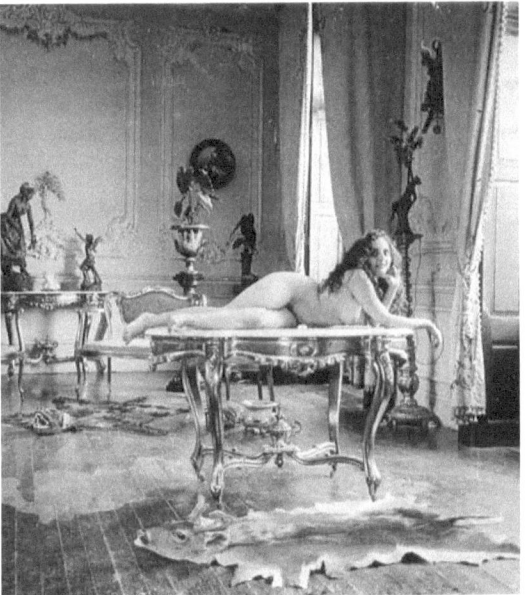

Figure 3.2. A prostitute as a table centerpiece.

photographs often could not go beyond their immediate physical world. Of course, there is a modernist current that achieved something like a precarious and even satisfactory amalgamation if the landscape was not too hostile. This is what we find in the most ultra-urban versions, where the built environment can effectively mask the New World realities of the background. One thinks of the achievements of the Belle Époque in Buenos Aires or Rio de Janeiro or the private chambers of the Colombian poet José Asunción Silva, as described in remarkable detail by fellow-Colombian Fernando Vallejo in his biographic novel *Chapolas negras* (Black butterflies; 1995).

But this is not the case with the photographs presented by Vargas. On the one hand, we have faithful re-creations of the luxury of the Mexican oligarchy/upper bourgeoisie. These are the palaces—or *petits palaces*—that are imitations of models seen in Paris and London, where the imperious display of luxury items creates something like a fantasy cabinet in which the body is inserted in poses that oblige it to adjust to the static dimensions of the setting. For example, in figure 3.1, the binarism of the objects and the boundaries of décor are reduplicated in the feminine body, whose two arms, two hands, two legs, two breasts, and two eyes are reinforced, in turn, by the stereoscopic contemplation the client receives from the photograph. The sexual odalisque is perfectly framed by the tapestry that extends outward toward the viewer as though inviting him (I used the masculine form, since the masculinist gaze is supposedly to be privileged here) to enter into the realm of the photograph and to enjoy through/ with his own body what the tableau has to offer. This image is timid in its provocation, but it matches many others in which the women spread themselves open before the spectator, and always with their bodies and corresponding anatomical details being framed by the setting of luxury.

In another image, the naked body of the woman lies spread out on a serving table. One supposes that this is a bedroom because of the presence of the chamber pot below and to the back of the table. Whatever the room's function is, it is replete with objects of décor that could fill an extensive, detailed list. Suffice it to point out the modern detail of the lamp to the right, between the two picture windows, which, although neoclassic in design, comes with an electric cord and tulips holding lightbulbs. What is, however, particularly notable about this photographic montage is how the woman, who is objectified, serves as one more detail of the décor. Her languid pose turns her into a table centerpiece, although the way in which she extends from one end of the table to the other makes one think that she is perhaps more of a table runner, especially in the way her hands and feet hang beyond the edge of the table as the ends of a runner might do. One cannot help but take in the phallic features that are part of the excess of the worked detail of the table that puts the naked woman on decorative exhibition.

While almost half of the images in *La casa de citas* place woman in this sort of fantasy box that is the interior décor of the architecture of modernity, the other half concern a surprising dislocation of décor, whereby the female nude is thrust into the hostile landscape of the central Mexican mesa. Bernardo de Balbuena could take pride, in his *La grandeza mexicana* (Mexican greatness; 1604), that this Valle de Anáhuac was another Tempe:

Al fin, aqueste humano paraíso
tan celebrado en la elocuencia griega, [. . .]
es el valle de Tempe, en cuya vega
se cree que sin morir nació el verano
y que otro ni le iguala ni le llega. (cap. VI, est. 16)[4]

Balbuena could be certain that none of his readers in the Spanish court possessed reliable photographs that might contradict him. Nevertheless, the shock is nothing short of jarring when the anonymous photographer or photographers come up with the brilliant idea of taking the women from the sporting dens outside to place them in the Mexican countryside (the place where many of the women in the photographs, one can well surmise, had come from, as in the case of Santa, the namesake country maiden forced by rape to become an urban prostitute in Federico Gamboa's 1903 novel). Although in many cases the women are simply arranged in poses with the landscape in the background, in other cases one takes note of the attempt to create an artistic composition that echoes the ones already described in terms of the metaphor of the fantasy box. For example, there is a series of four photographs in which the two women (always the same ones) are posed amidst the rushing waters of a rapids. They are aquatic nymphs, Mexican Nereids whose beauty interacts with the elements of nature. Although the fifty daughters of Nereus and Doris are often represented as inhabitants of the deep and turbulent oceanic waters (as in the case of the acclaimed masterpiece of sculpture by the Argentine Lola Mora), there are also many images of them as delicate fairies who splash around in serene pools of waters and streamlets.

In the case of the Mexican nymphs, we see them sitting on top of enormous rocks, some larger than they are, and in one case they are semisub-

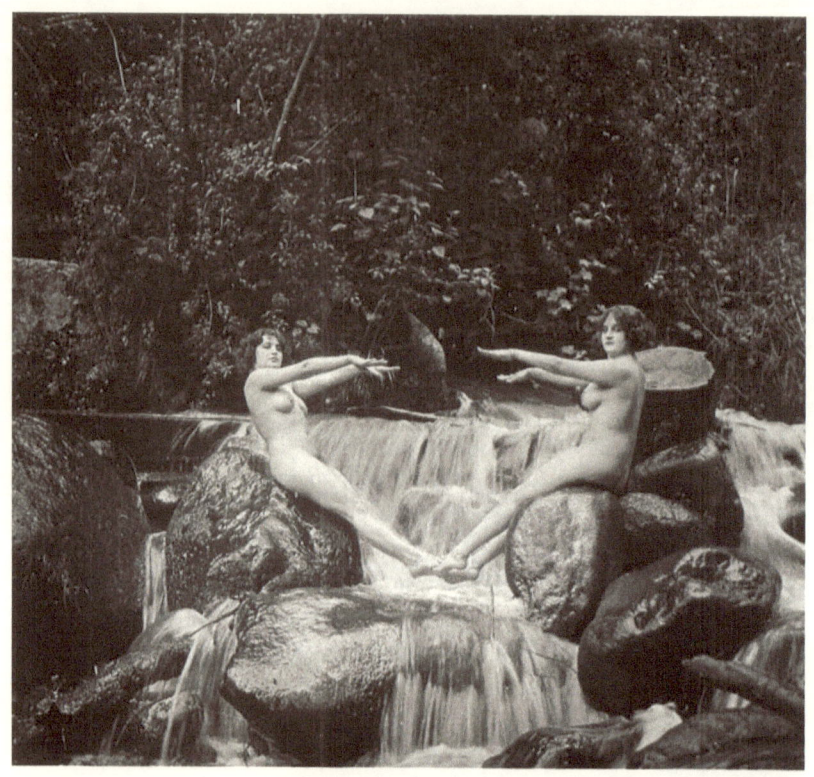

Figure 3.3. Prostitutes
posing as water nymphs.

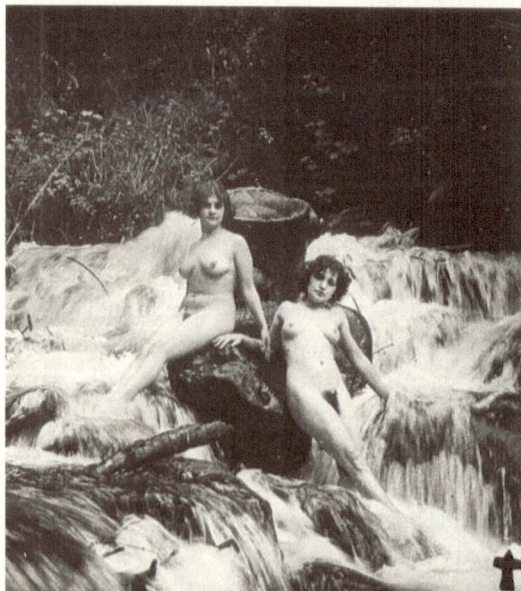

Figure 3.4. Prostitutes
posing as water nymphs.

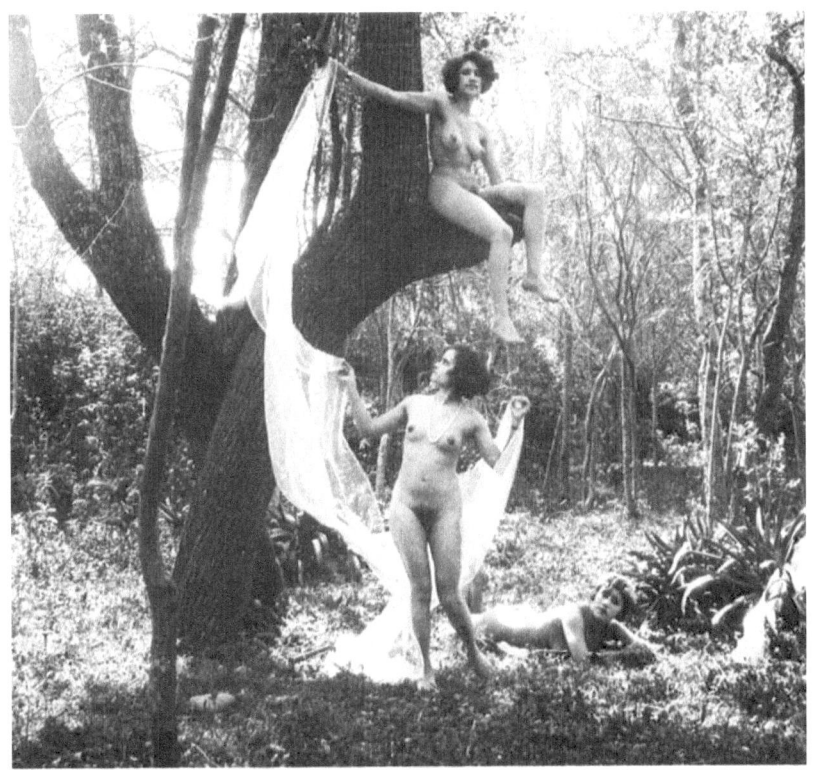

Figure 3.5. Prostitutes posing as forest sprites.

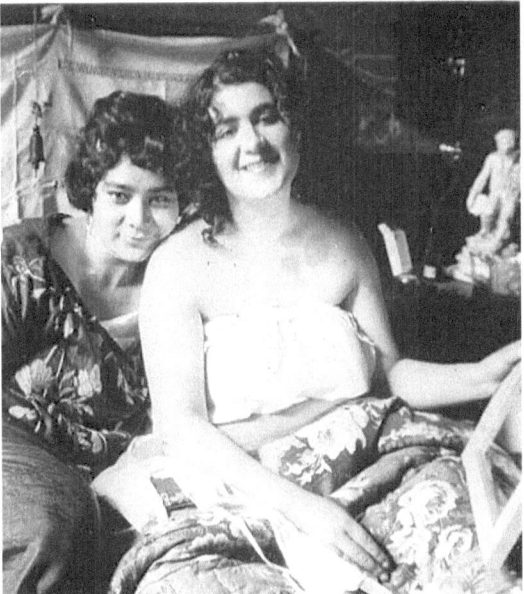

Figure 3.6. A moment of homosociality among prostitutes.

merged in the powerful currents of the rapids. In one of the four images, the attempt to achieve a classic tableau is apparent.

Despite all the efforts to direct the gaze of the viewer of this photography toward the paradigmatic models the women represent in contexts of the elegance to which high modernity aspired or against a Mexican landscape that is to be a remaking of Balbuena's new Tempe (yet the images of the women posed against the backdrop of majestic agave plants are in particular almost truculent), there is a fundamental characteristic that prevails above all else. It is the way in which the body placed on view is, once and for all, the body of a Mexican woman. Even if in the most highly priced brothels of Latin America the little French girls were the most highly prized object of attention for their delicacy, refinement, and erotic savoir, not all of the clients could aspire to such heights, and local flesh is what prevails, even in the most refined of sporting dens, with all the dimensions imposed by the ethnic origin, diet, lifestyle, circumstances of personal and collective health, and the personal story of each woman in terms of the trajectory that ended for her in *barrio galante.*[5] Each viewer will measure and appreciate in his own way the bodies of the women who gaze back at us across a century in Vargas's dossier, but in one photograph after another, these are bodies of women who are Mexican, regardless of the international privilege that the interior and exterior settings pretend to model. In this sense, one of the most eloquent photographs has to do with two women snuggling together on a bed, comfortable in their relationship of friendship and intimacy, with or without the lesbian dimension to be found in the back rooms of the women's world of the whorehouses. The Mexicanness of the two, and especially of the one on the left, is what most gives the touch of authenticity to these long-lost images.

BUENOS AIRES AND WOMEN IN CRISIS
The Photography of Silvina Frydlewsky

◆ ◆ ◆

I would like in this chapter to examine the photography by Silvina Frydlewsky included in *Crisis in Buenos Aires: Women Bearing Witness*, with the goal of providing interpretive comments for what I consider the most eloquent of the thirty images. There are also eighteen poems, all signed by Argentine women poets, included alongside these visual images. An important inaugural image is part of the cover of the book. This image, taken in the Café Tortoni, is subsequently paired with a poem, and I will discuss the poem below. Located on the Avenida de Mayo near the Avenida 9 de Julio and blocks from the Casa Rosada, Argentina's government house, the Tortoni evokes the rich social and cultural history of Buenos Aires. Along with the much-decayed Ideal, also located a few blocks away and now mostly a tango club, the Tortoni belongs to the tradition of elegant afternoon teas, posh cocktail hours, and late-night soirées. The café retains its Belle Époque elegance and is now an important stop on the thriving tourist circuit of a very much in vogue Buenos Aires (as part of that circuit, the Tortoni also includes a small theater space for late-night tango shows). The Tortoni evokes a bygone Buenos Aires, that of the so-called *vacas gordas* (fat cows), when Argentina was one of the strongest economic powers of the world and it was important for the elite to maintain the image of Buenos Aires as the Paris of the Southern Hemisphere. Little is left of that image and its material traces, and the Tortoni survives as a relic, as an archaeological find that indexes a way of life that disappeared something like eighty years ago.

Frydlewsky's shot is organized around two principal visual references. One is a depth shot that emphasizes the cathedral-like quality of this cultural icon. The mirror at the end of the nave-like passage between tables reduplicates the outlines of the café and amplifies the rich interior of highly polished woods; marble floors, columns, and tabletops; an abundant display on the walls of traditional art and photographs; impeccably maintained red leather chairs; crystal chandeliers, along with a lead glass skylight. Although the patrons do not seem particularly elegant (long into the 1960s, men were still required to wear coat and tie in such establishments), in one's eye one can envision what the place must have looked like populated with the denizens of Buenos Aires's long-lost café society. Indeed, the Tortoni can be read as something like a symbol of what Argentina once was (with all of the socioeconomic disparities of that epoch), what Argentina has become (perhaps with other but no less severe socioeconomic injustices . . .), and the self-image Argentina would like to maintain, which is what drives the current tourist interest. In truth, perhaps today more foreigners than Argentines frequent the Tortoni.

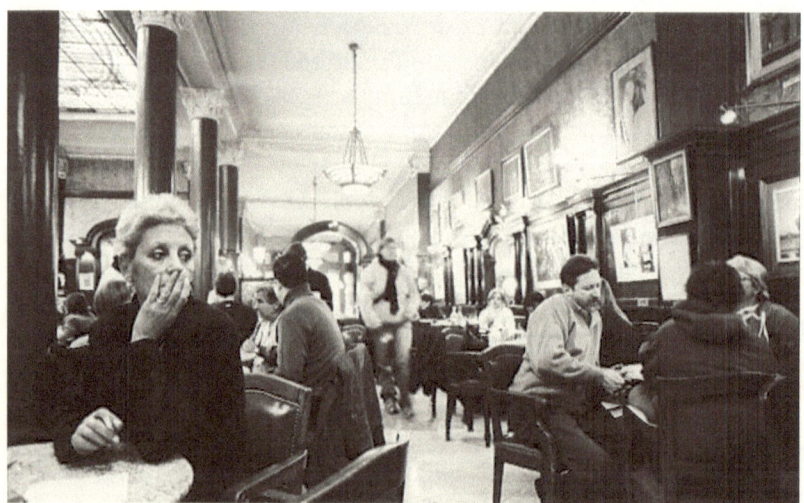

Figure 4.1. Silvina Frydlewsky, Café Tortoni, Buenos Aires. Used with permission of Silvina Frydlewsky.

However, there is another point of reference in Frydlewsky's photograph, and that is the middle-aged/late-middle-aged woman seated at a table in the left-hand foreground (because so many women of even limited means have plastic surgery in Argentina as a matter of course, it is often difficult to guess with any assurance the generation of "women of a certain age"; hair dyed blonde is frequent among women of all ages and social classes). It is not clear whether she is scrutinizing someone or something that lies outside of the frame of the photograph or whether she is staring off into space. In any event, she appears to be alone, enjoying a solitary cigarette, and probably espresso coffee, which is also outside the frame of reference; she also appears to have some sort of document before her, although she is no longer paying it any heed.

One of the major Argentine cultural motifs is the eponymous title of Raúl Scalabrini Ortiz's 1931 interpretive essay, *El hombre que está solo y espera* (The man who stands alone, waiting). Scalabrini Ortiz's essay, which references a major downtown street corner, Corrientes and Esmeralda, just steps away from the Ideal and blocks away from the Tortoni, invokes the silent, passive, blank despair of the Argentine who senses he has been excluded from the project of modernity that accounts for the city's much-vaunted Belle Époque (and Art Déco) elegance, a project that may have forged a solid financial and political elite, a solid middle class, and considerable social mobility for the children of foreign immigrants and, later, the children of those who migrated from the provinces to Buenos Aires. Yet something was always not quite right, and this is what Scalabrini Ortiz's protagonist embodies in his feelings of socioemotional dislocation. Of course, Scalabrini Ortiz is unrelentingly masculinist in his assessment of Porteño alienation,[1] and one searches his document in vain for any reference to the presumed "mujer que está sola y espera" (woman who is alone, waiting).

It is necessary to turn to feminist writing for such a recovery of the stories of the other half of Argentine society, and Martha Mercader's 1981 novel *Solamente ella* (Her alone) could well have borne as a subtitle the feminine version of Scalabrini Ortiz's now famous phrase. Indeed, the cover of Mercader's novel shows a woman posed almost exactly like the one in Frydlewsky's photograph, although she is much younger (yet equally blonde) and the café in question is much humbler and more of the neighborhood variety, of which there must be thousands throughout the city, sometimes three to four on the corners of an intersection, even in the most modest reaches of the streets. Mercader's novel carries, below the photograph in question, a publicity pitch: "Ser mujer en la Argentina, pavada de proyecto" (It's a cockamamie idea to even think of being a woman in Argentina). Although Mercader's novel charts, in a good feminist fashion, the perils of a woman's attempts at self-empowerment in the unrelentingly masculinist/*machista* network of Argentine society, it also speaks to the historic struggle for independence of Argentine women.

Now, it is important to note that Argentine women—at least those of a certain economic status and often of a certain age—do enjoy a considerable range of social independence, moving visibly in the city to a degree that is quite unique for most of Latin America. Yet the issue is the degree to which these women are, nevertheless, "alone and waiting" for a personal fulfillment, for a measure of significant social intervention and participation, and a true empowerment that, when all is said and done, never comes. They are there, but what really does that mean? What is Frydlewsky's subject thinking, and where does she have to go and what does she have to do when she can no longer abide remaining—since there is virtually no restriction on how long one remains at a table in an Argentine café, long after the dregs of the coffee have turned cold and the last cigarette has been smoked—at her solitary table in the Tortoni? Frydlewsky's subject may remain staring off into space at the Tortoni for virtually as long as her male counterpart held down the corner of Corrientes and Esmeralda.[2] To be sure, a woman holding down a street corner would always be considered a prostitute and treated accordingly, although today such a man, too, could well be a prostitute (prostitution, by the way, is legal in Argentina, though pimping is not).

There is certainly an important social distinction between a street corner man (who might have ended up in trouble with the police, who at that time strictly enforced vagrancy laws) and the female denizen of an elegant café. Yet the vacancy of their stare and the vagrancy of their social presence are metonymies of the Buenos Aires crisis.

The poem by Marjorie Ross that accompanies the reappearance of the photo from the Tortoni in *Crisis in Buenos Aires* underscores the way in which a space such as the Tortoni, while evoking a past national splendor, also, through the exceptionality of its value as a social icon, in reality also evokes the Argentina of critical social decline. Ross organizes her poem in terms of a then/now axis, supported by the juxtaposition of past-tense description and present-tense circumstance. Each of the four stanzas is organized around a major theme in Argentine social history: the legendary figure of General San Martín, the Liberator of the Andes; the so-called Guerra Sucia, the dirty war mounted by the military dictatorship against left-wing subversion, which was often more alleged than proven; the dissolution of the boundary between European Buenos Aires and reputedly more Latin American Argentina, defined by the province of San José to the north and Tierra del Fuego to the south; and, finally, the *corralito*.[3] Overlapping this historical trajectory is an opening and closing frame that makes reference to childhood and its passing: in this case the loss of innocent childhood correlates with the loss by the poet of any remaining sense of idealism for her native land. The reference to childhood is anchored in the patriotic images associated with General San Martín, but even more to the children's magazine *Billiken*, which is essentially an archive of Argentine concepts of childhood and the values and beliefs associated with it for, principally, the period 1930–1970 (*Billiken* continues to be published and is now available online, but it no longer bears the iconicity it had in the mid-twentieth century). By contrast, the *corralito*, in addition to representing material disaster to so many Argentines, is credited also by the poetic "I" with the definitive destruction of her infancy.

This is an eloquent poem about the loss of patriotic nationalism and idealism and the icons that represent such sentiments. The poem is not without flaws, because there is a problem associated with mourning the loss of the supposed privileged status of Buenos Aires, not that it *must* live like the rest of Argentina and, by extension, the rest of Latin America. Yet to the extent that Buenos Aires has always been synonymous with Argentina and, more importantly, with the Argentine dream of a unique modernity on the continent and the overall social and cultural benefits such modernity purportedly brings with it, the collapse of Buenos Aires is also the collapse of the nation. Hence, the image is of Argentina as a whole bleeding to death. Needless to say—and herein lies the conjunction with Frydlewsky's photograph discussed above—we are dealing here with the feminist motif of the particular status of women as emblematic of sociohistorical disaster. If one can invest in the principle that the world is engineered and activated through male privilege and the masculinist ideology that endorses such privilege, while men may "stand alone and wait" because they are excluded from that privilege, then aside from those who may enjoy the masculinist power of the phallic woman, the vast majority of women, while not always and forever totally bereft of power, are essentially tangential to it. Thus the woman in the Tortoni, wrapped up in the solitary waiting of her lost and vacant stare, is very much homologous with the poetic "I" of Ross's poem.

Yet women constitute only one, albeit major, social sphere of the many overlapping ones that make up those sectors of Argentine society that fall—and, most significantly, continue to fall—outside the domains of power and privilege in early-twenty-first-century Argentina. One of the dramatically visible new spheres that has emerged since the late 2001 collapse of neoliberalism is the *cartoneros*. The *cartonero* is a person who gathers and sells discarded *cartón* (cardboard), and the presence of such individuals throughout Buenos Aires from the early evening hours until well after midnight is one of the most striking social phenomena of recent years.

It is often difficult to know when to place the beginnings of a social movement, because the root causes are often so diverse and involve so much history that a phenomenon is more the coming together of diverse circumstances than it is the orderly growth of the phenomenon from specific causes. In the case of the Argentine *cartoneros*, however, roots may at least be found in the decision in early 1991, by the new Carlos Menem government, to establish parity between the Argentine peso and the U.S. dollar. Prior to that time, although Argentina had had moments of economic prosperity and had competed favorably in the international marketplace, the peso had fluctuated considerably and in the late 1990s had fallen enough so that the Argentine standard of living, especially as viewed from the perspective of the Buenos Aires middle class, was seriously compromised. The economy of the fluctuating peso was based to a large extent on the ease of access to foreign goods that allowed the feeling that Argentines were able to live more or less at the level of the First World. Parity with the dollar, which was accompanied by the slogan "Argentina is First World," allowed for the enormous influx of American and European products, for cheap travel abroad to buy these products and to consume the culture of the First World, and for sustaining an image of Argentine prosperity (again, at least when viewed from Buenos Aires) dramatically different from that of other Latin American societies, including the often equally prosperous Brazil.

One of the features of the economic boom of neoliberalism that was driven by parity (never dollarization, as the Argentine peso was always maintained as legal tender, although major business operations had long been conducted exclusively in dollars) was the massive importation of foreign goods. These goods not only displaced those produced by Argentine and other Latin American economies (resulting, therefore, in the disappearance of local industries), but they generated an enormous amount of garbage: not only the detritus of discarded "outdated" products, but also the trash of the packaging of imported goods (see Gabriel Valansi's photography in my *Urban Photography in Argentina*). One of the most visible elements of this trash was cardboard boxes, cardboard boxes of all sizes and shapes, in which foreign products arrived.

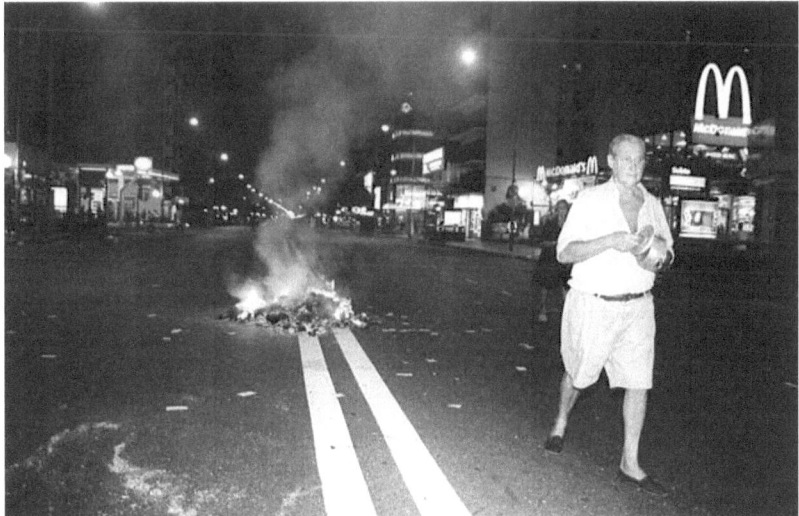

Figure 4.2. Silvina Frydlewsky, creating a public disturbance in downtown Buenos Aires to protest economic policies. Used with permission of Silvina Frydlewsky.

Neoliberal society pursued its course, driven by economic principles that seemed to many based on science fiction rather than sound financial policies, principles that, nevertheless, a middle class that benefited most from them subscribed to enthusiastically. Thus a rift arose between those who profited from neoliberalism and those who did not; that is, there began to emerge a radical division between economic classes. This was not unexpected by anyone able to examine objectively the workings of neoliberalism, which inevitably fueled a massive redistribution of wealth, with the equally inevitable emergence of a whole new—and, eventually, rapidly expanding—class of have-nots. Well before the precarious house of cards of neoliberal parity collapsed (which it did with enormous financial consequences and ensuing social violence and political instability in late 2001), Argentina was experiencing the presence of an impoverished class that was quite unique in its national history. This class notably included senior citizens, always a very large sector of Argentine society and one that the social security system and medical institutions had no longer treated in a beneficent manner. One very public response to the descent into abject poverty of senior citizens was a rash of public suicides to protest their marginalization. However, those benefiting from the stridently touted prosperity hardly took notice, as they opened more and more boxes of imported goods.

The production of trash by prosperity is one of the ironies of the improvement in living conditions that prosperity was supposed to bring. Neoliberal Buenos Aires may have, in general, become more and more elegant, but the streets at night were often mini-junkyards, and, as one might suspect, there was, ironically, a direct correlation between the quality of the garbage and the socioeconomic standing of a particular neighborhood of the city, with, concomitantly, a greater concentration of *cartoneros* in the more prosperous neighborhoods. At some point, the poor began to take advantage of what was being discarded, not only to incorporate the goods discarded by the prosperous into their own life, but also to initiate an economic process whereby trash could be exploited for its exchange value. One of the most significant items in both cases was the cardboard box, which could be used as building material and could relatively easily be recycled. Thus was born the *cartonero* phenomenon.

Today, the *cartoneros* are an organized lumpen workforce. They pour into the central core of Buenos Aires, where, despite the fallback of the economy with the collapse of the neoliberal enterprise, there is still a significant level of prosperity. They encounter much garbage awaiting disposal. Typically, these individuals—men, women, older persons, teenagers, and children—come in from the marginal suburbs of the province of Buenos Aires (the city of Buenos Aires is the so-called Federal District of the country, but it is geographically, if no longer administratively, a part of the province of Buenos Aires). Since Buenos Aires is a major port city,

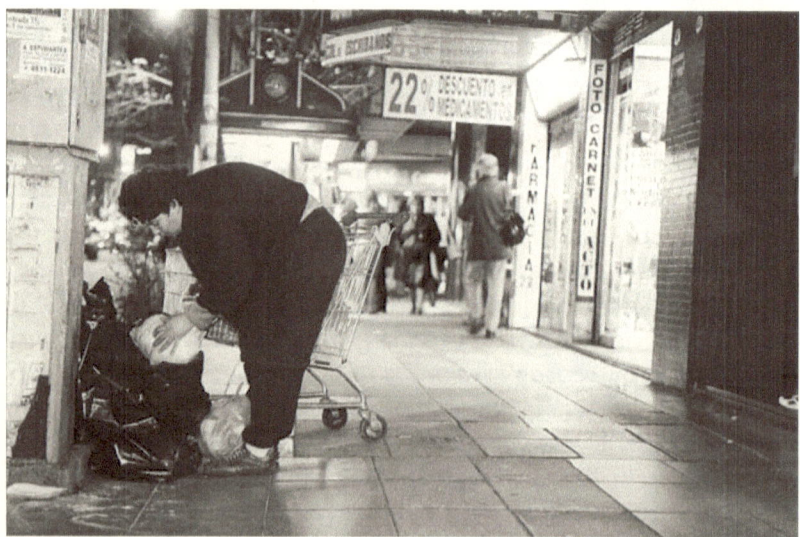

Figure 4.3. Silvina Frydlewsky, used cardboard gatherer in downtown Buenos Aires. Used with permission of Silvina Frydlewsky.

goods enter through the capital, and much of the garbage is, therefore, confined to the central core of the city (it should be noted that not all this garbage derives from foreign products; it is simply that foreign products brought the issue of the growth of garbage to the fore). *Cartoneros* often arrive by train, and a special train has been designated for them, not out of social concern but in order to segregate them from "decent" passengers. Made up of battered rolling stock, these trains have cars minimally configured to accommodate the carts of the *cartoneros*. Their carts arrive and depart empty, the contents being sold at distribution points before the *cartoneros* return on the train: El Tren Blanco (the White Train), as it is called.

The *cartoneros* are not to be confused with the *picoteros*, individuals who protest their un(der)employment and the way in which the banks defrauded them of their savings (thus, many are more middle class than the *cartoneros* are likely to be). The *picoteros* often disrupt transit and business, frequently in gross and disagreeable ways, while the *cartoneros* consider themselves to be gainfully employed social subjects. It is important to note, without disparaging the legitimate causes that motivate the *picoteros*, that, aside from enjoying the support of some political figures, they do not enjoy widespread social endorsement in Argentine society. By contrast, considerable public sympathy has emerged for the *cartoneros*. Undoubtedly, many comfortable inhabitants of Buenos Aires are not happy to have to maneuver around this highly visible workforce in the nighttime streets of the city (both Argentine café society and the large bohemian community have always considered the nighttime streets to be their privileged social space), but it is evident that the *cartoneros* are attempting to survive with the current economic system in an industrious and apparently effective manner. And they do make garbage collection much easier, since they themselves carry away trash that previously the municipality had to pay to dispose of.

Part of the support for the *cartoneros* has resulted from their recognition as a valid social movement by intellectuals and artists. They have grown to be seen by many not as a passing manifestation of an unstable economy, but as an integral part of an unexpected impoverishment of Argentina that is not likely to go away anytime soon; nor, indeed, are the *cartoneros* likely to go away anytime soon.

The Eloísa Cartonera publishing program is one of the ways in which the *cartoneros* have received recognition by the intellectual establishment, which has been concerned to provide them with acceptable visibility (as in Nahuel García's fine 2003 documentary film, *El Tren Blanco*, which allows several of the *cartoneros* to speak in their own voice), financial underwriting for establishing the infrastructure of the movement, and, more than anything else, legitimating dignity as valued social subjects.

Eloísa Cartonera (a name that is significant in recognizing the feminine—and perhaps even feminist—component of the phenomenon) allows established and newer authors (mostly Argentine, and mostly young, although some texts are by deceased figures) to donate short texts that are reproduced photostatically. The copies are then bound in cardboard covers, and the latter are hand-painted in multicolored acrylic. The clumsiness of this medium for lettering contributes to the unique appearance of these publications. Two hundred such publications are now in print, although only a handful has made it into library catalogs in the United States.

There are numerous photographs by Frydlewsky that capture the phenomenon of the *cartoneros*. Interestingly, these photographs also function in conjunction with images of middle-class citizens, often members of the so-called *tercera edad* ("third age," the Argentine euphemism for senior citizen status). They are images in which we see such otherwise invisible participants in the prosperity of modern Buenos Aires protesting their descent into economic marginality, if not outright poverty. They are present on the street, protesting individually or in groups, often assaulting establishments thought to be responsible for or complicit with the corruption of the economic collapse, or, on occasion, engaging outright in the imperatives of destitution, such as begging and garbage picking, these activities constituting a grim bridge between the haves and the have-nots of, to use a quite appropriate cliché here, the urban monster.

There is a cluster of Frydlewsky's photographs that supports the characterization of the *cartoneros* here. All three capture some of the most elegant sites of the city. The first begins with the Recoleta, famous for the colonial church where the elite of the country are baptized, married, and mourned before being buried next door at the European-style *città dei morti* (city of the dead). But the Recoleta is also one of the city's major museum, restaurant, and club areas, near the elegant shopping street of Avenida Alvear, which is anchored by the oligarchic Alvear Palace and the location also of the papal nunciature and foreign embassies like those of the Brazilians and the French. Here, during the nighttime apogee of the visible social life of the wealthy, the tourists, and sundry glitterati, the streets are shared with the *cartoneros* as well as the impoverished garbage pickers in general: as much as the practices of the privileged generate waste, so in like measure do those excluded from privilege avail themselves of the surplus value of what is thrown away. It is significant that Frydlewsky's photographs capture the terrible irony of the juxtaposition between the tattered appearance of the *cartoneros* as they rummage through the trash and the comfortable dress of those who participate in the nightlife of the Recoleta, who park their expensive cars alongside the mounds of garbage on the sidewalks, framed by the luxuriant verdancy of one of the most attractively landscaped areas of the city.

The second photograph features another of the most elegant venues of the city. The Teatro Colón, the Buenos Aires opera house considered to rank third internationally among such grand palaces devoted to the musical arts, is one of the signature buildings of the city. It has recently undergone renovation for its rededication on its hundredth anniversary. Buenos Aires is rightly proud of such a magnificent theater, but the Colón is, nevertheless, not exempt from history. Garbage may not litter its entryway or the sidewalk around it, but it is much in evidence in the spaces outside the frame of this photograph. Moreover, the entrance faces the Plaza Lavalle (whose other architectural monument is Tribunales, the seat of the Argentine judiciary), which, like most of the city's famous plazas, attracts the homeless and the destitute. In recent years, pensioners, who have been left to their own devices by the virtual devastation of the retirement system, have, along with others, taken to creating emergency abodes in the area.

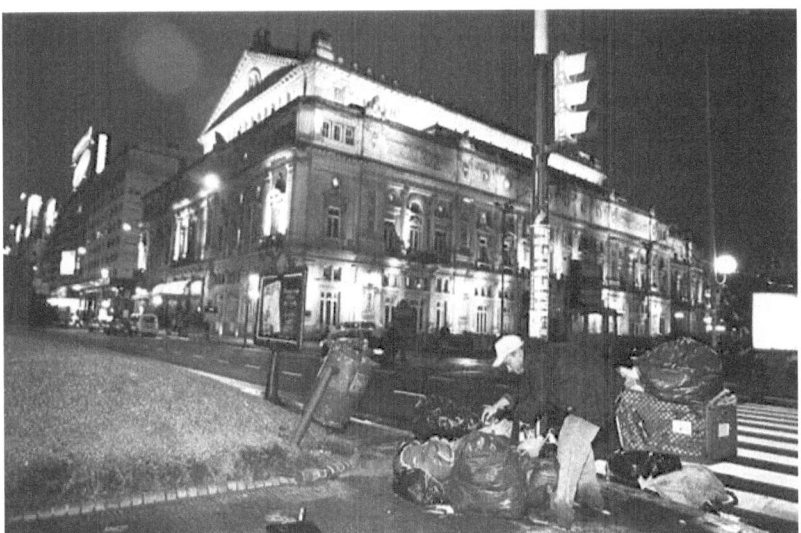

Figure 4.4. Silvina Frydlewsky, garbage picker outside the Buenos Aires opera house, the Teatro Colón. Used with permission of Silvina Frydlewsky.

The third photograph of this group captures the second-story café located in the public area of the Galería (sometimes called Galerías) del Pacífico. This extensive shopping mall is the remodeled central headquarters of the train system built by the British in the late nineteenth century, and it, like many other edifices along the kilometer-long pedestrian street Florida, is a monument to the Generation of 1880, which inaugurated the project of modernity in Argentina and gave it its first boom period of the *vacas gordas*. One immediately notes both the elegance of the accoutrements of the café and the comfortable socioeconomic status radiated by the seated clients, but also the fashion status of the boutiques to be seen in the background (this is a sector catering to male fashion). But like the Colón, the Pacífico cannot escape history. Florida is a pale shadow of its former splendor, and formidable private security agents must be stationed at each of the three entrances of the building to control closely who enters the mall. Outside, the street teems with beggars of all stripes, pickpockets, ragtag performers, assorted crazies, and, in general, a plethora of individuals (local citizens and recently arrived immigrants from the provinces and surrounding Latin American countries, where things are worse off socially and economically than they are in Buenos Aires) who stand no chance whatever of being given access to the commercially hallowed space of Pacífico. Meanwhile, outside the entrances to the side (Avenida Córdoba) and back (Calle San Martín), it is business as usual with the garbage the *cartoneros* rely on to survive. San Martín leads to the heart of La City, the main financial quarter, which is particularly attractive to the *cartoneros*, as well as to a host of individuals, many children, who take over the streets and doorways at night.

Frydlewsky's photographic triptych (there are many other images of *cartoneros* and the down-and-out elsewhere in the dossier) is accompanied by Gladys Ilarregui's poem "Buenos Aires: historia del anochecer" (Buenos Aires: a story of nightfall). For many, nightfall is always a particularly poetic time of day, with the transition it signals from workaday routine to the twin joys of relaxation and entertainment. It is a commonplace to say that a city like Buenos Aires changes character with the coming of night, precisely because of all of the intense nightlife the city has to offer, and even more so now with the burst of international tourism there. But the night has also always brought out some of the most unsavory elements of the urbanscape. Many would include the *cartoneros* among the latter, although as I have tried to argue above, their activities are related to survival in the city without, except in a symbolic way, interfering with the comfort of the privileged local or the tourist, whom they may discomfort with their presence but whom they do not otherwise molest. A greater threat is posed by roving gangs of muggers and flimflam artists dressed to look indistinguishable from their victims.

Ilarregui centers her poem on the omnipresent bags of garbage and refuse containers, to provide an aura for the city that is counteridyllic. The poetic voice identifies Buenos Aires as "la ciudad paris" (the Paris-like city), a denomination that echoes the legendary claim that Buenos Aires is the Paris of the South, while at the same time categorically diminishing that claim: not only is the phrase cited in lower case (and it is "paris," mockingly the French not the Spanish spelling), but also the syntax creates a false exocentric compound equivalent to the English "paris city"—that is, a city defined appositionally by whatever the lower-case qualifier "paris" might be taken to mean.

The poem goes on, like Ross's, to contrast a then versus a now, the then being the elegant, "imperturbable" city of old black-and-white photographs, as contrasted with the now of piles of garbage turned wild and murderous spectators driven by the devastations of a city where nightfall segues into nightmare, where the imperturbability of yesteryear is the "ira," the rage, of today. The night, in the end, reaffirming a symbolic meaning for the night that far antedates that of the glistening splendor of prosperity, records death through the image of refuse, "un objeto roto" (a broken object).

I would like to conclude this commentary on these juxtaposed poetic and photographic texts by returning to the urban stories of women. Another one of the images of a garbage picker involves a woman and, it would appear, her two preteenage children, a little girl and an older boy. The locale is recognizably Barrio Norte, near Plaza Vicente López. We see lovely residential buildings along with mixed small commercial establishments, a typical demographic distribution for the city; there is a handsome late-model car in the background. Somehow, the woman has obtained a grocery cart, and we can see how her daughter is sitting astride the successful pickings of the night; plastic bags containing other items hang from the cart, and a large plastic bag filled with cardboard cores leans against it. All three figures are cleanly dressed (not always the case with the *cartoneros*, as their work is often dirty), and the older child is holding what may be a bag of food, perhaps recovered from the garbage.

There is no way of knowing if the woman is a single mother, although this is a strong statistical likelihood. Even if there is a husband/father off somewhere else, working (which could involve picking garbage elsewhere) or not, there is no other choice for the woman but to have her

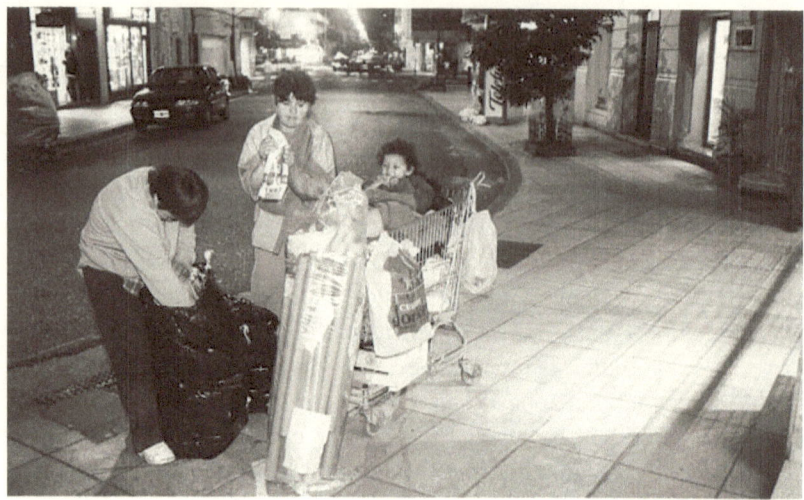

Figure 4.5. Silvina Frydlewsky, an impoverished street family garbage picking in an elegant neighborhood of Buenos Aires. Used with permission of Silvina Frydlewsky.

children with her. While the older child may assist her in sifting the garbage, there is no escaping the fact that the nuclear family here involves, unimpeachably, a mother and her children: to trope a religious assertion defending the nuclear (and fully parentally constituted) family, the family that picks garbage together stays together. A fair number of Frydlewsky's photographs depict women in the process of sorting through rubbish, as though this were somehow a gender-determined participation in the country's economic system. I particularly liked one accompanied by another poem by Gladys Ilarregui, "Regina/Reina," which evokes not only the image of woman as queen of the household (the two halves of the title are, respectively, the Latin and the Spanish words for "Queen"), but also the sanctification of women's lives by, in the vein of the traditional Catholicism relentlessly invoked by the elite when they have no other response to social and economic crisis, ascribing to women their inheritance as daughters of the Virgin Mary, Regina Coeli (the Queen of Heaven). This is specifically articulated by the poetic voice, which insists that these women (e.g., the one represented in the photograph and her sisters) lack the saintly halo of the Renaissance icons—and, one might add, the ones to be viewed in the churches found along the *via dolorosa* (painful route) that takes these queens of the contemporary Porteño streets from one sack of garbage to another.

The dossier includes two images of the same family taken at different moments in the same locale; the second one shows the mother offering food (undoubtedly pulled from the garbage) to her younger child, a little girl. Additionally, there is a third image of various women going through a large mound of garbage bags. Again, the locale is one of middle-class prosperity, which is, as I have insisted, what generates the garbage that provides a livelihood for these women.

These three photographs are accompanied by a poem signed by Delfina Muschetti. The poetic "I" speaks of being awakened during the night by the various sounds associated with garbage picking. The neighborhood is the upscale bedroom community of Olivos, which just happens to be where the presidential residence, with its vast private preserve, is located. There is a basic narrative concerning the privileged and private existence of the narrator, which involves her in generating the garbage that she subsequently, before going to bed, places outside her residence. Once asleep, the narrator is awakened by the garbage come alive through the agency of the *cartoneros*, who produce an array of noises characteristic of the manipulation of the plastic bags, the various forms of garbage, and the (usually primitive) cart on which profitable leavings are taken away. There is an interplay among various words and phrases relating to nothingness: garbage becomes a nothingness for the narrator by being discarded, but the garbage pickers also constitute a nothingness in their shadowy and underindividuated existence: we hear and see them for a moment, and then they are gone, moving on to another mound of garbage down the street. Too, the silence of the night is a nothingness that has been interrupted by the nocturnal incursions of people always from an unknown somewhere else, although the narrator perceives that the "ruido nuevo sorpresivo" (surprising and [entirely] new noise) is here to stay: given the reference to Olivos, it would be no stretch of meaning for the poem to insist that this noise has become a permanent fixture of the placid suburban setting. And Olivos, too, cannot exist outside the history being transcribed here.

One final note: Frydlewsky's photographs are presented in lush color, quite distant in their artistic, almost hyperrealistic, texture from grainy journalistic images or those of paradigmatic documentary filmmaking, of which there is a long inventory in Argentina (compare the gritty texture of color in García's aforementioned *El Tren Blanco*). One could even say that such heightened color here aestheticizes Frydlewsky's subjects and is, therefore, insulting to them and their struggle for survival. Yet Frydlewsky, I would maintain, cannot be accused of monumentalizing the impoverished and the miserable in the fashion of the Brazilian Sebastião Salgado's often strongly criticized photographic canvases. Rather, because so many of the images focus on marginal subjects surrounded by the opulence of a mythic First World Argentina, the contrast between that opulence—the streets, the architecture, the cars, the clothes, the spaces of privileged consumerism—and those who are marginalized by it is made all the more painfully manifest.

I have made much here of the continuity of women's life on the fringe because of their exclusion from the commercial and financial dynamics of their society. But it is also evident that, as with the woman depicted in the cover photograph, being able to partake of privileged opulence can be chimeric: both sectors of women are witnesses to a national crisis from which there, for the time being, appears to be no return.

GIRLS WILL BE GIRLS
Daniela Rossell's *Ricas y famosas*

◆ ◆ ◆

One of the most interesting Mexican imprints of 2002 was Daniela Rossell's notebooks of photographs, *Ricas y famosas* (Rich and famous women). A note that precedes them reads, in Spanish with an English translation: "Las siguientes imágenes muestran escenarios reales. Los sujetos fotografiados están representándose a sí mismos. Cualquier semejanza con la realidad no es una circunstancia" (no pag.).[1] This trope, involving a concluding litotes of the standard disclaimer of fiction, introduces approximately fifty high-density color images of the rich and famous women of Mexico City (a few men are featured, without explanation). These women inhabit—and rule over—the vast residential estates of various Mexican cities and the Mexican capital, in the case of the latter those found behind walls and tight security systems in the Bosques de las Lomas, San Ángel, El Pedregal, and Santa Fe, the poshest districts of the city. Some of the photographs were also done elsewhere, as it is possible to discern the New York skyline outside the window of the plush setting in a few of the photographs.

Much has been made of an alleged disingenuous and duplicitous nature of Rossell's work. Rossell, it has been maintained, comes from the same social class as these women, and they are supposed to have had no idea that she would publish the photographs they allowed her to take (many in very intimate situations within their homes), nor that her publication would be promoted as a form of social denunciation.[2] Press coverage, which was quite extensive in Mexico and abroad when the book first came out in late summer 2002, spoke of death threats against her and related how a double stood in for Rossell at the formal presentation of the book by the publisher, and one wonders if the enormous sales success of this expensive book was as much a matter of the curiosity of the general Mexican readership as it was a campaign of acquisition by the subjects, torn between their pride at being photographed in such a public way and a competing desire to make the book disappear from public view (since there is virtually no censorship in Mexico, one tactic is simply for the powerful to buy the entire press run of an offensive title).

A general reaction to *Ricas y famosas* has been the repudiation of the social image it represents: idle women with enormous disposable incomes such that they may dress extravagantly and bejewel themselves in an almost ludicrous manner, disporting themselves in domestic settings overflowing with the most expensive furniture and accompanying appointments, engaging in all manner of provocative attitudes, in general bordering on the outrageous, scandalous, and, in more than one case, the sacrilegious (see Camps's review and Brooksbank Jones's essay, which includes summaries of Mexican commentaries). These are women whose access to disposable wealth is matched by their surfeit of disposable time, such that they are able to fill their days with conspicuous consumption and the organization of playful activities such as the photographic sessions with Rossell; one supposes that these women must devote their nights to the *ricos y famosos* (rich and famous men) who support them, fulfilling the obligations of matrimony, a principal one of which is being a trophy wife to the plutocrats of Mexican society.

To be sure, there are many ways of reading these photographs in terms of social denunciation, whether intentional on the part of the photographer or as the unavoidable consequence of the juxtaposition of these images, via publication, with another, more universal, photographic record of the circumstances of daily life of the vast majority of the Mexican populace, whose only sustained contact with these women is to work for them as their silent and obedient servants. One might well wonder, however, what thoughts and feelings lurk behind the mask of the servant, compelled not only to engage in the customary tasks of service, but, as in the case of a striking illustrative image, to put on display for the camera his subservience and the material differences of his class and ethnic origin. In the image, a dark-skinned and sullen servant, with dark hair and the trace of facial hair surrounding his mouth, looks into the camera as he holds a silver tray containing what one assumes is a shot of tequila. His mistress is lounging on an expensive decorator couch next to him, framed by two portraits of women, which may or may not be her; perhaps in the case of one, it is her mother. Dressed in fire-engine red, her pale skin is complemented by her straight bleached-blonde hair. Both mistress and servant look into the camera, although it is as if the camera were triangulating a sexual tension between them: the woman's gaze is sexually seductive, and the viewer might well ask if the camera is intervening in the erotic demands the woman could well make on the man. Whereas the rules of service require a cluster of performance traits that can be captured, synecdochically, by the imperative of the downcast gaze, the presence here of the camera and the obligation to perform his service for the gaze of the camera require that the servant acknowledge the presence of the camera by directing his gaze, in a fashion that parallels that of his mistress, in its direction, thereby assuming a physical stance that is anomalous with that of routine attendance to his mistress.

Yet other commentators have detected a note of hypocrisy in the denunciations of such widely divergent sources as the chronicler of the elite, Guadalupe Loaeza, to *Proceso*, a weekly whose fine journalism is, nevertheless, devoted to being a major platform for Mexico's broad constituency on the intellectual left. Cuauhtémoc Medina, writing in the daily *Reforma*, observes that

lo radical de las imágenes de Rossell no es sólo abrirnos las puertas a casas vedadas por guaruras, murallas y rejas eléctricas, función que, sin que nadie se inmute, cumplen las secciones de sociales de los diarios y las revistas de cotilleo. Más que mostrarnos "cómo viven" los privilegiados, Ricas y famosas hace alusión a cómo quisieran vivir; no qué son, sino cómo se imaginan.

Las fotos de Rossell son siempre una puesta en escena de una multitud contradictoria de fantasías adquiridas desordenadamente en casas de antigüedades, tiendas departamentales, safaris, viajes e infinidad de supermercados. Lo que Rossell ha documentado es el esfuerzo desesperado de una clase por crearse un "otro lugar" distinto al collage de miseria campesina, industrialización bárbara y urbanismo parapléjico que los demás habitamos.[3]

However, it is not difficult to detect a note of hypocrisy in Rossell's photographs, as much from the point of view of the subjects as from that of the photographer herself.[4] The proposition that her images merely serve to capture a neutral reality and to show individuals in their own "homes and workplaces" and to capture them "photographed next to their personal belongings" sounds very much like this is Mexican social reality quite like and innocently parallel to any other when, of course, it is not. The social class represented by *Ricas y famosas* is able to create another, privileged space in counterpoint to the "real Mexico" because its members have the economic wherewithal to do so. Moreover, there is, as a consequence, a directly proportional relationship between the features of that real Mexico and those of the imaginary (concrete but inhabited as though located elsewhere than in Mexico) world of these individuals, who are, in fact, in a position to wall themselves off from any less palatable and more inconvenient life in Mexico. The note of overwhelming excess is proportional to the degree of misery in the country, and the splash, panache, glitter, and gloss, which might, from someone else's point of view, be viewed as the deepest of kitsch and the most wretched of taste, is the countervailing pole to the dull, mean, and dreadful misery to be found in the version of real Mexico portrayed in the first segment of Alejandro González Iñárritu's 2001 film *Amores perros* (in González Iñárritu's film, the misery of this segment is contrasted with the advertisement-set comfort of the fashion model's apartment of the second segment). For example, one of the recurring features of the photographs is not merely one adornment, but its multiplication almost ad infinitum, such that the living human being, literally submerged in the sea of the proliferating adornments, becomes one with them.[5]

The world that Rossell portrays is a model of what most Mexicans want in place of what most Mexicans get, and one can hardly believe that most Mexicans would not be content to trade the reality of their daily lives for a shred of the prosperity, no matter how one measures its aesthetic quality, of the privileged. At that, a few of the wretched of the Mexican earth do get to aspire to a modicum of that privilege, to the extent that they achieve employment as servants of these women and their husbands. This is evident in the way in which, discounting the colophon image of a woman holding a bar decoration that reads "He who dies with the most toys wins," the opening and closing images of *Ricas y famosas* involve the servants.

The first image features a servant with clear mestizo features, dressed in an almost hot pink uniform with saucy cutesy-face sandals, against the backdrop of fuchsia and purple upholstered furniture in a huge living room with walls painted in old rose. The color coordination of walls, furniture, and maid's uniform virtually makes her part of the décor, and her jauntily provocative pose makes it look like she is proud to be a part of this supposedly elegant montage. The final image is a double spread, and it features the entire assembled staff of one of the households where Rossell shot her photographs. There are no less than thirty-seven individuals ranged, as though in a school photograph, up and down, from one side to the other, along a marble stairway. Many are displaying the elements of their particular function within the household: one woman holds up the plug of an iron at her feet; another woman displays an adding machine; a man holds a pair of garden shears; another man, a pair of car keys; while there are no less than three men wearing chef's hats. The back, uppermost row is made up of four hard-faced men in guayaberas (three in dark glasses), who hold cell phones: they are obviously the bodyguards. One cannot say that the expressions of these thirty-seven servants (and it is apparent there is a hierarchy among them—for example, between those who are in uniform and those who are not) express the joys of servitude, but as the discourse of property goes, they should be glad they have a job, and one cannot be faulted for supposing they are. Some might reasonably be even proud to be working in the household of such a mighty family.

These two photographs frame the main body of Rossell's images of the *ricas y famosas*, and I would now like to detail what some of the interesting points of these images are.

In the first place, one is struck by the kittenish attitude of the majority of these women. By this I mean not only their relative youth: Mexico is, after all, a society with an extremely youthful base of the demographic pyramid, and there are few women here who look to be much older than thirty years old. To be sure, questions regarding the sexism of lookism and the paradigms of feminine beauty are involved here, and not all of these women are the *Playgirl*-type wives of captains of Mexican society. Some are, in fact, their daughters, who have been efficiently and effectively inscribed within the idle rich paradigm of their mothers. But these women are kittenish in a different way, in the specifically sexual sense of the word, as though the privacy of their own inner sanctums provided them with the license to engage in provocative body display of a sensual-to-sexual nature in a way that would not be possible in the decorous streets and plazas of the public façade of the Mexican bourgeoisie. But there is a third dimension of kittenish here, and that is the way in which the model for the Mexican trophy wife is the infantilized woman, more often than not a Barbie-doll bleached blonde. The projected insouciance of these women, where even explicit sexualization is framed in a baby-doll fashion, is the image of a world in which women may remain children because they do not need—or must pretend that they do not need—to face the harsh facts of life beyond the borders of their inner sanctums.

One of the most interesting dimensions of the display of these child-ish sex kittens lies in both the presumed scandal of their interaction with male servants and their potentially homoerotic interaction with each other. In various images, these women, lounging in a carefree fashion on the expansive stretches of their furniture, are being attended to by their servants, who are at stiff and obsequious attention. This is the nature of the wraparound cover image, in which a gold-lamèd, barefoot, blonde, and pink-skinned lolling Lolita is tended by her standard-issue mestizo servant, who nevertheless breaks her passiveness to look up, with some-thing like a face of bewilderment, at the camera, which looks down on this scene from the rafters. The sexual edge appears, however, when the blonde mistress is waited on by her young virile manservant, the sort of Mexican specimen that could expect to do well with the foreign tourists in any one of the city's many pickup bars.

The note of homoerotism is a projected segue from the necessary ho-mosocialism of so many of these images, although in a few photographs men appear who are a part of these women's world and are, presumably, their consorts. In one image a highly sexualized leopard-skinned woman teases the camera, while a handsome upper-middle-class man—one as-sumes, her husband—looks on skeptically from the patio beyond the lanai doors of the bedroom on whose bed, almost leopard-skinned, she is pos-ing. But these are women who are left during the day to their own devices, which includes making a life with other women, relatives or social co-horts, who are as equally abandoned by their toy-acquiring husbands. We see these women posing together in similar clothing, engaged in similar poses and similar feigned activities, such as in one blasphemous image in which they are breaking and eating Offertory hosts over Communion chalices (Camps in his review refers to the recurring religious images of these photos [168–169]).

One image that sees this homosociality reaching toward homoerotism involves the reaction, on the lower level of the furniture and floor, of those in a vast drawing room to a huge wall panel depicting an Orientalist ha-rem. The women are in various stages of dress and undress in imitation of the scene of the harem, which involves explicitly displaying to each other and to the feminine eye of Rossell's camera their bodily charms. Whether or not they are directly aware of the lesbian possibilities of the Orientalist harem, in which women had more opportunity for sex with each other than they did with their master, is immaterial,[6] since only the most culturally uninformed viewer of the photograph can fail to capture the homoerotic latency of this double image of the harem.

There are many images of *Ricas y famosas* that have an insinuation of an erotic content. A few are heterosexual: the aforementioned photograph of the *rica* with her hypermasculine manservant, as though he were yet one more of her expensive decorative items. Some are autoerotic, such as the image of one scantily dressed woman who rides a fancy Mexican tooled-leather saddle mounted on a metal frame. The décor of the room is replete with images of Mexican masculinity: a bust that resembles Pancho Villa; a large wall painting of Emiliano Zapata; a PRI political pamphlet featuring a conventionally masculine Mexican candidate, mustache firmly in place; another photo of a conventionally masculine man, this time with beard, against the backdrop of the image of a Mexican revolutionary. The woman is wearing a cowboy hat, and her arm is extended out, covering the forehead of the Zapata painting, with an appropriate phallic cigarette in her hand; her red-sandaled foot rests firmly on a stuffed alligator, another presumably phallic symbol. Her expression is one of starry-eyed defiance. Although this is perhaps the most overtly sexual, a good number of the photographs feature women alone in vaguely or suggestively erotic poses: one is in a sensual trance against a backdrop of crucifixes (this only one of several images that are, by traditional Mexican Catholic standards, blasphemous); another poses in a low-cut zebra outfit, seated on two different animal pelts, with a stuffed tigress prancing toward her; another is watching two dogs copulate at the foot of a fully appointed altar in what looks like the home chapel; the pose of another, breasts flowing out of her leather top, thumb hooked in her pants as if to drag them down, is juxtaposed to a conventional image of the Virgin of Guadalupe; another, dressed in a red outfit with plunging neckline, but wearing also a white fur coat and diadem, sits with her legs spread, her hands barely covering the pubic area of her taut panties. The woman in another image is dressed as an odalisque, surrounded by a medley of Orientalist images.

Finally, there are photographs of women together, such as the one of the harem enactment. There is a two-panel sequence of four women, seen first strutting their stuff in front of another home altar and then, in an image I have already referred to, breaking Communion hosts together. (Is this the most sacrilegious image, or is it the one of the dogs copulating at the foot of the altar?) One can read these women as a version of vestal virgins/temple harlots, with a query as to what bonds them together in their poses in unison. There is another panel of three women who assume come-hither poses, each at the doorway of a row of public toilets. If this is a ladies room, one wonders just who, within the realm of the photograph, is the object of their invitational gazes. I do not mean to imply that Rossell has captured her subjects in frankly homoerotic conjugations (although there is one image of women engaging in a wrestling match on a bed). While there is always the possibility of dalliances, heterosexism is unquestionably the order of the day in the world of these women. And yet, one can assume that these apparently restless women are likely to have lovers, and why would one assume that they are going to cheat on their husbands only with other men? However, one is willing to beg the issue by falling back on the general tone of *épater le bourgeois* that characterizes *Ricas y famosas* in general, and accept that any insinuation of lesbian relations is only part of the "let's be outrageous" quality that is the overall stamp of Rossell's collection.

One of the notably outrageous dimensions of these photographs, in addition to the five or six that play with overt blasphemy, is the investment in the baby-doll look that seems to be a feature of femininity in the world depicted. Not only is there an abundance of dolls and stuffed animals (alongside full-sized taxidermy specimens), but there are photographs of women lounging among these toy animals (for example, one image of a woman plunged in her bed in a sea of such toys—little-girl pink dominates) and dressed in such a way as to correlate—either directly or in an inverse sense—with the dolls. This is the case with the woman in a fur coat, her legs spread to the camera: she is seated on a couch and flanked by dolls in an old-fashioned dress. In another photograph, an older woman is surrounded by all manner of stuffed dolls and animals, decked out in a glossy chiffon-pink leather outfit, with matching backpack. Next to her on the wall is the painting of a young girl, also done up in pink; perhaps it is a childhood portrait of her. The depiction of women as toy dolls is complemented by several images of young girls dressed to resemble sex kittens, as is the case with one lounging child, with pouty lips and an inviting stare, dressed in mesh stockings and wearing a short skirt decorated with a six of hearts playing card—although from the way she is posed, the six reads as a nine. Another photograph is that of a woman or young girl—it is difficult to gauge her age—who is pulling herself up what appears to be a scale model of the Eiffel Tower. The girlish note comes from, in addition to her teenybopper clothes, her dirty feet. Given the other overt sexual images in which *Ricas y famosas* abounds, it is not too far-fetched to see the tower as another phallic symbol.

Ricas y famosas is neither great photography nor is it—intended or otherwise—eloquent social criticism. It is mostly what it superficially seems to be: a photographic romp through the world of the Mexican superrich, who are only too willing to collaborate in posing themselves in mostly outrageous ways. While it might be worth imagining a measure of social criticism on Rossell's part—or, at least, subscribing to a reading of these photographs that constitutes a denunciation of the women of Mexico's leisure class—the element of playfulness that drives Rossell's camera is to be found in her self-portrait on the back flap of the book: Rossell poses in oversized glasses against the backdrop of a symbol of the PRI, the political party that, for the most part, sustains the wealth of her subjects. The green, white, and red orb of the party symbol frames her head like the conventional halo around the head of Catholic saints.

PEDRO MEYER

Constructing Masculinities, Constructing Photography

◆ ◆ ◆

Pedro Meyer, of German-Jewish descent, was born in Madrid in 1935. He is, at present, one of the most esteemed photographers of Mexico and Latin America. Breaking with a long tradition—passionately defended by masters such as Henri Cartier-Bresson—of photography as strictly and objectively documental in nature, Meyer, like his American counterpart Joel-Peter Witkin or the Argentine Marcos López (see chapter 10, on López, in this volume), sees in a photograph's composition and frame an open field for an intense semiotic elaboration of the image.

To this end, the camera's eye, far from being an ascetic observer of human life, encompasses a world that is arranged, created, and interpreted by the artist-photographer. It is fundamental to distinguish between the photographer who arrives fortuitously to capture what has already been made in and of itself or by unknown agents who are no longer present and the photographer who first creates a fragment of the world and who later takes a picture with his camera. In the first case, the photographer, presumably, puts the world, as it is, without interpretation, before the spectator who is not present, while, in the second case, the photographer sets before us a world he has already interpreted, inviting us to interpret his interpretation.

As much as there cannot be a completely objective, observant, and neutral photograph in the first case, there is an attempt to rigorously maintain the pact of nonmediation between the photographer and his audience. In the second case, the pact is precisely that the audience reflects upon a preordered world that has been interpreted by the photographer, who invites the audience to be an accomplice with him in the contemplation of possible worlds. If there is a pact in the second case, it is one that recognizes certain significant coordinates of the world of photography, while at the same time recognizing the legitimacy of the multiple combinations of said coordinates.

There will be those who maintain that, at the end, there is more of a continuum between these two positions—that of the absolute verism of the photo and the one that offers the photo as a "creationist" object—but one's sociocultural understanding of photographic work becomes strained when one recognizes the validity of both pacts, and of the hybrid combinations that may exist between them.[1]

As founder and president of the Mexican Consejo de Fotografía and director of Zone Zero, Meyer plays a prominent role in creating new tendencies for a national and continental photography that, in the wake of various guiding practices of sociopolitical commitment to Latin American "reality"—as much in the hands of autochthonous photographers as in those of foreign photographers—has been seen as a strictly verifiable document of historic experiences. Maintaining that "reality" and "truth" are not trivially and plainly present in realistic photography, Meyer and the artists that may be associated with him hold to an artistic ethos that aims to make the spectator understand that truly profound access to genuine reality lies in the interpretive efforts of the photographer, in which new transformations of signs cast and facilitate a more meaningful comprehension of history.

It is important to remember here that a word like "history" is fundamentally ambiguous, for it alludes to what one assumes "is really there," and, at the same time, it points to the interpretation that one can summon of that "really." That is why it is said that history never "is really there" and that one only has access to interpretations of it, some more scientific and eloquent than others; this is the deconstructionist moment in which one loses confidence in the certainty of accessing, transparently and without difficulty, what "is really."

It is not that one ends up constructing historic reality, but rather that one resynthesizes the scarce and fragile signs that one has access to in order to understand the world. Edward Weston must have thought that Mexico was spread out before the lens of his camera, waiting to be photographed with the best techniques of his time. For Meyer, it is not about improving the technique and the material elements of the photographic process with which Weston experimented throughout his career, but rather about constructing a subject to be photographed and manipulating it with all the resources that the digital process affords.[2]

Since Meyer's photographs point concretely to a historic reality that the audience can recognize, it is senseless to speak of a "creation of reality," a "surrealist fantasy," or any other parallel reading. No one can assert that Meyer does not portray a historic reality that is immediately grasped by the spectator. It is that, instead of recording, his camera collaborates in the project of transmitting the profound fact that reality is always a construct and that interpretation is a construct of a construct, and contemplating the process of said constructions is much more productive than witnessing a state of reality that does not exist as is.

It is inevitable that Meyer, while occupying himself with the profound reality that is Mexico, dedicates a significant part of his work to the grand actors who stand upon the stage of said reality. However, they are not grand actors in the sense that they are the illustrious figures of the national pantheon, but rather because they are those who exercise the most agency in Mexican society. I am referring to men. Much can be said about the gender hegemony of men in Mexico, beginning with the fact that such hegemony has been exercised in a multitude of societies throughout the human universe. Nevertheless, I will not expand on the details of whether Mexican gender hegemony is different, more or less significant, or more or less efficient, or whether the preponderance of masculine agency in Meyer (in comparison to the major agency of women in the photographs of Graciela Iturbide, for example, which are examined in chapter 8 of this volume) is representative or not of a sexist posture on the part of a masculinist photographer. I prefer, rather, to leave such considerations aside because, although they are pertinent in an important way to the global sociohistoric sense of Meyer's production, they are not directly involved with an analysis of his artistic ideology, which is what occupies me at present. Much has been written about the role of man in Mexican society, along with the interpretation of man in cultural production. Meyer's photography can be taken as another example of this discriminatory emphasis.

Nonetheless, where Meyer's photographic work represents a truly innovative posture in relation to man is the way in which, when being photographed through Meyer's constructivist processes, man and his masculinity end up being framed like another construct of social and photographic processes. That is to say, Meyer's photographs allow us to see that man and his masculinity—that cluster of material characteristics that define, in an axis, his way of being in the world—are constructs.[3] If Meyer can do without essentialisms in the field of interpretive construction, likewise he can disregard them in relation to the actors/agents of said field.

Although the principles they elaborate are not universal, theoretical studies of gender accept as a guiding axiom that gender identity is a construction and that it is, also, a mimicry of a model that does not exist, but that, on the contrary, the mimicry of gender identities constitutes models that end up being accepted as platonic ideals to be competently represented by social subjects. Such a stance does not deny so-called biological differences, but rather it highlights how these are identified and managed by bodily practices—or technologies, to use a Foucauldian term—while becoming involved in current and hegemonic social semiotics. Nor does it deny the possibility that the social subject may formulate a subversive and resistant attitude in the face of the gender script that he/she is expected to follow. Precisely, one of the ways in which the word "queer" and the agency that it carries ("to make queer," "to queer") is understood goes directly back to the potential of the subversive and resistant.

There are many *queer* elements in Meyer's work, not so much in the sense of capturing and illuminating so-called homosexual lives, but rather in the perception that sociosexual identities, far from being inherent and universal, are representations that refer to a hegemonic scheme, not invariable or inevitable. One of the sites upon which an investigation about Meyer's artistic production could likely unfold is whether Meyer subscribes to the unquestionably constructivist representation of gender—especially the masculine one—and the strategic binaries that it implies, or whether his interpretation of gender constructions in Mexico's sociohistoric reality is more nuanced.[4]

A strategic play of gender identities is immediately evident in *The Arrival of White Man, Magdalena Peñazco, Oaxaca, 1991/92* (Meyer, *Truths* 91).[5] An unquestionable fact about the Spanish conquest of the Americas is that it was an exclusively masculine phenomenon. Even though the Spanish Crown was shared by the royal couple, and in spite of the fact that primary myths have taught us that Queen Isabella was more cunning than her husband in the endeavor of the so-called discovery of America, the project of getting to the West Indies in and of itself was carried out within the most rigid parameters of masculinity, beginning with

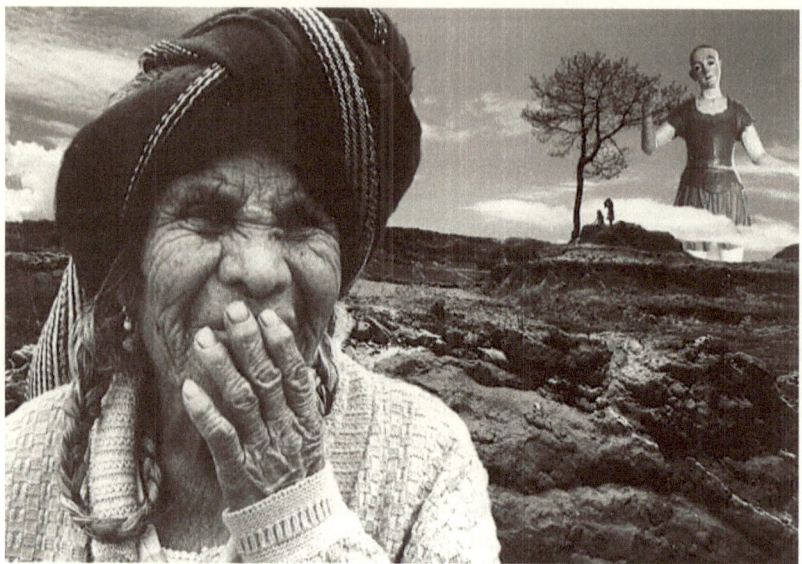

Figure 6.1. Pedro Meyer, *The Arrival of White Man, Magdalena Peñazco, Oaxaca, 1991/92*. Used with permission of Pedro Meyer.

Columbus, its iconic figure. If the burgeoning infrastructure of the empire was the exclusive dominion of men, the agents of the vanguard were also theirs, in spite of the spectrum of sexual preferences that there could have been among them in the lengthy maritime journey. The officers, soldiers, priests, and even the infamous cabin boys were all of masculine "gender," and they were united by the work that was suited for and worthy of men only. If there was, occasionally, a Catalina Erauso among them, it was an absolutely exceptional case; furthermore, the autobiography (1959) of the female second lieutenant leaves no doubt that she saw herself as a man like any one of her comrades who carried the categorical marks of their gender identity. The world of men of government and their official expedition became complete and confirmed by their ecclesiastical companions, whose hegemonic masculinity rested on the arrogant conviction that their authority and power came directly from a divinity that was the Man among men, the Supreme Father.

In Meyer's image there is a juxtaposing of two human figures that confirms the binary of gender: a close-up of an indigenous woman occupies the entire left half of the photo, and a white man occupies the upper right-hand corner. This binary is duplicated by the barely visible figures of a man and a woman under a tree on the right side of the masculine figure. It is possible that they allude to Adam and Eve under the proverbial tree of wisdom, a human framework that, allegedly, founds all conflicting narratives of human history, among them, of course, the conquest of America.

The distinction between the characters of the two main figures is the most telling aspect of the photo. On one hand, the indigenous woman does not present any uncertainty about the prototypic identity associated with her social sector; even the hybridity of her clothing made up of the autochthonous turban, the woven braid, and the embroidered blouse is complemented by the modern cardigan of obvious industrial fabrication. The expression of consternation—the squinting eyes, the wrinkled face of an elderly woman contorted in horror, her hand over her mouth as if suppressing what can surge from deep within—and her size make her the focal point of the photo: this woman is seeing and reacting to something profoundly terrifying. As the title of the picture tells us, it is about the arrival of the white man. She does not know the extent of the tragedy that this arrival signals, but there is no doubt that her reaction reveals that nothing will ever be the same.

On the other hand, the figure of the conquistador is dull—and almost androgynous. It looks more like a plaster or wood statue of a saint on a pedestal, dressed in a tunic that can pass for either a woman's dress or the clothing of a conquering soldier. Lacking the armor that the Spanish are presumed to have been wearing when they stepped off the ships to face

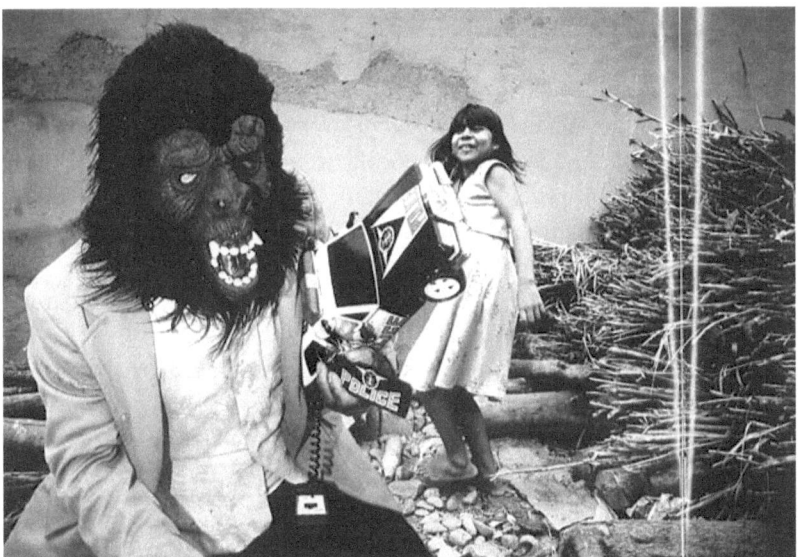

Figure 6.2. Pedro Meyer, *The Sheriff, San Juan Mixtepec, Oaxaca, 1991/93.* Used with permission of Pedro Meyer.

potentially hostile enemies, this figure, of smooth and extremely white skin and the gaze of a languid child, is precisely unsuitable for a poster commemorating the victorious manly men of the West Indies. Despite insinuating that the Conquest was carried out by barely adolescent soldiers, of stilted and bewildered appearance—one remembers the guiding question of Todorov's study (1987): How could so few men decimate organized empires and tribes of ruthless warriors?—and making one recall that the Spanish made the indigenous surrender as if they were only bands of terrified women, the picture points to an ominous result: the destruction of this woman's world.[6] This destruction is summarized in the old woman's cardigan: this apparently insignificant detail is a masterful metonym for the subjugation of the indigenous culture by the white man.

It is important to point out a recurrent characteristic in Meyer's photography that appears in this picture: the representation of feminine figures, even when they are mythic as in the case of the Virgin of Guadalupe, conserves their features within traditional parameters of women's identity. It is the masculine figures that represent "turbulent" details, as is the case with the fearful conquistador, taken to be Quetzalcoatl revived or not, reduced to a little saint in a church wall alcove, the object of the veneration of none other than old spinsters who are, as the Spanish saying goes, left to dress saints.

The photographic montage entitled *The Sheriff, San Juan Mixtepec, Oaxaca, 1991/93* (Meyer, *Truths* 106–107) takes on important significance given the almost certain involvement of the Juárez police in the disappearance and murder of an estimated thousand women in the last twenty years in the context of the foreign sweatshop system. These are the women photographed by Lourdes Portillo in her important film *Señorita extraviada* (2001; Missing young woman). However, the case of Juárez is only the most internationally recognized face of the gender violence that exists in Mexico.[7]

Once again, Meyer takes advantage of a variety of means in regard to the respective images of social actors, although this time the "man" is the foreground and the woman is reduced in scale. Furthermore, by placing the masculine actor's name between quotation marks, his identity is put under erasure. In terms of gender violence, even though the age of the aggressor does not really matter—as long as he puts forward symbolic and real power in order to exercise and legitimize his exercise of violence—in the case of women it is common for them to be "fresh" like the women of Juárez, who ranged in ages from fifteen to twenty-five years old.

Meyer's image presents a paradigm of the purportedly defenseless and innocent girl. She wears a pretty dress of a recognizably feminine color and print, and, by the position of her feet and the swaying of her hair, it seems that she is dancing with a joy that confirms the happiness on her face. It is the face of a childish ignorance that does not allow the girl to perceive the danger that haunts her, although the audience of the photo, like the powerless photographer of Julio Cortázar's short story "Las babas del diablo" (Devil's drool), is terrifyingly aware of the inevitable assault that is about to happen.

In the foreground, still more threatening because of his relatively larger size (not because of his age, but rather because of the artist's graphic placement), is the "sheriff," summation of the police's abuse of power in our societies. The only objects that indicate that he is a man are not his clothes, but rather his toys, those toys that teach boys to be social aggressors at the expense of women and other "womanized" social subjects. The grotesque details of his fingers, with their filthy skin and nails, would seem apish when one makes the visual synthesis with the gorilla costume that the supposed aggressor is wearing. In various Spanish dialects, the word for "gorilla" (gorila) is also used to describe the agents of police brutality, the "black-mustache men," the thugs who impose order by force. With the pardon of real gorillas, it can be said that this mask serves the purpose of encapsulating the cruelty and physical violence against which the victims have no recourse: secure in the legitimacy of his exercise of power, the "sheriff" and his thugs fulfill their functions, without fear of having to justify their actions to anyone.

I place the nomenclature "man" between quotation marks, precisely in order to facilitate Meyer's deconstruction in regard to the supposed distributive balance between sex roles. Even when one does not attempt to see the two paradigmatic gender roles as equal, even when one subscribes to the belief that men rule and woman obey, one evokes a distribution of roles that tends to confirm an effective social functionality; gender role arrangements, be they what they may, facilitate the tranquil side of life.

On the other hand, a reinterpretation of said roles, in which men assume the power to violate and rape women, constitutes, literally, a mortifying force for life, especially in the case of preadolescent girls, who have not yet reached the age of their supposed reproductive obligations. It is true that patriarchy is also perpetuated by a certain exercise of violence by women. However, it is also true that such violence is "corrective" in some way; it does not serve the purpose of raping a minor, which is what motivates the gorillas of the so-called social order. It is in this sense that a deconstruction of man operates: in spite of being part of a continuum, the self-affirmed macho is one thing, and the agent of death is another thing altogether, and more so, when one speaks of state terrorism carried out by police who function outside of the law.

One last comment about this image: the spectator would have noticed that the toys of police power that the masked agent holds do not say "policía," but "police." This is a clear allusion to the American model of the "sheriff."[8] It is how the photo alludes, in some way, to the violence in Juárez. As Portillo's documentary shows, the sweatshop system, which is owned mostly by Americans, is an accomplice, in a direct or indirect way, to the deaths of disappeared young women.

The last image to be analyzed here is possibly one of Meyer's most known works: *The Strolling Saint, Nochistlán, Oaxaca, 1991/92* (Meyer, *Truths* 79).[9] Latin American Catholicism—and, in particular, Mexican—is characterized by subtle and significant fractures between official dogma—defended by the incontestably masculine hierarchy—and a tradition of beliefs that breaks away from dogma on essential points, contradicts it, or, in a fashion one can almost call Derridean, supplements it in clever ways. Although this Catholicism—more popular than institutional—can include large sectors of the population, it is typically a phenomenon associated with women, being that women, at least at the popular level, are the ones who most turn to religious beliefs and practice, a phenomenon that

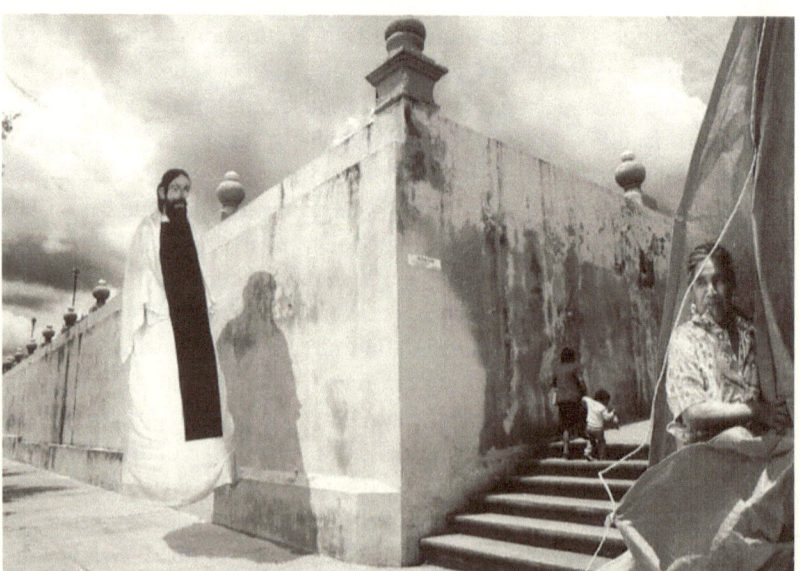

Figure 6.3. Pedro Meyer, *The Strolling Saint, Nochistlán, Oaxaca, 1991/92*. Used with permission of Pedro Meyer.

is seen in particular in Mexico with the feminine cult of the Virgin of Guadalupe. As a matter of fact, the prompt official recognition of the Virgin of
Guadalupe contrasts with the popular support of the Indian to whom she
appeared in 1531, Juan Diego. In spite of the support given to Juan Diego's
sainthood by popular fervor, the official Church did not understand until
2002 the value and merit of recognizing him in the institutional canon.
At the popular level there are Mothers, Saints, Children, Fathers, Broth-
ers, Sisters, and Widows whose saintliness is subscribed to uncondition-
ally by the people, but who do not ever enter, not even in a lesser form, the
institutional canon.[10] It is in this disjunction that Meyer's photographic
montage can be found.

Constructed at the entrance of a church in Nochistlán, the montage is
separated into two parts by one of the angles of the stone walls. Nonetheless, the blue/bluish-purple tones give the image a structural unity, reinforcing the way in which all the elements come together in one single experience that can be called dreamlike. However, the division of the image
produced by the angle of the stone walls echoes the schism between the
masculine and feminine in Meyer's other work. This rupture is anchored
in a concrete material experience; the masculine figure is converted into a
deconstruction of the elements of its masculinity. That is to say, the figure
of the woman is revealed when the drapes are drawn back so that she can
peek into the ethereal realm. This distinction is confirmed by the fact that
her image appears in ordinary hues, as is the case with her complexion
and the colors of her blouse, hair, lips, and earrings.

It is as if she belongs to another realm of existence, as she peeks, with
visible caution on her face, into another dimension of reality. Furthermore, in this second reality there appear—like a reduplication of the real
feminine sphere—two figures that climb the steps leading to a street that
passes by the stone wall. The purple color of this second woman's blouse
echoes the other hues of the image, but it is part of a conventional composition of her and the boy (girl?) that accompanies her, whose hand she
is holding. The sex of the child is not important. It is a feminine composition in that, up to a certain point, boys and girls in Mexico, as in most
parts of the world, are pieces or extensions of their mothers.

In addition to these two women—one who peeks in directly and the
other who is walking by circumstantially—there is juxtaposed, in large
scale, the form of a saint who floats by. Meyer notes in his own analysis of
the montage process (Meyer, *Truths* 117) that it is not uncommon to find
in the small villages of Mexico stories about the figures of saints that roam
the streets. The image that Meyer reproduces in his analysis makes one

see that he is referring to giant figures that people intentionally parade down the streets. However, Meyer claims to base his work on the figure of a saint of larger than life proportions that he discovered in a local church and decided to use in his montage. The difference between the real practices and Meyer's montage is how it represents a saint who floats in the air. In contrast to the figures displayed by people in the street, the apparitional saints are not tied to solid ground, and in this way they appear to be, literally, floating in the air.

The reconfiguration of the masculine figure that is implied by Meyer's photographic proposal is the manner in which man is disconnected from the material world. One can see the realistic contours of the muscular calf of the woman who is in the act of lifting a foot while climbing the steps. Likewise, one can see the realistic features of the woman who pulls the drapes aside with her tense fingers. However, the masculine saint figure is made of wood. In addition to its washed-out complexion, the statue's gaze seems vacant, like that of a figure made out of cardboard or another similar material. Without arms or feet, the figure is reduced, from the head down, to being no more than a hollow shape.

Unlike the gorilla man who threatens young innocence, unless one can discover invisible masculine attributes in him, the saint floats innocuously through a concrete world inhabited by flesh-and-bone women who are busy in their daily activities: one is walking up the street with a specific destination, while the other is carefully observing her immediate surroundings. Whether, in women's reality, men float impotent and empty in the world, or whether they belong to a dreamlike dominion that one woman chooses to remain outside of, while another contemplates cautiously—it all comes down to, in both cases, a dematerialization of the material man. It is clear that men—the conquistadores and the child molesters of the first two montages analyzed here—are painfully historic facts. However, the unrealistic representation of the man who is observed by one of the women—and about which the other woman couldn't care less—is grist for some feminine/feminist fantasies of power capable of making a lateral incision into hegemony.

The images studied in this essay are far from constituting Pedro Meyer's photographic production. Nonetheless, photographic montages made possible through the technical capabilities afforded by digitalization and computer programs used to manage details place Meyer in the avant-garde of contemporary Latin American photography. At the same time that his artistic work addresses the power of art as a construction, elaboration, and deconstruction of the elements of the so-called sociohistoric reality, it intersects in a particularly eloquent way with similar propositions regarding sexual gender, specifically those related to the ground zero of masculinity upon which myriad dogmas related to biology and society have been conventionally founded.[11] Questioning the aforementioned dogmas and the imperatives of reality in photography inspires Meyer's artistic work.

DISCOVERING THE MALE BODY
Marcos Zimmermann's *Desnudos sudamericanos*

◆ ◆ ◆

The female body has long been photographed in the nude as part of an abiding tradition of the fetishizing of her body by the masculinist gaze of the camera, a gaze that wanders all over the erotic map in the many ways, the many perspectives, the many close-ups available to imagining the female body. There is now some tradition of a lesbian photographic gaze at the female body: the work of Annie Leibovitz comes immediately to mind, especially with regard to her highly controversial dossier on Susan Sontag and her dying body.

In the case of male nudes, while there is certainly an art tradition that would accord an aesthetic beauty to the male body, it always comes off as distinctly marginal: most Western cultures have some version of the Mexican saying "El hombre debe ser feo, fuerte y formal" (A man must be ugly, strong, and dependable) or the Spanish proverb "El hombre es como el oso, cuanto más feo, más hermoso" (Man is like a bear: the uglier he is, the more attractive he is). The proposition that there is inherent beauty in the male body comes off, for most, as masked homoerotic desire, and the fact is that the display of the male nude in all art forms, and especially in photography, can ultimately be traced to an interest in a fetishizing of its homoerotic parameters. To be sure, there is an unabashed homoerotic/pornographic gaze at the body, in which the subject, either naïvely or with professional aplomb, displays pertinent attributes for a gaze that could only disingenuously be labeled as anything other than purposefully erotic.

Zimmermann's eighty-one plates, however, constitute a much different project, although, as with any form of cultural production, it is up to the reader/spectator to complete the meaning in terms of the needs of personal interest, "artistic" or otherwise. Zimmermann is most known for spectacular art photography featuring the Argentine wilderness, particularly in its most dramatic natural forms. By contrast, *Desnudos sudamericanos* is, as stated in its prologue, intended to capture the Latin American male in his most immediately material form, deprived of any attempt to glamorize or objectify him for ulterior symbolic purposes. One thinks in the latter vein of ideologemes such as the noble savage, the natural man, the Edenic/Adamic/prelapsarian native, the family of man figure.

Zimmermann photographed men in seven countries: Argentina, Chile, Bolivia, Brazil, Paraguay, Peru, and Uruguay. Men of all ages, including children and the elderly, are represented, although the emphasis seems to fall basically between the mid-twenties and early fifties. Each model is represented against the backdrop of his daily life and the specific attributes of his occupation. Most are completely nude, although some are clothed to various degrees. The latter, however, are all represented with their primary masculine attribute in full view, while as for those that are fully nude, in a few cases, they either sit or hold an article of their livelihood that covers their penis. Since, except in one case, none of the occupations involved is customarily conducted in the nude (although some, such as tropical fishing or surfing, require minimal clothing), Zimmermann's gaze acquires a double resonance.

In the first place, his stated goal is to accomplish a representation of the meager circumstances of life of the Latin American inhabitant, totally alien to the circumstances of modern life that from the time of the arrival of the conquerors to the present day of late capitalist exploitation have contributed to the "denuding" and "stripping" of, first, the original peoples and, later, their descendants of natural and artisanal riches. The fact that most of Zimmermann's men appear to be mestizos captured in rural, nonurban settings underscores the attempt to echo the pillage of the original peoples and their possessions. If most of these men engage in occupations that derive from various versions of modernity, that too is part of the consequence of their domination: the clothes that some do wear

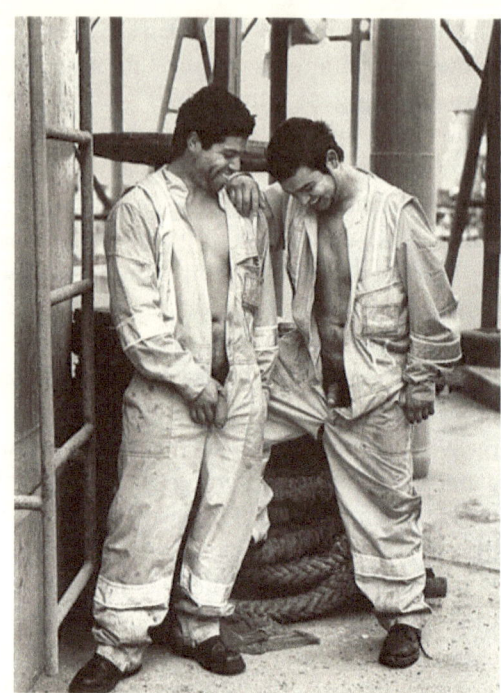

Figure 7.1. Marcos Zimmermann, *Juan Andrés y Héctor Antonio, estibadores, Puerto San Antonio, Chile* (Juan Andrés and Héctor Antonio, stevedores, Puerto San Antonio, Chile). Used with permission of Marcos Zimmermann.

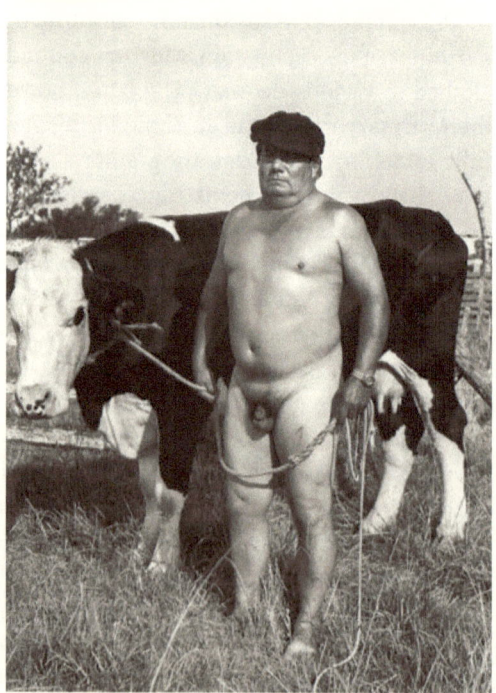

Figure 7.2. Marcos Zimmermann, *Ramón, gaucho. Ruta 2, provincia de Buenos Aires, Argentina* (Ramón, gaucho, Route 2, Province of Buenos Aires, Argentina). Used with permission of Marcos Zimmermann.

and the backdrop of the elements of their livelihood index their incorporation, albeit in a most impoverished way, into the web of modern life.

Yet there is a second resonance, and that is the sense of the material
body that is sufficient unto itself beneath the trappings of social or socioeconomic circumstances. There is no force of idealization at work here,
since there is never the implication that there is the putatively real or pure
or integral body hidden by the trappings of contemporary life, no matter
how impoverished. The sort of close examination of the body these high-
resolution photographs provide (the sort of high resolution, although in
black and white, reserved for artistic, fashion, or pornographic modeling) reveals bodies marked by lived human experience. There are not only
traces, presumably, of chosen inscription in specific social codes such as
tattooing (professional and amateur) or circumcision, but the scarring
produced by the process of life: the traces of malnutrition and bad eating
habits, accompanied, in the case of the elderly, by the inevitable decay
of the body; scar tissue from apparent accidents, burns, and abrasions
and hands and feet worn by harsh use. One detail marks eloquently the
absence of any intention on Zimmermann's part to re-create Edenic individuals: many who are otherwise completely naked wear bracelets, rings,
and necklaces that, with only a few possible exceptions, are part of modern body adornment.

These black-and-white portrayals of males bodies have been formed
by hardscrabble work and differ notably from the air-brushed perfections
of the models to be found in Buenos Aires beefcake photography, not to
mention those of the idealized and far more widespread Argentine macho
who populates commercial advertising. The latter are both ideal (because
hegemonic) and real men (air-brushing and other strategic enhancements
aside), but Zimmermann's male models are the systemic refutation of the
urban paradigm.[1] Some of Zimmermann's models are fishermen, while
others are industrial workers. But they are all peripheral to the idealized
urban body of Buenos Aires–based male modeling.

Several of the men, as one might suspect, do correspond to parameters
that can be called beautiful, erotic, or seductive. Most of the individuals
photographed stare neutrally into the camera or look away from it, but a
few are clearly aware of their opportunity to engage the viewer playfully
and even, indeed, coquettishly. One photograph is particularly notable
in this regard. It is the image of Leonardo, identified as being from Llavallol, in the province of Buenos Aires. This is a fully posed beefcake shot,
as Leonardo looks back over his shoulder, with an enticing glance, from
his fully extended body on a bed. His body is notably fleshy in contrast to

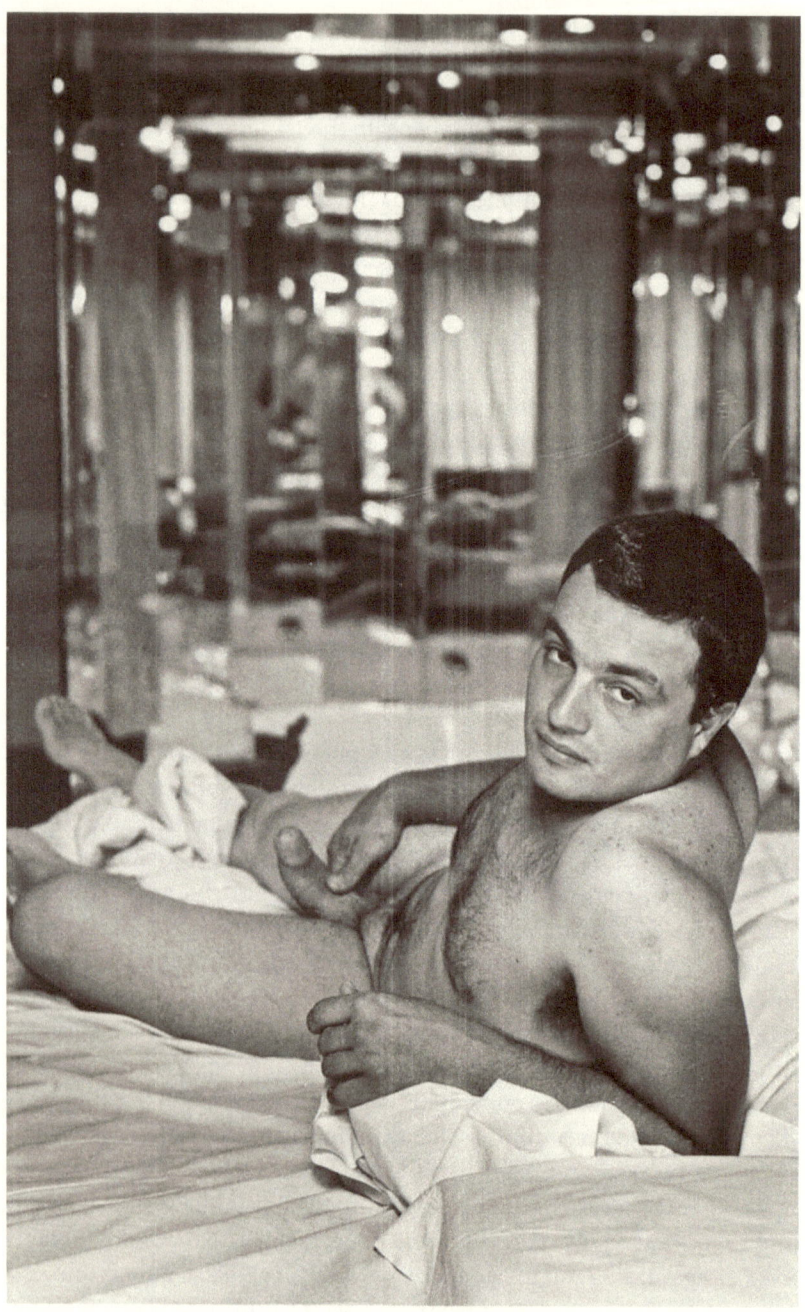

Figure 7.3. Marcos Zimmermann, *Leonardo, taxiboy, Llavallol, provincia de Buenos Aires, Argentina* (Leonardo, hustler, Llavallol, province of Buenos Aires, Argentina). Used with permission of Marcos Zimmermann.

the bodies of the men who have spent their lives in occupations of hard work, often in strenuous working conditions and in contact with inclement weather or the polluted air of the factory workplace. Of all the men in *Desnudos sudamericanos*, Leonardo is the only one portrayed with a full erection, which he holds in full view with his right hand. This photograph makes sense when we read that Leonardo is a "taxiboy," a male prostitute who quite reasonably displays in full view the instrument of his livelihood in the world.

Erotic response is, of course, a relative proposition, and there is no way of saying that there is anything more or less sexy about Leonardo than there is about the image elsewhere of the eightyish Héctor and his almost skeletal body. Whatever the response of the viewer to these South American male nudes in artistic and erotic terms, Zimmermann's basic proposition would appear to be that it must always be tinged by the political, in the sense that, unlike the unabashedly pornographic, with its frequent blatantly false settings and poses, all of these men are contextualized in ways that permit the contemplation of the business of everyday male lives in the countries represented.

QUEERING GENDER IN GRACIELA ITURBIDE'S
JUCHITÁN DE LAS MUJERES

◆ ◆ ◆

Juchitán has had the good fortune to maintain its integrity as a Zapotecan city, while at the same time taking advantage of the opportunities
the outside world has provided to it. This is in no way a common occurrence in Mexico or anywhere else in Latin America among the countries that have considerable indigenous populations (Royce 203).

"The women of Juchitán": hardly any other phrase in Mexican culture—at least feminine/feminist culture—enjoys greater resonance than
this one has. The phrase conjures up images of the so-called profound
Mexico, of a Mexican Other that, many would insist, is threatened with
disappearance under the unsustainable weight of globalization, neoliberalism, the effect of hybrid cultures, new border realities, and so on. The
image Iturbide provides is of these often hefty women taking care of the
business of their world as they see fit, preserving something like a primitive communism that is in strident disaccord with the national narrative,
with Zapotecan roots and inhabiting a socioeconomic space in which the
elements of capitalist society are episodic and precarious. There is a certain romantic or sentimental patina surrounding the cultureme (the min-

imal unit of cultural knowledge) identified as "Juchitán" that the afore-mentioned considerations continue to promote. The social, political, and economic singularity of Juchitán de Zaragoza has provided much work for anthropologists, and it is recycled in the popular, and international, imaginary. Juchitán has been the subject of a considerable scientific bibli-ography dealing with the remarkable lives of its women.[1]

The popular imaginary holds on to the images of women who enjoy a close-knit homosocialism in their lives that allows them to dance together as though they were sweethearts or lovers, a homosocialism that would seem to hold traditional Mexican machismo at bay but permit, in turn, a behavior in and among men that questioned the law of masculinity far before the phrase "crisis of masculinity" was first formulated. Much is also made of the strong matrilinearity between mothers and daughters and between young women and their grandmothers that would seem to model and solidify a version of the bonding between women (*comadris-mo*) that exists elsewhere in Mexico and among Mexican women in the United States, even when the latter is often now much more a matter of traditional formalisms without the extensive transmitted social language attributed to the women of Juchitán. In this way, the Juchitecan woman stands out as something like a ground zero for an alterity that is deeply seductive for a society characterized by the homogeneity surrounding the project of modernity.

When *Juchitán de las mujeres* was first published in 1989, with pho-tography by Graciela Iturbide and texts by Elena Poniatowska, two of the most outstanding women producing culture in Mexico today, not only was a long-standing enthusiasm for this Mexican microsociety rekindled, but it became the most sought-after photographic dossier in Latin Amer-ica. *Juchitán de las mujeres* not only struck a chord in the long process of questioning the projects of modernity in Mexico, but it also connected with an enormous feminist current in Latin America, especially what we might term a "radical" current that called into question in a particularly intransigent way patriarchal paradigms. Feminism and postmodernism can be two sides of the same coin, which becomes, perhaps, somehow tri-dimensional when it incorporates the ideological parameters of the queer. It is a matter of a feminism that not only questions masculinist privilege, but also challenges additional concepts of being a woman in Mexico by undermining the postulates of heteronormativity that are part of the so-cial hygiene of Mexican society. Based on the refocusing of the gaze of two female artists from the iconic Latin American megalopolis to an almost inaccessible corner of the country, the book portrays a world that, even if it is not definitively matriarchal, stands at a considerable distance from prevailing national patriarchal values. And in examining closely other allegiances and alliances of gender, sexuality, and desire that are markedly different from the narratives of metropolitan heterosexuality, *Juchitán de las mujeres* is perhaps a unique book in Mexican culture.

All one has to do is to consider the title, which is an eloquent trope of the anthropological phrase. The latter serves to identify a demographic subcategory writing the semantic universe of Juchitán. It is a subcategory that, despite the theoretical conclusions that can be drawn from fieldwork grounded in questions of gender and sexuality, remains grounded in the binarism of gender identity. Since anthropology has mostly concerned itself with men, women being seen as appendages of men, the creation of a field of research relating to women, with or without the implication that women constitute the most important group socially and with or without the implication that, in this event, men are seen as appendages of women, constitutes in and of itself a marked emphasis on the importance of women, something that is confirmed significantly in the large bibliography that now exists, especially in Mexico, where feminist anthropology has been diligently pursued. In the case of the Iturbide-Poniatowska project, the insistence on a trope of the anthropological phrase affirms precisely the way in which women predominate in Juchitán and how Juchitán is either a subcategory of the semantic universe of women (one supposes that there will be other subcategories, all related to the same concept of "place," even when they have not yet been discovered, such as, perhaps, the Paraguay of women) or another interpretation of the preposition "de," whereby the particle is not locative but first and foremost possessive: Juchitán belongs to women and they dominate in that place.

Such a conjugation of terms, and even more so when it is the matter of a trope that refers to something that has been as consecrated as "las mujeres de Juchitán" has, is necessarily destined to produce a frisson of understanding. From the point of view of a feminism oriented toward the revindication of the real power of women, the proposal that such a place might exist in the country—and strategically from the national optics of a book produced in Mexico—can be quite encouraging. From the point of view of any social subject who would maintain, consciously or unconsciously, the "naturalness" of a sexual binary that favors men, the verbal construction here either will come off as simply strange or will only be meaningless. Poniatowska's texts function to characterize the existence of a social setting in which it is possible to contemplate some other ordering of things:

Juchitán looks like no other town. It has the destiny of its indigenous wisdom. Everything is different. Women like to stroll along in an embrace and they show up in force at marches, thick-calved, their man like a kitten at their feet, a puppy that needs to be scolded: "Be still." They provoke each other as they stroll along, swaying. They invert the roles, groping a man who looks at them from the side-lines, pulling on him and fondling him as they curse the government and even the man himself. The women are the ones who turn up for the marches and hit the police. (Poniatowska 79; a version of this characterization is found in Campbell et al. 133–135)

Look upon these women as towers in motion, their bellies broad, their hearts a window, their night-time girth that visits the moon. See how they come, they who are now the government, they who are the people, the guardians of men, the distributors of provisions, their children astride their hips or reclining in the ham-mock of their breast, the wind blowing their skirts, florid ships, their sex a honey-comb spilling forth men. There they come sashaying their bellies, dragging along their machos who, by contrast to them, wear plain shirts and pants, huaraches and a straw hat that they raise on high as they shout "Long live the Juchitecan woman." (Poniatowska 82)

One of the most well-known images of *Juchitán de las mujeres*—in a certain sense, the master photo of the collection—is *Nuestra Señora de las Iguanas* (82; Our Lady of the Iguanas).[2] One immediately notes the evocation of Mexican Catholicism, especially in its dimension that allows for the ongoing creation of new popular saints, with or without the ap-proval of the official church. In this case, it is more exactly the evocation of the Virgin Mary, with an explicit intertextuality with the paradigm of the Catholic religion in Mexico, Nuestra Señora, la Virgen de Guadalupe, who not only has a privileged place in the constellation of venerated holy figures, but also enjoys an official position within the identity of the Mexi-can people that goes far beyond her basically religious identity. To put it in a different way, the religious quality of this figure constitutes an essential nucleus of Mexican national identity that transcends the official church, and one need not be Catholic to understand how the Virgin of Guadalupe also functions as a founding myth of Mexico as a sovereign nation.[3] In the case of a woman from Juchitán, this circumstance in turn connects with the legendary political dissidence of the area (which, if we are to believe Poniatowska, is woman-grounded) and its sustained opposition to the capitalist central government, especially in its version, still unwavering at the time these photographs were taken, as the Partido Revolucionario

Institucional, which for seven decades, until its first loss in 2000, was, in Trinitarian fashion, President, Party, and State. There thus emerges an overdetermined triangulation of national signifiers: the Virgin of Guadalupe as founding myth; the PRI and its rigorously lay and anti-ecclesiastic expropriation of national myths, including religious ones (the material Church in Mexico is part of the national patrimony whose most imposing possession is the Basílica de Guadalupe, both the original one and the newer edifice); and the political culture of Juchitán, in which a historical community disassociates itself from institutional power.

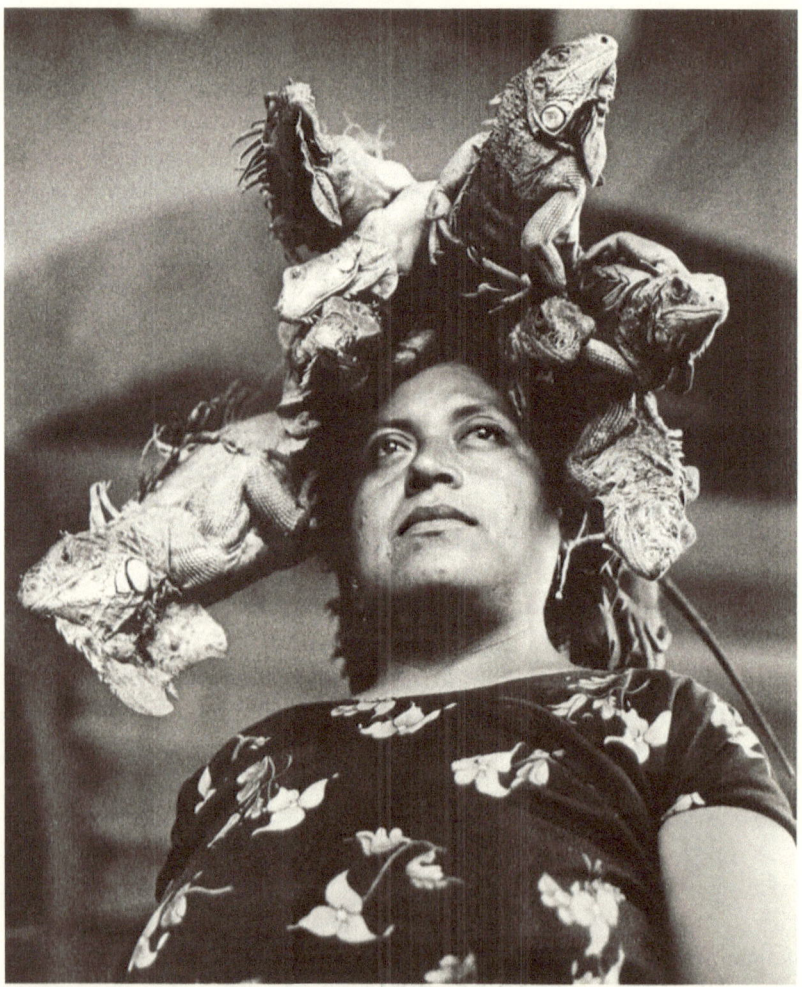

Figure 8.1. Graciela Iturbide, *Nuestra Señora de las Iguanas* (Our Lady of the Iguanas). Used with permission of Graciela Iturbide.

In terms of a configuration of gender, the Virgin of Guadalupe assigns to Mexico, despite centuries of machismo transmitted in a sustained, undiminished fashion throughout Mexican popular culture, a matriarchal resonance: angels are perhaps not one sex or the other, but Nuestra Señora, everyone's sainted mother, enjoys a feminine identity designed to serve as the paradigm for all women. And, in its masculine version, in the form of the men of Guadalupe, among all men. Iturbide's image is that of an imposing woman, whose gaze is as haughty as it is peaceful in her sense of self-assuredness. There is no doubt that the photographer was interested in portraying one of the millennial matriarchal figures of Juchitán, and this is one of the organizing principles of the dossier, whose cover is emblazoned with the hefty presence, one of the bottles of her commerce held on high, of one of the female Coca-Cola vendors who work the fishing beaches of the area. The image Iturbide gives us with *Nuestra Señora de las Iguanas* is virtually a holy card in the way it engraves a human presence that transcends the quotidian, an image that projects itself as an icon of the eminence of woman in Juchitecan society.

If the woman who appears on the cover of *Juchitán de las mujeres*, the Coke vendor, stands for the commerce that sustains the daily life of the area, *Nuestra Señora de las Iguanas* engages a spiritual transcendence. This is not really for any pose reminiscent of a holy card Virgin, but lies in the fact that her head is adorned not with the customary halo of the canonical saints, but with a crown of live iguanas. It is not the crown of thorns of Jesus Christ the martyr, a crown that is extended to other martyred saints of both sexes, but a living halo that constitutes the materiality of Juchitecan life. We don't know if this woman is a vendor of iguanas (a tasty meat dish when prepared, for example, with *mole poblano*, a chocolate and chili paste made with an array of other spices) or if it is a question of the representation of a ritual with some sort of religious implication, such as one finds among other peoples in the case of serpent handlers and viper trainers. The iguana is a poisonous reptile despite being a prized meal, and it must be no easy task to weave them together—and one can see by the image that they are very much alive—as though making a straw sun hat. It is left open whether the telluric powers of this woman are capable of taming them by her very feminine presence. If the poisonous reptiles index the hostility of the natural setting the human being must confront in order to survive, and one considers also the legendary force of the reptile in Jewish-Christian symbolism, the power of the Juchitecan woman comes across as enormous in her incorporation of the small animal (little more than a nuisance for the urban viewer) into her daily wardrobe.

But there is another resonance that we cannot help but comment on here, another turn of the ideological screw that underlies the Iturbide/Poniatowska dossier. I am referring to the genital aspect of the reptile, which is well established, not only in Freudian interpretations, professional or armchair, but also in a particular reading of the history of original sin. What the serpent offers as knowledge to Adam and Eve in the Garden of Eden is sexual knowledge and power, which signify the human fall from grace, and thus the serpent is a sign of the phallus. Moreover, the iguana, as one of the reptilian species, is particularly thick in body, as should be the penis of every self-congratulatory macho. Nuestra Señora de las Iguanas, by converting the masculine phallus that is the iguana into a detail of her dress as a feminine patron saint, is affirming the primacy of woman in the management of the relations between the sexes. This is not an asexual woman such as we might expect to encounter on a holy card, where the very absent, transfixed gaze of both female and male saints removes them from the realm of erotic desire. Quite the contrary: the profundity of her gaze, the smooth quality of her skin, the chunky nature of the only arm we see, the sculpted and symmetric nature of her lips, and the apparent softness of her skin are all very concrete and for many are more desirable than the firm or even scrawny body of the urban model. This is an imposing empowered woman who handles her sexuality as she pleases, with the same dexterity as she handles the poisonous iguanas.

We don't see the hands of Nuestra Señora de las Iguanas, but there is the recurring motif of women's hands in *Juchitán de las mujeres*, of the "powerful hands." This is not surprising not only if we take into account the traditional role of women in handling the trivial but so essential duties of housekeeping, but also if we see them in terms of what is still a premodern society, where almost everything is done by hand. These hands are assigned reliquary status, and they represent for us the transmission of matrilineal relations within this society. Within the enclosure of what looks like a ramada, as though it were a niche for venerating a saint, two women each hold in her hands pedestals containing carved wooden hands (*Manos poderosas* [Powerful hands]). They are a girl and her grandmother, a young woman and an old woman, the latter the former's mentor. The carved set of hands each holds matches her age, since the hands of the grandmother are three or possibly four times larger than her granddaughter's. Each hand is open to its maximum reach as though an offering to the faithful who come to adore them: the hands of women are powerful and are at the service of the community or humanity to undertake the tasks of survival. The magnified value of the feminine hand (that is, the hand

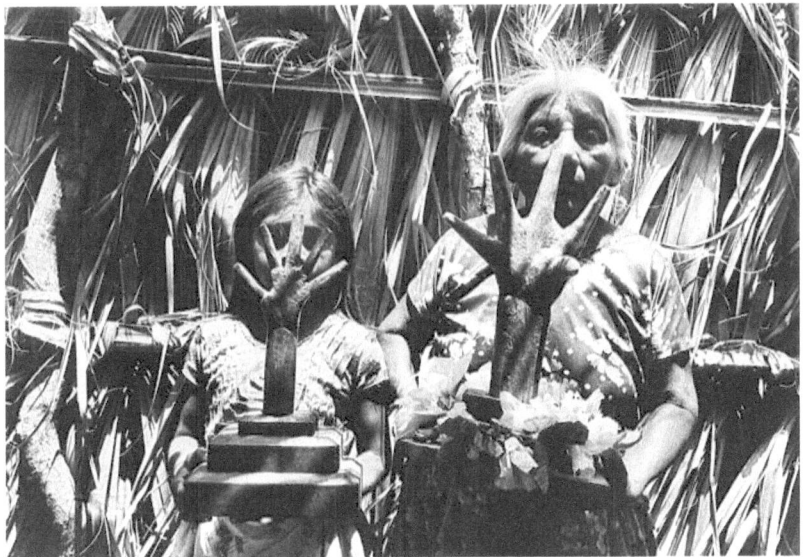

Figure 8.2. Graciela Iturbide, *Manos poderosas* (Powerful hands).
Used with permission of Graciela Iturbide.

as a feminine noun that corresponds to a woman, the hand that, with the philological symbolism the Spanish language allows, is that of feminine identity) is embodied in the way the two women, whose dress, hairdo, and stance before the camera are similar, hold the small pedestals such that each one is essentially hidden behind the wooden hands. We more clearly see the eyes, although they almost disappear among the shadows produced by the niche in which the two are standing, of the older woman. This gives the grandmother greater control, leaving her granddaughter more relegated to the secondary plane of dependence in the face of the woman who is older and, therefore, more experienced with life, wiser, more powerful. The relative difference of degree between the two women, with respect to their age, their stature, their presence before the camera, and, what is most eloquent, the size of the hand that each one offers, is a measure of the hierarchy that we are to understand exists between them, a circuit of power where, just as one hand reaches for another, they transmit the wisdom associated with their sex.

Leafing through the pages of *Juchitán de las mujeres*, one is struck by the status of men. If men were absent from these photographs, one might understand a focus on women as representing something like a "correcting the balance," in the sense that so much feminist production is devoted to recovering women, in their social and, by extension, their artistic representation, from marginalization and oblivion. The concern for giving representation to women and showing how they can be rescued from symbolic and, consequently, real subjugation by men is a worthy feminist undertaking that has borne fruit like the anthologies of women's writing, not to mention the array of artistic representations—especially photographic, as in the case of the great New York photographer Annie Leibovitz's *Women* (see also Neumaier)—of women "as they are."[4] But men are not at all absent from the Iturbide/Poniatowska dossier. There are a couple of images in which men, in a completely conventional sense, with no highlighting, are present in conjunction with women. But what are most notable among Iturbide's images of Juchitecan men are those of transvestites.

I am using "transvestite" here as sort of a wild card to cover the sense of the English word "queer."[5] "Transvestite" is also preferable here because the manner in which the men of the three photographs I wish to discuss are queer is the way in which they dress in clothes that are conventionally considered to be feminine. The images in question are titled (again, in subsequent editions, but not in the 1989 original) *Magnolia, Magnolia* [bis], and *La cantina*. If what one understands "queer" to describe is any transgression against the social space in which the norms of the heterosexism of the hegemonic patriarchy are in force, transvestism is one of the most glaring transgressions. This is so because of the importance clothes have historically played in the imposition and maintenance of a binary sexual identity: in many societies transvestism has been a capital crime. One could even wonder if so much importance attributed to clothes and the hysteria[6] provoked by the failure to respect the customarily rigid disjunction between so-called men's clothes and women's clothes do not have more to do with the fact that the difference between the sexes is less pronounced and more precarious and ambiguous than it is said to be, with clothes and other such attributes therefore being a formality designed to affirm categorically what does not exist.

For example, in the case of the men in these photos, what most marks them as "feminized" (and I avoid the word "effeminate," because it's not a matter of behaving like women, but of having themselves pass as though they were) is not their clothing in the basic sense of the word—a specific basic item and accessories (a dress and shoes that match, for example, or a skirt and its corresponding blouse)—but rather a pearl necklace that is attached, as though it were a brooch of some sort, to a seashell or the shell of a sea animal such as a crab. In fact, the presence of the same collar in the three images allows us to deduce that the individual on the left in the

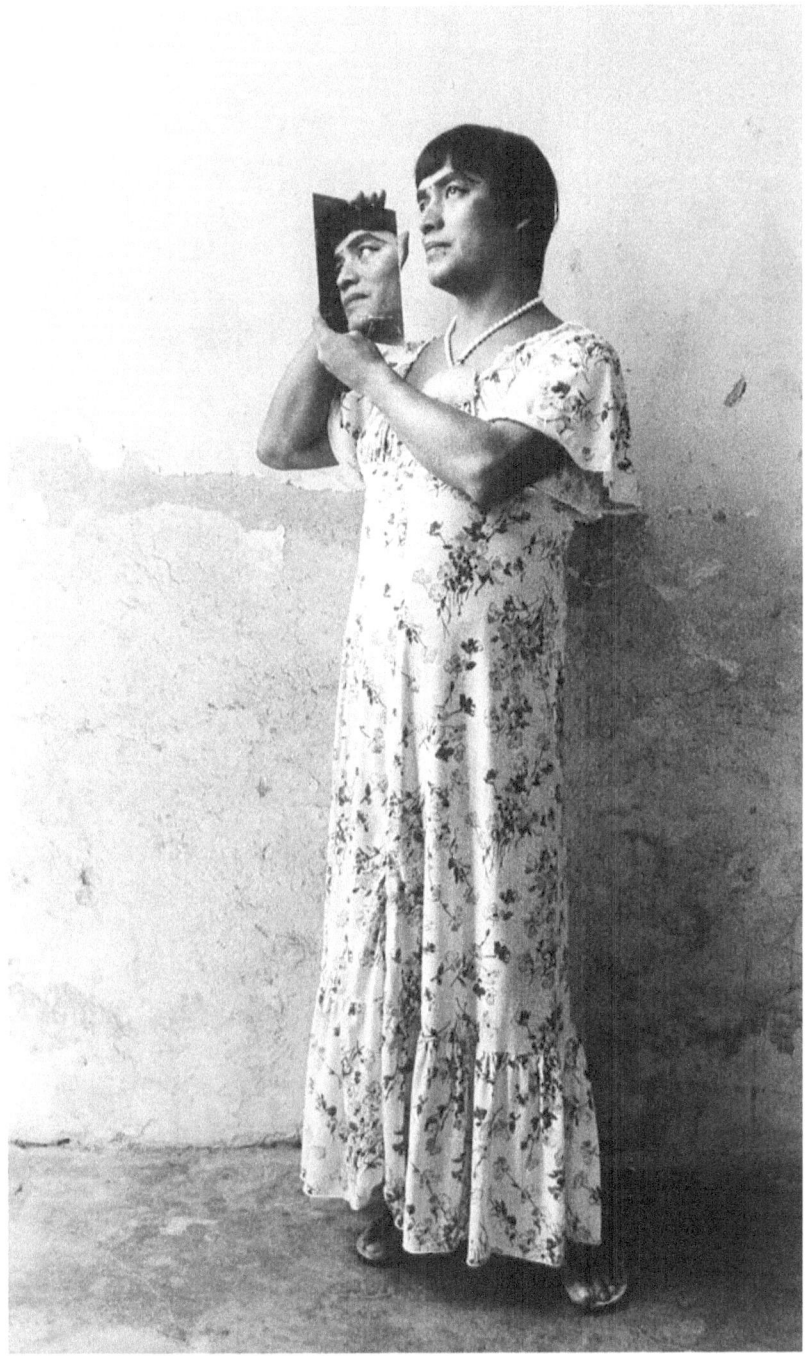

Figure 8.3. Graciela Iturbide, *Magnolia*. Used with permission of Graciela Iturbide.

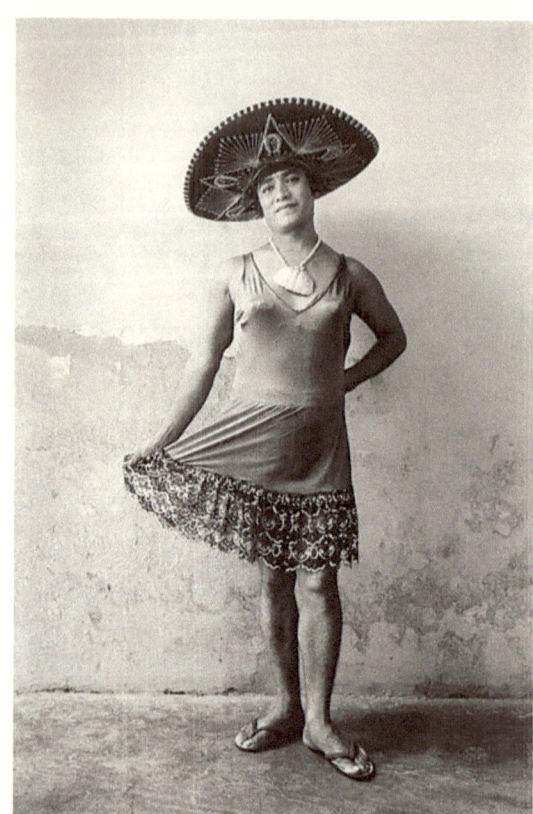

Figure 8.4. Graciela Iturbide, *Magnolia* [bis]. Used with permission of Graciela Iturbide.

Figure 8.5. Graciela Iturbide, *La cantina* (The cantina). Used with permission of Graciela Iturbide.

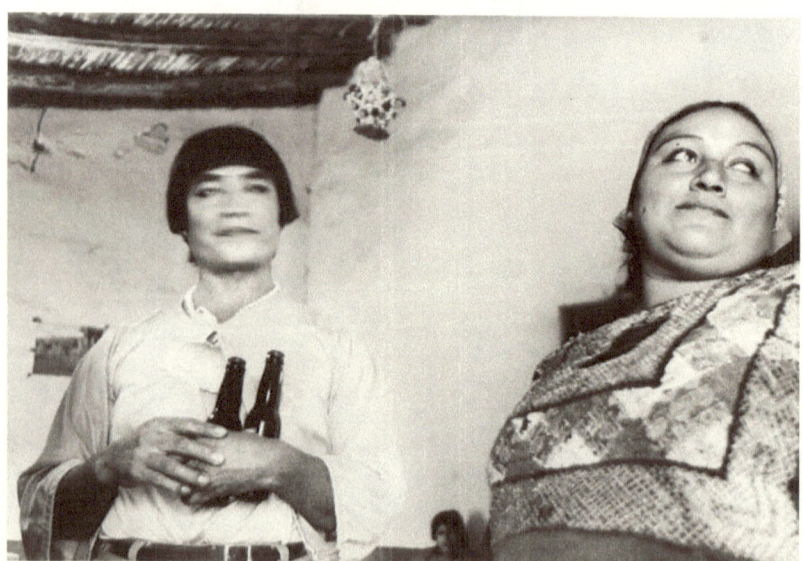

image labeled *La cantina* is also the man called Magnolia in the other two images in question (it is not completely clear, though, that the person on the right is necessarily a woman, given the fact that the cantina in Mexico is paradigmatically a homosocial space:[7] the only women customarily admitted are prostitutes or transvestites, who are normally taken, in every sense of the word, as prostitutes). Nevertheless, the Magnolia of *La cantina* (The cantina) is not wearing women's clothes exactly. Aside from the pearl collar, he is wearing tight pants with what is a potent symbol of masculine power, a leather belt, the preferred instrument for the imposition of the power of the macho, via punishment, over children, women, and other men. He is also wearing what appears to be a loose peasant shirt of the sort one frequently sees in Oaxaca, a region of south central Mexico of which Juchitán is a part. This image is somewhat fuzzy, especially as regards the man's head. Thus, it is difficult to see if he is wearing a wig or if it is his own hair cut in a pageboy style. The same is true as regards his gaze, in the sense that it may be either the neutral smile of a "man" or the sweet inviting look of a "woman"; this is also true of the individual, whether man or woman, to the right in *La cantina*.

But it is in the two images of Magnolia in women's clothes where we especially see the quintessence of the queer, as much in the quality of the human situation captured by the photograph as in the subject's own gaze in it. For example, in the case of the two images specifically identified as focusing on the man named "Magnolia" (I will continue to use the masculine pronoun for reasons that I clarify in a moment), we see him in a full-body pose, and he is indeed an imposing man. He is wearing a long flowered dress, with something of a plunging neckline, a ruffled hem, and puffed sleeves, all of which give the impression of a relaxed dress characteristic of a Sunday afternoon party. Yet he is wearing huaraches, or sandals typical of the Mexican male peasant, that permit us to see the thick toes of a grown man. In addition to the pearl necklace that appears in all three images, Magnolia has his face and hair arranged with a very feminine look, with the expressive gaze of a woman who is very much in control of her own body, with her eyes looking off in profound self-absorption. This is not a stare, vacant but not empty, aimed at the camera, such as one might associate with the somber Mexican macho, a gaze that is to be found, for example, in the vast bulk of the photos of the revolutionary machos from the early twentieth century (for example, many of the stock images of Pancho Villa or Emiliano Zapata). The bywords for the Mexican man are that he must be ugly, strong, and dependable, and Magnolia's cosmetics speak eloquently against such a triple imperative.

Moreover, the gesture of self-absorption is one that the Mexican man can never give in to (self-sufficiency, yes; self-absorption, never), and we see Magnolia examining himself in a mirror held in such a way that the image of his face is repeated for the camera. It is transgressive enough that we see Magnolia's muscular arms revealed (and note that in *La cantina*, the man's blouse-like shirt has the long sleeves demanded by traditional Mexican machismo),[8] and the narcissism of contemplating himself in the mirror carries the transgression of his transvestism to a second level.

It is important to retain the masculine pronoun when referring to Magnolia in these two images, because there is no good reason to claim that he is attempting to pass as a woman. If this were his intention, he would attempt to mask any detail of his masculinity, such as his feet and muscular arms. It's not that a woman might not have muscular arms, but in attempting to pass as a woman, the transgender male wishes to eliminate any doubt as to his femininity. And too, he would enhance in a redundant fashion the signs bespeaking "woman."[9] Thus, it becomes necessary to ask how we ought to characterize Magnolia's transvestite project, if it is not the sort of transvestism of the man who wishes to pass as woman, such as we have, for example, in Arturo Ripstein's important film *El lugar sin límites* (1978; Place without limits), in which La Manuela goes all out in her feminine array (beginning with a long red dress) in order to dance flamenco for her client/suitor, the very macho truck driver Pancho, in the brothel run by La Manuela's daughter and where La Manuela also works.[10] La Manuela wishes to pass as a woman, and it is only when she publicly lets it be known what Pancho always knew (that is, that she was a transvestite man) that the latter has no choice but to kill her: the fiction regarding the construction of gender has been unpardonably revealed.

Yet such a scheme is not at issue in the universe of Iturbide's photography, because it would be difficult to envision anyone making the "mistake" of thinking Magnolia is a woman. No, Magnolia is a man, and this is very much in evidence, a man who likes to deck himself out as a woman. This type of undertaking, which is what is understood in street English as genderfucking, is an assault on gender binarism that is in large measure sustained via the tertiary characteristics of clothing,[11] in contrast to transvestism properly speaking, in which one aspires to pass for the other (binarily speaking and predominantly masculine ▸ feminine) gender. It is an aspiration, to be sure, that maintains the binarism of the sexual system.

Magnolia combines the masculine and the feminine, in a paradigmatic intersexual gesture (i.e., the third sex of the *muxé*) in which the feminine and the masculine are combined, and this is also very much evident in *Magnolia*

[bis]. In this image, Magnolia is wearing a sort of silk or satin petticoat, material that is considered very feminine. There is a complicated design that might be considered flowery, although this is not clear in the photograph. The petticoat is held up on Magnolia's shoulders by delicate straps, and the bodice appears to have some sort of stuffing to form barely pubescent breasts. Finally, Magnolia is holding up and out to the side the edge of the petticoat in the gesture of a runway model, and his head is turned to the side and he is looking off in the distance, in accord with the recommendation for women dancing *danzón*, which is a popular form of Mexican lower-middle-class ballroom dancing. (See the recommendations to this effect given by the protagonist of María Novaro's 1991 film, *Danzón*, to her transvestite friend who wishes to learn to dance the *danzón* as a woman.)

Nevertheless, despite all these details of feminization—and I would want here to underscore the element of agency, because what is involved is the effort to deck oneself out as a woman and not the circumstantial situation of being effeminate—Magnolia is still very evidently a man, and one with an otherwise very virile body: muscular, hairy legs, strong hands, large feet with a suggestively chunky big toe, and the firm arms of someone who has done hard labor. Besides, Magnolia's waist is thick, and the size of the petticoat, if it was not made specifically for (by) him, is likely that for an imposing woman. Finally, there is the added effect of the ostentatious hat of the Mexican *charro* (landowning horseman), one of the great symbols in Mexico of male virility. The sum total of these details is that Magnolia does not, in any of these three images, achieve the transvestite's goal of passing as a woman. Magnolia, as a man, assumes and assimilates to various womanly features, beginning with his name: there is no name more paradigmatically feminine than that of a flower, except possibly for the primary holy personnel of the Catholic pantheon.[12] In general terms, in Western culture, if not in all cultures, where women, if not marginalized radically, occupy a position secondary to that of man, masculine transvestism, involving men passing as women, is considered an abjection susceptible to discrimination and persecution that is at times unqualifiedly violent: why would a man wish to humiliate himself to the extent of identifying with the belittled gender? In this sense, transvestism is taken as a first step in a process of transsexualism that culminates in the surgical reconfiguration of the masculine body to make it that of a woman. If the foregoing question transmits a profound perplexity for macho society, in the case of the women-based society of Juchitán, things are quite to the contrary: the man who decks himself out as a woman can be seen as aspiring to assimilate to those social subjects who wield the greater material and symbolic power. Thus, Magnolia's transvestism cannot be a circumstance of abjection (except perhaps in his failure to assimilate to that power), but rather serves as an honorable tribute to the potent feminine Other. And by engaging in such a tribute, the Magnolias of Juchitán, far from maintaining a rigid heteronormative binary and far from erasing the ostensible material differences of human bodies, seek to incorporate into theirs the signs of the powerful Juchitecan woman.

As a consequence, the photographs that predominate in *Juchitán de las mujeres* are those that have to do with the society of women, with all its homosocialism and with the exchange of symbolic, corporal, and affective communication they maintain in their domain, which lies beyond Mexican machismo in general.[13] The image *Marcha política* (Political march) reminds us of the political militancy of Juchitecan women, and with *Quince años* (At fifteen) is another of the many photographs that emphasize the transmission of culture between generations of Juchitecan women (it is interesting to note that a little boy spies on the world of women in the photograph from behind a grated window). *Limpia de pollos* (Cleaning chickens), in which the faces of the working women are not seen, only their plucking hands working in concert, suggests the ritual communitarian labor they exercise, while *Doña Guadalupe* is a portrait of a dignified matron of the town who is contemplated in awe by a little girl. *Images of the Spirit*, the photographic collection from which I am quoting, does not reproduce two major images from the original 1989 edition of *Juchitán de las mujeres*, one in which we see four women, dressed as though for a grand festival or an important saint's day, dance without the presence of a single man. In the other one, in which no man is present either, six women have come together to chat among themselves: one rests her arms clasped together by her hands in a very tender fashion on the neck of another woman, both of them with a gaze of mutual trust. I do not wish to insist on any measure of homoeroticism in these images. It may well exist in the social and personal exchanges between the women of Juchitán. But what Iturbide does capture unquestionably with her camera, and what Poniatowska emphasizes in her accompanying texts, is the profound extent of the homosocialism among them, a relationship that affirms the real and symbolic power of the domain they inhabit. As the photobook makes abundantly clear, it is a sort of domain in which the greatest fascination for the two authors had to do with a universe of sex and gender in which things were not as "they were supposed to be" in hegemonic Mexican society.

One of the ruling maxims of queer studies is that the world exceeds, in the reality of human experience, the anemic version provided by compulsory heterosexism. Iturbide/Poniatowska's Juchitán does not correspond, one might say, to the Mexico of the country's bourgeois television (see my study in chapter 11 of this volume on Stefan Ruiz's photographs on Mexican soap operas). Nor does it correspond to the romantic Mexico marketed by the country's vast tourist industry. This Juchitán is some Other Mexico, a Mexico in which it is possible to see the dynamic of sex and gender functioning in a decidedly different way. It is no wonder that *Juchitán de las mujeres* has become one of the most prized works of contemporary Mexican culture.

GUILLE AND BELINDA
A Protolesbian Arcadian Romance

◆ ◆ ◆

The dossier of photographs by Alessandra Sanguinetti entitled *Las aventuras de Guille y Belinda y el enigmático significado de sus sueños* (2007; The adventures of Guille and Belinda and the enigmatic meaning of their dreams),[1] on the two young female playmates Guillermina (shortened to the sexually ambiguous Guille; Guillermina is the feminine form of the male name Guillermo) and Belinda, is, at the very least, a protolesbian romance story.[2] It is a romance story set in the provincial Argentine heartland, legendarily the Arcadian paradise of Argentine national and Creole/nativist values, and the stronghold of the paradigm of heteronormative values as embedded in the gaucho and his descendants, the rural farmhands and their bosses. It is a love story that involves two young women who are cousins, one a conventionally attractive country sweetheart and one an obese woman of the sort destined to be a combination of a social outcast and an object of sexual exploitation: to the degree that the obese woman is less likely, conventionally, to be anyone's sweetheart, she is consigned to be an object of sexual abuse precisely because she belongs to no man.

I do not mean to imply that Guille could not find a husband in the setting of rural Argentina (where, in fact, she might be prized for her heft);
rather, in this story she plays the outcast who finds love with her cousin
Belinda, and the two of them enact a family unit with child that is a fantasy, a dream, in terms of the likely sociological profile of the Argentine
family as evidenced by the rural heartland.[3]

Indeed, one of the immediately significant features of Sanguinetti's
dossier is the focus on the rural setting, in a medium that has in Argentina been relentlessly urban and is likely only to be displayed in an urban
setting of gallery photography.[4] The rural subjects of these photographs
are likely to see themselves portrayed in the published dossier, but not
in images hung in a gallery in their own rural setting. I make this point
because a significant dimension of Sanguinetti's narrative is the turning
away from the urban setting as quintessential for contemporary love stories, particularly those that involve the transgression of traditional heteronormative values. Certainly, much that is nonheteronormative occurs
in the countryside: as has often been observed, if Saint Thomas Aqui-
nas had spent more time on a farm, he would have realized that there is
nothing theologically natural about the primacy of heterosexuality, and
that the animals of nature he believed to model heteronormativity just
as much engage in modeling the "sodomy" he considered to be theologically unnatural. Concomitantly, there is no reason to believe that the other animals of the fields, those of a human kind, adhered to compulsory
heteronormativity any more than their nonhuman animals did. It's just
that, with the exception of a smattering of narratives and a smattering of
critical readings of canonical texts (such as Geirola's queer reading of the
urtext of gaucho cultural narrative, the *Martín Fierro* [1872, 1879]), one
associates with Argentine literature, as with the bulk of Western narrative, the emergence of a queer consciousness, one involving as legitimate
same-sex marriages,[5] in an intransigently urban context. The social movements, in the face of a homophobic dictatorship (1976–1983) that echoed
overall homophobic sentiment in Argentina, began as urban phenomena,
the marches and other protest manifestations are urban phenomena, the
out gay culture that flourished after the return to constitutional democracy in 1983 is an urban phenomenon, the by-now vast queer cultural record (especially in film and television) is an urban phenomenon, and the
research and teaching on queer theory/issues/culture are an urban phenomenon.[6] To be sure, it is reasonable to assume that nonheteronormative love is taking place in all sorts of human spaces in Argentina. However, the primacy of the urban matrix in the national imaginary ("God is

everywhere, but he only holds office hours in Buenos Aires") has always been an erosional threat to that other prime of national(ist) culture, the transcendent meaning of the heartland. As much as Argentina, perhaps more out of ideological inertia than real conviction, holds onto the icon of the heartland (very much threatened by recent neo-Peronista govern-ments, which are steadfastly urban in their populist and even demagogic politics), Argentine cultural production remains hegemonically urban in nature and, more significantly, urban in its thematic commitments.[7]

Thus, Sanguinetti's preference for the rural is particularly noteworthy, not only in general, but also within the specific genre of a highly profes-sional photography. Her photographs of rural animals, *On the Sixth Day* (2005), are superb in their artistry and in the affective dimension the se-miotics of the photographs deploys. Sanguinetti is not the only Argentine photographer to focus on the nonurban. The inimitable Grete Stern (who was German-born) was doing rural/folklore-oriented images in the 1930s, and there is, of course, an extensive bibliography of tourist-oriented pho-tography that focuses on the rural imaginary and the gaucho figure. San-guinetti, then, has a very ideologically committed focus in her story on Guille and Belinda's amorous relationship: it is as much meaningful in its anchor in a specific rural setting as it is in its homoeroticism. That meaning is clearly, in essence, paradisiacal: Guille and Belinda inhabit an Argentine heartland Garden of Eden, a Pampas Arcadia in which a com-munion with their natural setting is a consolidation of their erotic attach-ment. The cover photograph (titled *Ofelias*),[8] which is also one of the last images in the dossier, shows the two women dressed in something like spring princess outfits (there is elsewhere the portrayal of more tradition-al wedding attire), and both girls are clutching bouquets of seasonal flow-ers. They are stretched out side by side in the shallow waters of one of the many rivulets that dot the Argentine Pampas, especially in the spring. The Pampas in general is a perpetually humid grasslands, but in the spring, year-round rivers are supplemented by many rivulets that form ponds and lakes that both water the animals and irrigate the fields. Water imagery is frequent in feminist and lesbian writing, a sensory trope for the liquid-ity of feminine erotics, the fluids associated with the maternal role that much of lesbian sentiment remains integrally attached to, and the sense of floating free that is both a part of female orgasm and a transcendence of masculinist/heteronormative society.[9] In a word, it is the confirma-tion of the bond between woman and Mother Nature, a fundamental ground for her legitimate dignity in the face of the homophobia of the heterosexist paradigm.

Because of the shallowness of the body of water, Belinda and Guille are only partially submerged, which allows for the spectator to appreciate the splash of color of their spring dresses, which in turn complements the color of the bouquets they are grasping, as they lie carried away in a dreamlike state in the gently flowing water. The *sueños* of Sanguinetti's title plays off of a fundamental lexical doubling in Spanish, since the word means both "sleep" and "dream."[10] Here, the women are asleep, to the extent that they lie in the water in a relaxed pose with their eyes closed; Guille's dress even floats beyond her feet as though it were a sort of fabric cocoon, suggesting, in turn, that at last she is to emerge in the spring from the larva of her body as a butterfly as colorful as her dress. But *sueños* also means "dreams," and here, as throughout the dossier, the dreams of Guille and Belinda are those of their love story. They are dreams that counter the harsh reality of the heterosexist narrative of their salt-of-the-earth environment. The sharing of a dreamlike stage, stretched out side by side in a meadow, is found also in *Dos desgracias* (Two misfortunes/Two disgraces), in which their bodies, dressed in everyday clothing—Guille in a man's shirt, Belinda in a cutoff top—are stained with some sort of liquid. We don't know if there is a suggestion of violence here, homophobic or otherwise, but Guille's eyes are closed, while Belinda's are wide-open in an intent stare beyond the camera.[11]

The sleeping/dreaming of the two women is not always benevolently portrayed, and there is certainly the risk that viewers might discern a measure of parody in the images or at least feel at liberty to mock what they are seeing: two naïve country bumpkins, one of whom displays her unseemly fat, playing at being a married couple and, in fact, in one set of images, pretending to be pregnant and then mothers whose babies are only cheap plastic dolls. Sanguinetti defies viewers, it would seem, to think she sees their love as a parody of the so-called real thing, defying them equally to exercise a privilege, as much heteronormative as it is urban-biased, to view these two women as ridiculous hicks.

For this reason it is significant that the women are shown as part of a constituted society, at least as far as their relationship with other women is concerned. Belinda may react in an alienated fashion in the assembled company of men, presumably some of whom are her relatives, in *La jineteada* (Horsemanship), but in *Jaulas* (Cages), the two are accompanied by two older women, relaxing on the veranda of a modest country house. The title refers to the bird cages affixed to the exterior walls of the house, a common practice in Argentina in both the country and the city, and not to any sense of caged women or even women in the rural equivalent of the urban motif of the "woman in the gilded cage." All four women are in a relaxed pose, the epitome of a lazy rural summer afternoon. There are other images of the women interacting with the older women of the household: one of the images of Guille as a girl shows her being bathed outdoors in a tub by an older woman, perhaps her grandmother, who is also one of the women in *Jaulas*.

But the most striking set of images refers to the strand of the romance between Guille and Belinda that involves courtship, maternity, and infant death, a veritable narrative trajectory of a love story. Let me focus on just a few of these images, which make up approximately half of the dossier.

In *El casalito* (Argentine Spanish: loosely translated as The lovebirds), we see the only image, aside from a rather androgynous-looking Belinda in *La jineteada*, in which there is any manifestation of heteronormatizing cross-dressing. De Lauretis's "the lure of the dyke" is here tenderly evoked in an image in which Guille, in her feminine if not conventionally erotic underwear, is embracing her "man" Belinda, who is something like cross-dressed as a young gaucho, at least as far as the rural farmhand's baggy pants are concerned (there is something that looks like the farmhand's scarf around her neck). Although topless—her body has yet to develop feminine traits—she wears a false mustache, the primarily visible sign, of long standing, of mature masculinity. The disconnect between her childlike body and the full mustache is gently comical, especially given Belinda's stare (again, as in *La jineteada*) off into space, apparently enacting the macho imperative to be manly and not display responsive emotion, beyond the concession of holding Guille's hand. If some viewers might see Guille's body as grotesque here, in its near nudity, the following sequences naturalize this staged image, as the protolesbian relationship between the two women, without the need for the confirmation of any pseudoheteronormativity, is affirmed.

The following images show the two women enacting stages in the arc of the romance narrative: Belinda dressed in a short, plain white dress holding a bouquet—she is, however, blindfolded; and Guille, beneath a sign reading Felices Fiestas (happy holidays),[12] dressed also in a long, plain white dress—more like a bridesmaid's gown—with a garland in her hair, seated on a bench next to a table festooned with a traditional wedding cake. Subsequent images show Belinda playing at being pregnant, holding what one presumes to be a balloon under her dress, while Guille contemplates her swollen belly as she holds a balloon herself in one of her hands, as though either to feign pregnancy herself or to enhance Belinda's. Their dress now is of a peasant, perhaps even gypsy, variety, and their faces are smeared with what appears to be the rich, fertile Pampas mud. This image is titled *La inmaculada concepción* (The immaculate conception). Then there is the image of the two women, two years previously, *Madonna*, enacting the adoration of the Christ child. Lost in rapture, the seated Guille (apparently in a garage where animals are kept) clutches a plastic doll, while Belinda, dressed as an angel, holds her hands in prayers and stares up to heaven (not at the child, as in customary poses of the adoration). This image is dated three years prior to the scene of pregnancy.

What is noticeable about these images, which can be called playful, a more detailed staging of the sort of so-called playing house most children engage in (although in expected heterosexual rather than, as here, queer paradigms), is that there are no fixed roles. If the first image mentioned has Belinda holding a bouquet as though she were the "male" suitor, Guille, in the next image, is dressed as though she were the bride. But then Belinda is the one who is pregnant, while Guille, albeit dressed as a woman, contemplates Belinda's belly, in a traditional macho image, as though she were the proud father contemplating his success in inseminating the woman in strict conformance with patriarchal norms. Roles are reversed again when it is Guille who is the Virgin Mary, whose archetypal motherhood is adored by Belinda. The achronology of the last two images is also a factor in disrupting the narrative arc.

Finally, many images later, the couple, dressed in funereal black, wails over what we can presume to be a coffin, draped with a white sheet and topped with a bouquet of wildflowers and a simple cross fashioned by tying two sticks at right angles. *El funeral de Archibaldo* (1999; Archibald's funeral) could depict that of the doll-child in *Madonna* of the same year, or it could be that of a beloved pet. Coming as part of the story of Guille and Belinda's relationship and marriage, it is also, reasonably, part of the narrative arc of romance, the segment relating to the loss of the blessed child that confirms the legitimately constituted family's compliance with the patriarchal imperative of reproduction. The emotional shock of loss is as great as the despair of having failed in completely fulfilling that imperative, which is to see the child brought to maturity and, in turn, secured in a matrimony that will reiterate the heteronormative cycle. This, to be sure, is striking for what Guille and Belinda are *not* doing, since they can never be a heteronormative couple, and even if one were to become a biological mother, they could never be enacting the legitimately constituted patriarchal family. The mockery of the legitimate narrative is reinforced here by the way Belinda is gripping, so that the viewer clearly sees the cover, a copy of the Santa Biblia (Holy Bible).

Sanguinetti's photobook is, I believe it is safe to say, the first narrative in Latin American culture inscribed through photographic images that allows for anything approximating a lesbian interpretation. Graciela Iturbide's *Juchitán de las mujeres* (1989) is a significant photographic investigation of queer gender identities, particularly involving women, in Juchitán, in the western part of the Tehuantepec region of Mexico.[13] But Iturbide's famous images do not inscribe any specific narrative. Done in extremely high-resolution and brilliant color photography, Sanguinetti's *Las aventuras* does involve something like a specifically visible romance narrative reminiscent of mass-circulation photonovels. Moreover, it is a romance that is anchored in a specific sociohistorical space, the Argentine heartland, which is incrusted with the supposedly simple virtues of traditional farm life, by contrast with the sophisticated customs of the metropolitan center of Buenos Aires. Those simple virtues, as opposed to the Sodom-and-Gomorrah sexuality of the metropolitan capital, center on the narrative romance of the heteronormative patriarchy. The force of Sanguinetti's narrative photobook, however, lies ultimately in the disruption, via a privileged woman-woman relationship, of that paradigm.

One might well argue that it is stretching a point to call this relationship lesbian or even to attenuate that designation with the prefix "proto." Of course, there are many definitions of what constitutes lesbianism, one of them being the privileged bond between two women, a bond that does not necessarily include anything that can conventionally be considered sexual, genital or otherwise. One might, furthermore, say that what is at issue in Sanguinetti's dossier (to which a sequel is forthcoming) is the innocent playacting children engage in, especially young girls thrown together in a solitary environment. To call such playacting "lesbian" or even "protolesbian" becomes, then, veritably outrageous. But is it? When children play house in mixed company, enacting prescribed mommy-and-daddy gender roles, one applauds their enactment of heterosexuality and, conversely, were their roles inverted, we would not be surprised to find that the adults would be alarmed: not even in play can the heterosexist norm be transgressed, as it augurs ill for future sexual identity. This heterosexist norm is still energetically enforced in Argentina, and nowhere more so than in rural settings. Why, then, are same-gender enactments by children, playing at romance, engaging in crushes, somehow "innocent" of sexuality, especially when cross-dressing, wedding scenes, and pregnancy are involved? To be sure, girls' fantasies and dreams (escapist or otherwise) about what their lives will become are involved. But whose fantasies are these, the girls' or the photographer's? Those of the child's world? Those of the adult's world? Or are they those of human relation-ships that segue from one into the other, without any necessary break between the innocence of children and the knowledge (in the biblical sense) of adults? Clearly, these are not Henri Cartier-Bresson's "found" and unmediated photographic opportunities, as there is very much an element of careful staging about them, enhanced by the high color density not customarily associated with photographs captured by chance. This is high art, not journalism, and part of high art is calculated composition. The fact that, at least for part of the period of their lives in which the im-ages were made, Guille and Belinda are "children" does not render their portrayal innocent of the matters of the adult world. They may not be les-bian lovers in the sense of, say, Annie Leibovitz and her famous subject, Susan Sontag, but there are here very many of the contours of a privileged woman-woman communication between them that Sanguinetti's camera captures so suggestively. What they might become in their subsequent lives is not of interest here.

HOMOSOCIALISM ◀▶ HOMOEROTICISM
IN THE PHOTOGRAPHY OF MARCOS LÓPEZ

◆ ◆ ◆

The photography of the Argentine Marcos López has attracted enormous international attention. Working in sometimes garish colors (his prints routinely include hand coloring), López mixes a parody of postmodern commercial advertising with an acerbic critique of the kitschy detritus of contemporary globalized daily life, especially in its urban Argentine version (for general characterizations of López's photography, see the chapter on him in my *Urban Photography in Argentina*). Whether focusing on specific commercial products, often ones that are icons of modern living like Coca-Cola, or on patriotic and quasi-patriotic symbols (the Argentine flag, Che Guevara, respectively), López relies on his audience to understand the clever, surprising, and often jolting utilization of pop art and kitsch as an artistic strategy for critiquing the morass of conflicting ideologies and their motifs that engulfs—assaults—our visual perception of the world. López's employment of forms of hyperrealism as found in one range of glossy advertising transforms the ideal/idealized universes of the latter into outrageous interventions, in common domestic spaces, of staged parodies of the quotidian, whether the latter is a com-

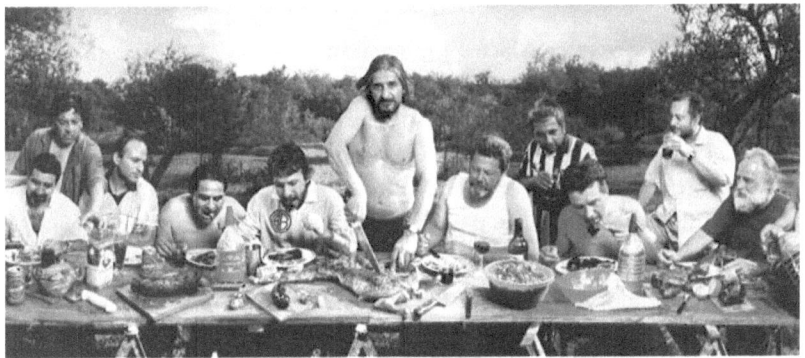

Figure 10.1. Marcos López, *Asado criollo* (Argentine barbecue).
Used with permission of Marcos López.

mon object, like the Coca-Cola bottle, or customarily trivialized motifs like
those of religion, sociopolitical commitments, routine cultural values, and
contemporary life: the "stuff" of our systems of identity and understanding.

One of López's most recognized images is *Asado criollo* (Argentine
barbecue),[1] which is a recasting of Da Vinci's *The Last Supper*. In place of
the sacred Last Supper of Jesus Christ and the Twelve Apostles, the founding event figured in the Holy Mass of the Catholic Church as a commemo-
ration of Christ's sacrifice for the salvation of mankind, we have the virtually sacralized ritual of the Argentine barbecue, where the blood-bathed
sacrifice of edible beef is the privileged figure of Argentine communal
identity. If, wherever Catholics assemble, they will celebrate Christ's sacrifice for the salvation of mankind, wherever Argentines assemble, they will
celebrate the sacrifice of beef for the affirmation of "Argentinity."[2] This is
all a pretty hilarious and irreverent network of associations, part of whose
resonance is the way in which so many Argentines are not particularly
overtly religious, on either a formal or folkloric level—not, at least, in the
way in which one associates popular Christianity as so essentially a part of
the fabric of everyday life in a society like Mexico, for example.

Images like *Asado criollo* (*Carnaval criollo* [Argentine carnival] is an-
other) have contributed to López's growing reputation, and, besides in
Argentina, his work has been shown in Spain, Mexico, and elsewhere in
Latin America, and in New York, in a show February 25–March 14, 2005,
at the White Box gallery (www.whiteboxny.org) called *Al sur del realismo /
South of Realism.*[3]

I have examined elsewhere López's use of kitsch in order to critique
globalized values through parody (Foster, "El kitsch argentino"), but here I
would like to address issues of homosocialism, homoeroticism, and their

interrelationship in López's images, particularly in those that appear in a small portfolio, *Marcos López*, published in Mexico City in 2004.

Let us first define our terms. By "homosocialism" (one could also invest here in the term "homosociality"), one understands the strong and exclusivizing bond between members of the same sex. Such a definition, and its implied or overt sanction—and implied or overt disapproval—by various intersecting social institutions, is predicated on a conception of stable sex identity, such that there is a clear-cut separation between male and female. This is a stability that is maintained, in the main, by both transgendering (the movement from one sexual identity to another) and by transsexuality (the anatomical reconfiguration of a body such that it migrates from one sexual identity to another); homosocialism becomes problematical wherever queer theory destabilizes binary sexual identity. In Sedgwick's famous formulation, which originally applied only to late-nineteenth- and early-twentieth-century British literature, but which has been extensively adapted to a wide array of societies by masculinity studies (see Connell for one early survey; Gutman for pertinent research in Latin America), homosocialism is the pact, the so-called gentlemen's agreement, whereby power is circulated among men, who are bonded together by a number of social networks and practices: marriage, business, fraternal associations, guilds, secret societies, shared initiations and acculturations, and the like. Women are not only excluded, but used by homosocialism as a token or shifter of masculine power. Two typical narratives are the accession to the realm of the boss by marrying his daughter or the use of the sexuality of women as a way of displaying to other men one's legitimating heterosexuality. Such narratives depend on an interaction with women to demonstrate the male's appropriate participation in the hegemonic codes of a male-dominated society.

It is significant to note that, while homosociality may be sustained by an undercurrent of (weak) homoerotic desire, as in the simple comfort of being with other men in an all-male sphere, strong homoerotic desire and the acting upon that desire through the enactment of a number of specifically genital and orgasmic scripts are taboo and would disrupt the homosocial pact.[4] But there is unquestionably a segue between homosocialism as the approved assembling of men and homoeroticism as what might happen among assembled men under the "right" conditions, such as having had too much to drink or sharing traumatic experiences.[5] To be sure, another dimension of this issue is exactly what constitutes homoeroticism: that is, exactly when is it present and how might we detect it (beyond manifest signs such as penile tumescence or specific acts we can agree to call homoerotic)? This is the problem of what to make of frater-nity initiations, especially where practices like spanking are involved (see Mattoso's extensive analysis of these phenomena in German, American, and Brazilian university societies), or of the hugging and butt-slapping of team sports, not to mention the display of the male buttocks promoted by tight-fitting uniforms, as in American baseball, and the fetishizing of the legs of soccer players (Manrique); also legendary are the display of the male body in bullfighting (see Afanador's photography and Foster's study of it, "Toreros de moda") and the way in which the all-male world of bull-fighting has always involved a dimension of homoeroticism, as Lorca so eloquently captures it in his famous "Llanto por Ignacio Sánchez Mejías" (see other references in my study of Afanador's photography).

Thus, if we reserve the term "homoeroticism" for a series of acts and their accompanying narratives that confirm the possibility of the fulfill-ment of sexual desire between same-sex partners, it is, nevertheless, evident that the homosocialism that cements the personal relationships between men in the exercise of patriarchal authority may often (perhaps always?) contain an undercurrent of the physical, but customarily tabooed and therefore unfulfilled, attraction between male bodies.[6] Such weak ho-moeroticism can rarely be the subject of overt social discourse, although one does occasionally hear calls for the boys to cut down a bit on the butt-slapping, while homosocialism—"getting together with the guys"—is an accepted and promoted intercultural norm of modern society.[7]

There is, then, an interesting vein of male homosocial imagery in the recent work of López that has unmistakable homoerotic overtones, even if it is only a weak homoeroticism that the viewer can "strengthen," so to speak, in an attentive contemplation of the insinuations of and the insertions into real-world experience that López's images put on display through parody.

Certainly, the homosocial is an issue in López's by-now rather legend-ary *Asado criollo* composition. In the first place, it evokes the founding or grounding homosociality of Leonardo Da Vinci's depiction of the Last Supper of Christ with his disciples. Leaving aside the question of whether or not there is a feminine presence in the painting in the person of Mary Magdalene, as touted by Dan Brown in his controversial and transgres-sive 2003 best-selling novel, *The Da Vinci Code* (which also expounds on Mary Magdalene as the wife of Christ), the assemblage of the thir-teen men of Da Vinci's painting and the endless reproduction of it, which the concept of kitsch helps us to understand, confirm a monumental paradigm of homosocialism in Western culture. Now, it is important to stress that López does not simply plug in substitutions for the arrangement, clothes, gestures, and interactions of the participants in the Da Vinci painting; this would be rather facile and the essence of noncritical or unreflective kitsch. Rather, he retains the six-against-six balance of the men on each side of the central figure, but has them more in the postures of consuming food and drink than is the case with the Da Vinci original. Moreover, while the latter is encased in an idealized Renaissance banquet room, López's denizens surround an improvised open-air table, with the unmistakable humid Pampas landscape of central Argentina in the background: that is, where Da Vinci's image is stylized and dehistoricized, López's photograph evokes a specific, gritty sociohistorical texture, that of the Argentine barbecue.

I use the word "gritty" here advisedly, because the texture of the carefully staged image is that of a casual, real-life weekend convocation of men to eat, drink, and enjoy each other's company. They are all dressed casually, some so casually as to project an offensive image to straightlaced Argentines, especially given the sacred context evoked by the image. Both the man we can call the Jesus stand-in and two of his "apostles" appear shirtless, one other wears a sleeveless undershirt, while two others wear shirts open to reveal more chest than some would consider decorous. One man, who bleeds off the left margin of the image, appears to be wearing a short-sleeved undershirt, leaving six men whose torso is respectably clothed. Undoubtedly, a major Argentine cultural referent here is the humorous drawings *Buenos Aires en camiseta* (Buenos Aires in an undershirt), drawn by Alejandro del Prado (Calé) for Guillermo Divito's popular magazine *Rico tipo* (Swell) in the late 1950s and early 1960s. Calé, in satirizing broadly the tics of the Argentine petit bourgeois male, also captured the way in which his habits veered from the rigorous standards of the sartorially perfect English gentleman the national upper middle class and oligarchy aspired to emulate. Also, Da Vinci's painting represents Jesus and the apostles as impeccably clothed or robed, and López's image subverts as much the decorum of the Renaissance work as it evokes an alleged Argentine careless vulgarity.

Of special note is the way the Jesus stand-in does specifically evoke the Savior where his companions do not merely replicate the apostles (beyond their balanced six-by-six distribution). The stand-in, who stands imposingly above his companions, has both the long hair and the beard of the Jesus original, just the sort of hirsuteness that was what the Argentine neofascist guardians of public morals in the late 1960s and again in the 1970s considered a sign of effeminacy and homosexuality. Da Vinci's

Jesus is seated, with his hands outstretched in the sign of the first offering of his sacrifice, but López's counterimage is masterfully wielding the knife in the central ritual of the *asado*, the cutting and distribution of the cooked meat. Not only is the latter shirtless, but his cutting action emphasizes pectoral muscles, which are complemented by what for some might be the erotic nature of a fleshy belly button and pants that ride just low enough to be right at the nevertheless concealed pubic line. While there is little here that one can call (homo)erotic beyond the possibilities inherent in the unkempt display of the bodies of the guests at this table and the physicality of dedicated eating and drinking that is crucial to a good *asado*, this assertedly homosocial gathering reminds one that the ur-homosocial drinking and eating party is Plato's *Symposium*, where one of the crucial topics of conversation is human sexuality, including Diotima's explanation for and defense of what we have come to call Greek homosexuality. These convivial Argentines might well discuss the women, the *minas*, but never at the expense of the ritualized shared physicality of their meal.[8]

One detail of the cultural horizons of Da Vinci's *Last Supper*, so pregnant with meaning as to the founding event of Christian homosociality, is Da Vinci's own homosexuality, a detail that the Vatican, and popular art history, would choose emphatically to ignore. Yet no serious art historian can overlook this dimension of the Italian Renaissance artistic giant's biography and, therefore, its appearance, if only latently, in his work.[9] Therefore, it would be rather risky, if not outrageous, to suggest that there is a hidden homosexuality about Da Vinci's painting, although viewers are always entitled to see what they (want to) see. Since no "protective veil of the sacred" envelops López's photography, and since, indeed, one of the licenses of parody is to encourage outrageous meanings, one may feel more comfortable with teasing out the latent homoeroticism of what one might call *Asado criollo*'s "la gran comilona de los muchachos" (The guys' real pig-out). Boy-men will be boy-men.

The homoerotic is more clearly evident in the cover image of *Marcos López*, where the same model is used for both the carefully groomed hospital aide and his long-haired, severely injured patient (the image in turn has a definite intertextuality with Frida Kahlo's signature work, *Las dos Fridas* [The two Fridas], which need not necessarily evoke Kahlo's well-known bisexuality/lesbianism).[10]

This image titled *Hospital* would be relatively uninteresting—serving, perhaps at best, as a poster for a national nurses/hospital orderly association—if it weren't for the bonding between the two men that is underscored by their both being enacted by the same model: photography

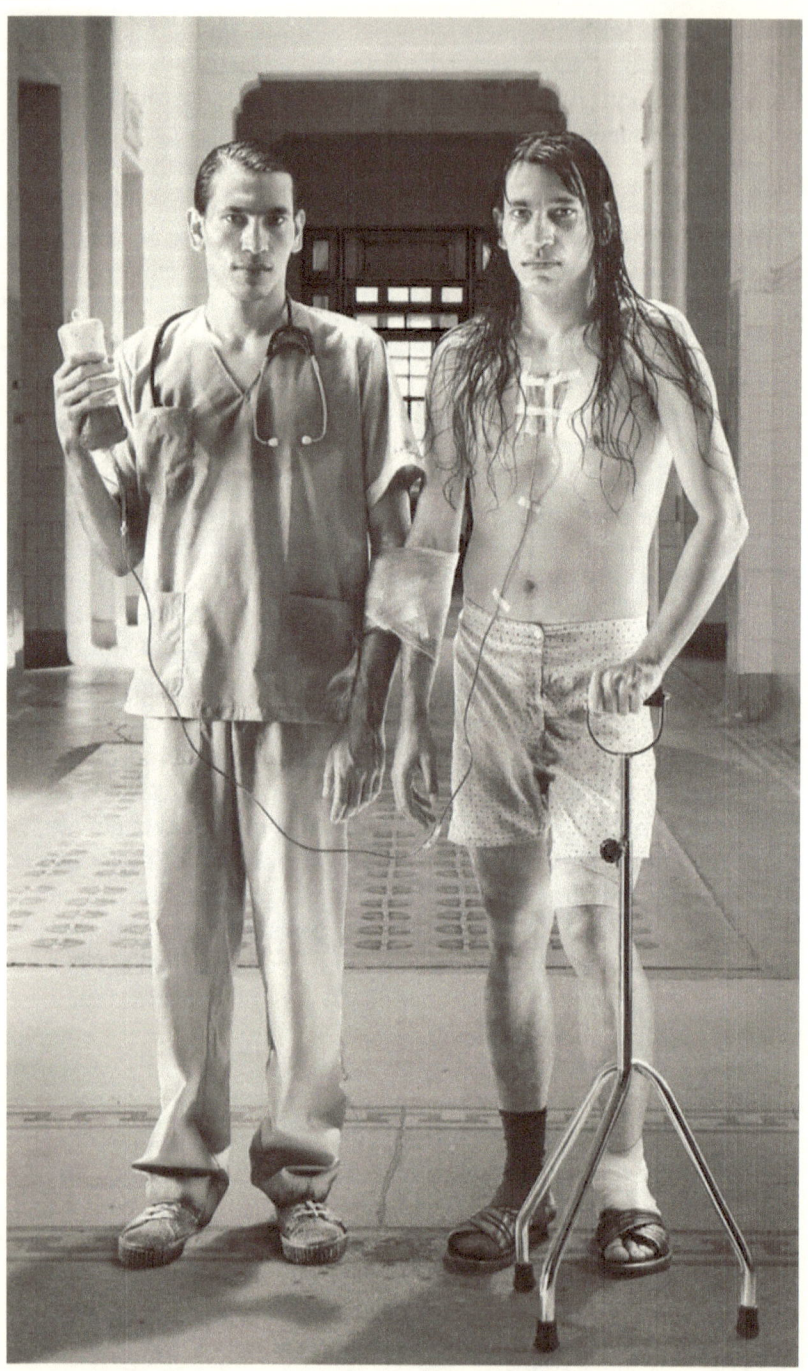

Figure 10.2. Marcos López, *Hospital*. Used with permission of Marcos López.

and cinema have a venerable tradition of dual (even multiple) parts being played by the same actor, often around the ages-old motif of the evil twin, as in Bette Davis's 1964 *Dead Ringer* (dir. Paul Henreid) or Jeremy Irons's 1988 reprise of the Davis film, *Dead Ringers* (dir. David Cronenberg).[11] Got up differently—the long-haired, partially nude patient; the soberly neat aide—they are also differentiated by the accompanying details of their role. The patient, of course, has the trappings of his treatment (bandages, the IV connection, the walker to support the traumatized right leg), and the aide of his role (the simple green cotton scrubs, the stethoscope worn around the neck, the IV drip). The pair is photographed in what appears to be one of the halls of an antiquated hospital from the generation of the Rivadavia or the Ramos Mejía.

But where the expected is disrupted, wherein lies the Barthean punctum that hooks the attentive viewer's gaze, is in the fact that the right forearm of the patient is bound to the left forearm of his aide by a tightly wrapped bandage of bloody gauze. There is no indication of why the patient should be wearing such a wrapping, since the patient's contusions appear to be confined to his left side, and it is left to the curious speculation of the viewer as to why the patient should be bound to the aide in this fashion. Of course, one could attribute an allegorical function to this detail: the patient needs the assistance of the aide in order to mend or even in order to survive. But that bond is already allegorized by the presence of the IV, which the aide holds (and will subsequently hang from the appropriate suspension apparatus) for the patient, ensuring the continued administration of whatever the bag contains. Again, there is nothing directly erotic about this image, except for the handsomeness of the actor, part of whose body is minimally revealed in the enactment of the patient. Much more suggestive would have been an image of the aide dangling an enema bag whose hose is inserted into the patient's rectum, although this would be an unlikely occurrence in the sort of transfer from one place to another that might be the "real-life" circumstance of the event captured by the photo.

Yet the disruption of the everyday occurrence of a transfer from one place to the next in the modern hospital that comes with the detail of the shared bandage provokes speculation as to the figured relationship between the two. The hospital is the setting for frequent (homo)erotic fantasies, and playing nurse/doctor is one of the ways in which children first discover each other's bodies: nurses and doctors are customarily the first nonparental authority figures who manipulate and invade our body in what can be later resemanticized in erotic terms (see the topic of rape by medical instrument as it is developed in the Irons film mentioned above). The intimacy with the body of the patient required in many routine medical procedures, in turn, is one of the reasons, even before the threat of STDs, why some medical personnel are uncomfortable with treating patients they know or suspect to engage in same-sex acts; for others, this will be part of the pleasure of the other's body.[12] Even when the body of the patient is neither manipulated nor invaded literally or metaphorically (the insertion of an IV or even an ear examination), the proximity between the two bodies (unquestionably where the vagina or the rectum is involved), the one ministering and the one being ministered to, can be suggestive.[13] The fact that such a proximity is sealed here, one might say, by the bloody bandage cannot, therefore, be dismissed as a quirky disruption of naturally occurring circumstances.

Two other images in the volume equally allow for the displacement from naturally occurring circumstances to the homoerotic. It is questionable to what degree the homosocial is involved in the hospital scene, except for a general policy whereby male patients are tended to by male aides and female patients by female aides. However, one of the most homosocial spaces in modern society is the locker room, which is closely associated with other athletic and gymnasium spaces like the shower, the steam room, the Jacuzzi, the massage room, and the infirmary. The bathhouse/sauna was, before AIDS, one of the great meeting places for gay men, and the fancy gym is, for today's guppy, one major site for same-sex cruising (American university sports centers are notorious in this regard).[14] The homoerotic dimensions of sports have long been maintained (Prongher), and it is difficult to forget that the original Olympics were performed in the nude; homoerotic overtones have also long been associated with European soccer, and Bazán recalls the 1995 controversy surrounding the Argentine national team (433–434). The sociologist Juan José Sebreli first broached the subject in print in a book from 1981, *Fútbol y masas* (Soccer and the masses), but develops it as a major theme in his 1998 *La era del fútbol* (The age of soccer; see also his "Historia secreta" [Secret history]).

In López's image titled *El vestuario* (The locker room), one is particularly struck by the fact that none of the seven men (athletes and trainers) whose faces can be seen (there is an eighth man stretched out on a massage table, his face hidden by one of the other players) looks anywhere else but directly at the camera: no one peeks out of the closet here at the body of another man . . . Moreover, all of the men visible are hypermasculine, confident in their pose before the camera, with marked secondary sexual characteristics well in evidence, such as hairy chest and legs, heavy beard, mustaches, muscular torso and legs, with appropriate tertiary ac-coutrements, such as athletic wear, soccer ball, the ankle bandage, and what appears to be a tube or container of ointment, that are metonymies of strenuous physical activity. The file of identical lockers against the back wall iconicizes the continuity between these men, where the sameness of their macho presence guarantees the easy circulation of the norms of homosociality without any trace of the discrepancy from these norms that would signal the countermasculine, the effeminate, the threat of homo-sexuality. True, one of the men, to the left of the image, somewhat older than the others, is fleshier than one associates with a sustained athletic life, while, in the right-hand background, there is a frankly paunchy individual with long hair (he is, nevertheless, properly uniformed for athletic play). But these are minor discordant notes that only serve to affirm the overall conventional hypermasculinity of the men we see in the foreground. In short, this is a world of men and for men, and if resolute homosociality were ever to segue into homoeroticism, it is not likely to include any sign of the feminine. It is precisely the homoerotic undertones of the hyper-masculine universe of soccer that both Bazán and Sebreli speak of, and, while Archetti underscores the way in which soccer—like many all-male sports—transculturally serves to assimilate young men to the codes of masculine homosociality, there is no way of categorically specifying when the frisson of the homoerotic will occur.[15]

One of López's most outrageous compositions is *Tomando sol en la terraza* (Sunning on the roof), which was used for the invitation and pub-licity for the early 2005 exhibit of his work at the White Box. Unlike the images I have discussed up until now, this image and the next one to be discussed involve a single male model; hence, there is no immediate ho-mosocial context. Yet, by contrast, the two images both more readily evoke the homoerotic, which is located here in the display of the partially naked male body. Although the image of the partially naked male body is legiti-mated in certain contexts, such as that of athletic locker rooms, it does not customarily involve the privileged exposure of the penis.

Tomando sol is constructed around the common occurrence of sun-bathing, which in an apartment-dwelling metropolis like Buenos Aires often means stretching out on a towel on the terrace of one's high-rise building. Certainly, the majority of sunbathers are women, and sports and other physically active undertakings are the most appropriate way for the male body to gain whatever are considered the beneficial aspects of direct exposure to the sun; concomitantly, to lie inert in the sun is a female/womanlike activity. True, López's male sunbather is surrounded by the details of a masculine world: various bottles of beer and a bottle opener, along with a half-consumed glass of brew. There is an ashtray with two butts of two consumed cigarettes, and a carton of Marlboros (unquestionably a real man's tobacco of choice).[16] A stack of magazines is also at hand, the top one of which appears to be a sports magazine, as its cover carries a routine soccer image. One rather whimsical detail is the garden hose (often laughingly referred to as a penis substitute), which runs alongside the reclining man and loops its way around one of the beer bottles, as though it were a sunning serpent; its two tones of green partially match the colors of the blanket on which the man lies sunning.

The model here is, in all regards, one of López's by-now familiar hypermasculine bodies: trim and muscular, with firm and hairy legs and a nicely matted chest, his strong facial characteristics manly in every regard. In sum, he is a man's man. What is jarring, however, is the way he is dressed and what that dress leaves exposed. Nude sunbathing on a private terrace may be preferred by some men, although heterosexual men are less likely than women (or homosexual men) to worry about tan lines: indeed, the tan line on a naked male body might be viewed by some as sexy, since it frames the now exposed but usually concealed genitals or

Figure 10.3. Marcos López, *El vestuario* (The locker room). Used with permission of Marcos López.

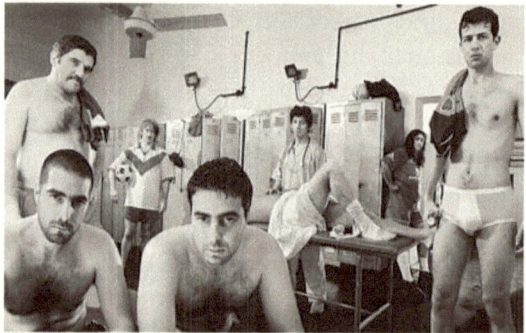

Figure 10.4. Marcos López, *Tomando sol en la terraza* (Sunning on the roof). Used with permission of Marcos López.

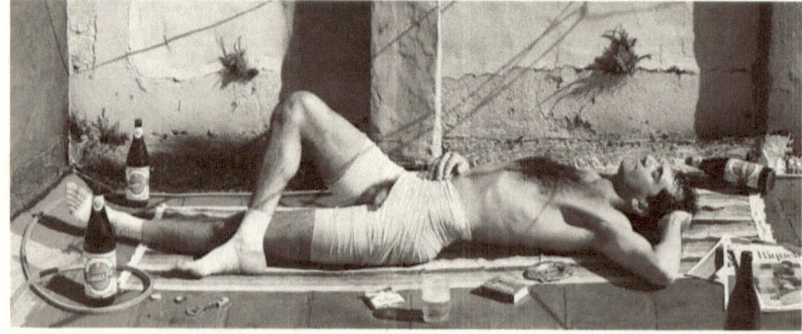

buttocks. But the covering of the lower regions of the body means wearing a swimsuit; even underwear might be permissible. However, López's model is swathed in athletic bandages from his midriff to halfway down his thighs, something like an improvised locker-room version of surfing shorts, although tighter and neutral in color, as opposed to the often colorful and baggy original. Moreover, the athletic bandage around the model's middle draws attention to the more reasonable presence of the wrapping around both his ankles and instep, such as one might find on an athlete's foot to prevent or remedy a sprain from action in sports.

But what is specifically transgressive about *Tomando sol* is the way in which the model's penis is exposed. The athletic bandage is wrapped around the man's waist, buttocks, and upper thighs in such a way that, although some minor glimpses of skin are allowed, his genitals are exposed, with his penis (notably uncircumcised from the point of view of a North American viewer) resting on the edge of a strip of the bandage. One does not normally sunbathe the penis without the rest of the lower body being exposed, and, not to mention the medical inadvisability of such exposure, I am unaware of any known fetish of the sunbathed (or sunburned) penis. López is known for his over-the-top whimsicalness, and it is amply evident in this composition, with its showcasing of the model's respectably sized penis and the echoes of the strongly masculine phallus in the beer bottles, the cigarettes, and the garden hose. The contemplation of the male body required by this composition, one that underscores the phallic, disrupts the heterosexist homosocial convention whereby the male body is masculine (a condition of the appropriateness of the homosocial pact), but it is not erotic: the genitals are assumed to be there, and with acceptable potency, but they can never be the object of confirming scrutiny. Whenever the male body is the occasion for the spectacular gaze, as the female body routinely is, it is placed at the disposal of a homoerotic interest that is inadmissible within the manly homosocial pact.[17]

I would like to close with what I think is López's most brilliant composition, the *Sireno del Río de la Plata* (River Plate male siren), a revision of one of the tritest motifs associated with the sea. The *sireno* of the title of the composition is the nonoccurring (at least in terms of academic Spanish) masculine form of *sirena*, the siren of the sea or, in its more domesticated form, the mermaid.[18] If one may use a queer designation, López's masculine mermaid is very much a parody of the siren of the sea motif.[19]

Whereas standard images of the siren (most commonly evoked is the sculpture that is the symbol of the city of Copenhagen) center on a series of ultrafeminine features—long blonde hair, firm and full breasts (but

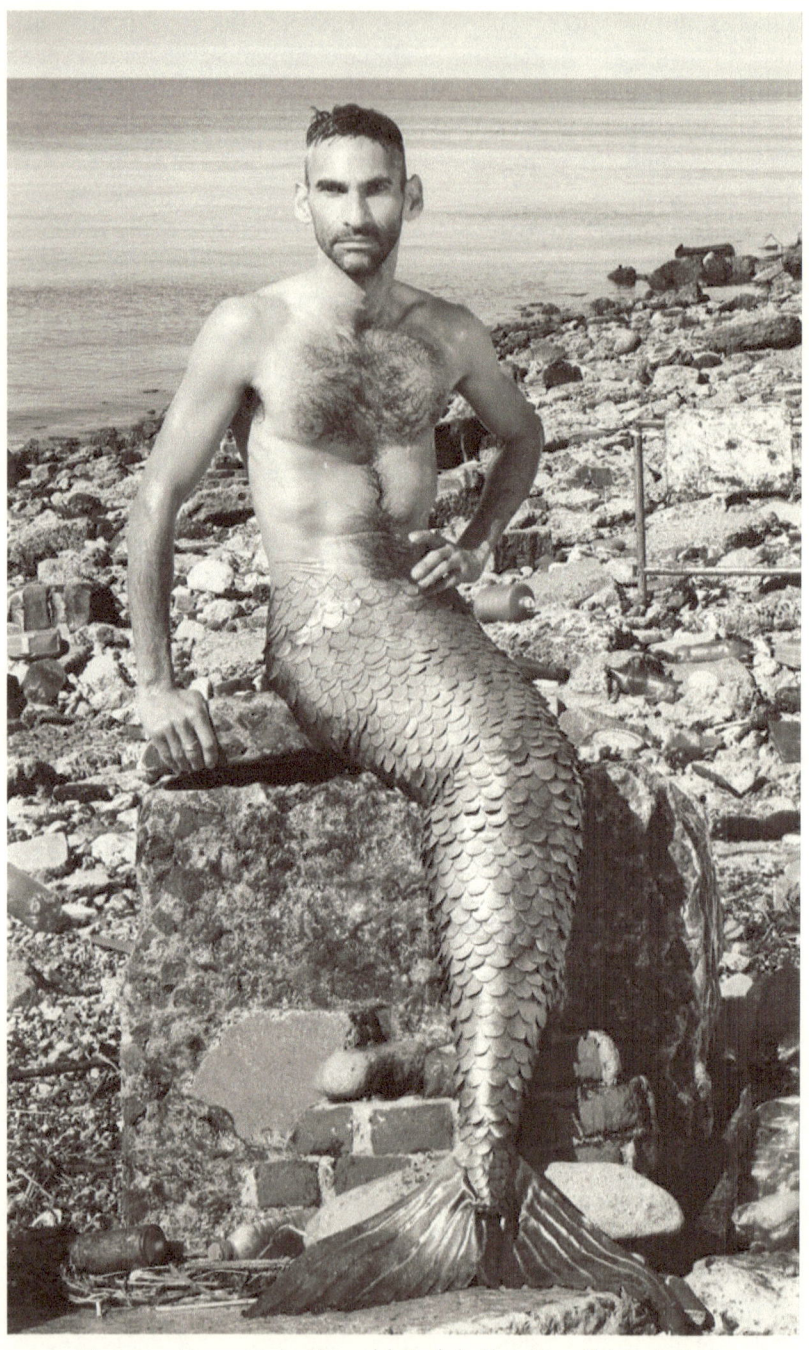

Figure 10.5. Marcos López, *Sireno del Río de la Plata* (River Plate male siren). Used with permission of Marcos López.

without being bosomy), curvaceous figure, languid pose—López's model is both a refutation of the feminine and an inscription of the hypermasculine. It might be a matter of taste as to whether this male model is grotesque in his masculinity or whether he is the male equivalent of female allure. The model is, without a doubt, as hard and trim as the conventional female figure is delicately curved, and his hairy torso constitutes as definitive a display of sex characteristics as the former's breasts. But his pose is anything but languid, as he strongly grips part of the stone shelf on which he is seated, with an arm assertively akimbo. His jug ears, unshaven face, almost scowling eyes, and unfriendly line of mouth may, in fact, suggest the way in which the mythological mermaid was actually no friend to those who became seduced by her fateful presence.

López's *sireno* suggests the threat implicit in male sexual attraction, whether addressed to a woman or to another man. The fact that the landscape of the masculine mermaid is a crumbling and garbage-strewn beach also undercuts whatever conventional artistry there is about Disneyesque depictions of this version of idealized feminine beauty. The effect of coming upon this figure washed ashore is not that of the sensuous swoon, but rather the shock of the most radically disruptive of artistic conventions. Of a whole with the men represented in images such as *El vestuario, Tomando sol en la terraza*, and *Asado criollo*—that is, men with unquestionably rigorously masculine bodies, with nothing of the conventions of the idealized bodies of gay pornographic visual art, such as Ruven Afanador's previously mentioned bullfighters—López's *sireno* mocks the motif of the mermaid, while offering in its place an aggressively masculine token. But to whom is this *sireno* offered? With its tapering tail replacing the sexual attributes of the lower male torso, the masculine mermaid calls out implicitly to the conventional audience of the siren—men. And to the extent to which this male body is not the androgyne of so much of gay male art,[20] López is offering the (homo)erotic gaze of his spectator exactly the sort of image that confirms the all-male universe of the homosocial pact.

PERFORMING MASCULINE HETEROSEXUALITY IN STEFAN RUIZ'S PHOTOGRAPHY OF MEXICAN SOAP OPERAS

◆ ◆ ◆

S oap operas in Mexico,[1] especially the vast programming undertaken by Televisa, which dominates the Mexican market and exports its products extensively, have replaced film as the mirror of a hegemonic social ideology in that country.[2] The great chroniclers of Mexico City, Carlos Monsiváis and Carlos Bonfil, maintained, with considerable eloquence and a persuasive documentation, that Mexicans during the Golden Age of Mexican cinema, following the Mexican Revolution of the second decade of the twentieth century that created contemporary Mexico, went to the movies to learn how to live and love as good citizens. Imposing a rigid code of morality, unswerving nationalism, and unquestionable heteronormativity, Mexican filmmaking, no matter what social class was dealt with in a specific film, conveyed a social model that unambiguously rewarded the faithful and punished the deviant.[3] While recent work on the filmmaking of this era, which began to crumble in the 1970s and effectively ended in the 1980s, has now begun to point out fissures in the edifice and suggest the compelling consequences of unresolved contradictions (such as the lesbianism of the redoubtable Sara García, who made almost fifteen films touting conventional heterosexist Mexican motherhood), Mexican filmmaking of the Golden Age nevertheless presents an ideological unity integral to the confirmation of revolutionary (i.e., post–Revolution of 1910) Mexico.

U.S. filmmaking was also ideologically hegemonic during the thirty-year reign of the Hayes Code (ca. 1930–1960). But in Mexico the government closely controlled film production in a direct fashion, allowing for an enormous range of artistic creativity and experimentation (one thinks of the magnificent camerawork of the ubiquitous Gabriel Figueroa), as long as filmmakers did not deviate from a conception of the revolutionary integrity and unity of a greater Mexico, the primacy of the Spanish language, the cult of mestizo identity with its roots in a rural, nonurban primeval tradition, and the unreflective heterosexist imperative ("Haz patria, ten hijos" [Be patriotic and have children]), with its equally unreflective sexism and macho primacy.[4]

However, by the early twenty-first century, there is very much a sense in Mexico that the hegemony imposed in the early twentieth century has become severely fragmented. Certainly, as has been noted, that hegemony in Mexican filmmaking had been very much undermined by the work of a new generation of independent creators who chose to defy and work outside the government-sponsored studio system, with the admirable results of the New Mexican filmmaking of recent decades, including directors (important women and queers among them) who have gone so far as to work in English outside the national confines of Mexico, giving rise to serious concerns about where, exactly, the locus of contemporary Mexican film is to be situated. In any event, filmmaking in Mexico during the past fifty years has yielded some outstanding, internationally recognized works in terms of themes and cinematographic experimentation, along with a host of vibrant actors, directors, and support personnel, all of which continue Mexico's important place in the realm of Latin American filmmaking. Yet, while that filmmaking unquestionably addresses itself in the main to the vital issues of contemporary life in Mexico, especially in terms of urban tensions, political corruption, emigration to the United States, and the matter of narcotrafficking, Mexican film no longer enjoys the status of being, in Monsiváis's words, the mirror of Mexican society. That role has been largely assumed by the soap opera genre.

Evolving out of radio and assuming importance in the 1960s–1970s, precisely at the time the hegemonic edifice of filmmaking was crumbling, the Mexican soap opera may be said to enjoy a prestige and influence second to those of no other entertainment medium in Latin America. To be sure, soap operas are an important staple of television programming throughout the continent, and in major markets like Argentina and Brazil they have displayed many innovative features, accompanying the return to constitutional democracy in those two countries (in 1983 and 1985, respectively), and modeled significant changes in social values, particularly with regard to sexual ideologies (especially in Argentina) and racial and ethnic ones (particularly in Brazil), as well as major urban issues in both countries. But it is in Mexico that the soap opera has attained the role that Monsiváis originally attributed to film, that of being a mirror of Mexican society and constituting a ground for the contestational representation of what the dominant social ideologies are in Mexico today. While soap operas in Argentina and Brazil have unquestionably been involved in similar debates, they do not enjoy the privileged status that soap operas have in Mexico and are only one genre among many others that constitute local programming and cultural exports. By contrast, Mexican soap opera not only dominates television programming—and, hence, viewing—in Mexico, but it is a significant aspect of exports to the Spanish-language market in the United States, and dominates as well the Central American and Caribbean market and enjoys a wide reception in translation in other parts of the world. In a certain sense, the paradigm of the Latin American soap opera today is that of the Mexican soap opera, and especially that of the Televisa production enterprise.

But what I want to do here is not engage directly in a characterization of the Televisa production enterprise, as excellent work has been done on that by others. Rather, I wish to explore the world of Televisa soap operas as recorded in Stefan Ruiz's dossier of production stills, *The Factory of Dreams* (2012), with particular interest in the way these images involve a problematical representation of male heteronormativity, insofar as there is a systematic implication in these stills of a disruption of a normalized or naturalized heterosexist gaze at the body and the insinuation of a range of homoerotic potentials that are intolerable with respect to the heterosexist imperative.

To be sure, there are both a systematic confrontation with the privilege of heteronormativity inherent in the soap opera, and the interest, excitement, frisson of the soap opera in the way it sustainedly engages in dramatizing the transgression of sexual and social decency in the representation of outrageous and defiant women, rebellious youth (who, in more recent years, indulge in drug consumption, although this was never part of the long-standing image of disobedience to the Father), adulterous activity on all sides, and class warfare (e.g., noncompliant and treacherous servants), accompanied by incest and a host of abusive behaviors. Homosexuality, however, was rarely a component of the traditional soap opera (and rarely a component of the Mexican film of the Golden Age); wherever it might have been suggested, it could never exist in any fashion other than as the loathsome sin (*el pecado nefando*), with sure punishment coming swifter and more conclusively than in the case of any of the multifaceted inventory of sinning in the universe of the soap opera.

I cannot enter here into the far-reaching issue of the essential queerness of human nature (Freud's propositions with regard to the inherently polymorphous perversity of the animal body) and the "civilized" policing of Eros that it entails, a policing that results in the presumed naturalization of the heterosexist imperative.[5] Nor can I entertain here a discussion of the queer substratum of Mexican society (or what came to be identified historically as the Mexican nation), which is overlain by the Counterreformation-inspired and Inquisition-enforced heterosexist ideology of the Spanish conquerors and reinforced by nineteenth-century concepts of sociosexual hygiene, other than to point out the fragility of the heterosexist norm, which can, arguably, be one reason why the enforcement of that norm must be so energetic and virtually hysterical, despite its reputed universal naturalness and eternal veracity. The Mexican male is called upon to be ugly, strong, and dependable, and this tripartite basis of character is understood to be a sufficient bulwark for him not to fall into the temptation of sexual practices disconsonant with the macho ideal. But it is, indeed, the overdetermination of the macho ideal that provides one thread for entry into the labyrinth of a range of sexual desire beyond the confines of the putatively natural. It is an overdetermination that raises the question of the excessiveness of protestation that things are not other than what they appear to be, as much as it serves to highlight, in a compelling exaggeration, what might, in fact, be the possibilities of forbidden fruit. If machismo is more performed between men, in the game of marking territory and establishing hierarchy (including the exclusion of those who reputedly perform poorly), than it is for the benefit of women (who only supposedly gain from being possessed by machos as an integral part of their performance), there is the inevitable segue into a circumstance whereby that performance leads to mutual allurement. Once those who perform poorly are excluded (and often, as a consequence of their ineptitude as machos, used as women to seal their exclusion),[6] the realm of the macho can lend itself to codes supplementary to heterosexism whereby the excess of performance becomes transformed, if not in practice, at least potentially, into a dynamic of mutual attraction and a reinscribed sexual dramatics that derive from that attraction. Sexual dramatics (that is, the scripts of actual erotic practice) are reinscribed because they now lie beyond the heterosexual and are now driven by homoerotic desire.[7]

Significantly, the cover photo of Ruiz's dossier of some one hundred images corresponds precisely to the process whereby the macho almost segues into the homoerotic. The image is of Daniel Cortés from the Televisa Acting School. As in all of Ruiz's photos, this image is framed within the confines of one of the sets for the array of *telenovelas* produced by Televisa in its studios in the upscale San Ángel neighborhood of Mexico City. Since Televisa has such a large production program and aspires to a recognizable artistic uniformity with its products, the acting school (in Spanish, the Centro de Educación Artística), established in 1978, grooms young men and women in a three-year program specifically for the Televisa market. In Ruiz's photography of, in this case, CEA student Daniel Cortés, or elsewhere of the established names of the Televisa stable, what viewers see is the fabricated reality that the soap opera represents. Hence, the title of Ruiz's dossier, *The Factory of Dreams*, a title that emphasizes not only the function of the soap opera to tie in with a specific spectrum of the Mexican imaginary regarding social life, but more important the fabricated quality of both that imaginary and the artistic product that engages with it, sustaining and reduplicating it through the seamless sameness of the Televisa product.

Ruiz might well have chosen to photograph his subjects in such a way that they are framed by no more than the conventional, neutral confines of the photographic frame as though their "natural" or "real" world extended infinitely beyond such confines of the image. This is the case with much advertising photography: either subjects are placed against the backdrop of the actual world they are presumed to inhabit or they may be situated to some degree in terms of the trappings of the photographer's studio, reinforcing what the spectator already knows, that they are being presented to us via a photograph that we know has been achieved in terms of a high degree of sophisticated technology.

But in the case of Ruiz's images, subjects are placed against a discontinuous backdrop, one that emphatically calls attention to the artificial invention of the universe of the soap opera. My understanding here of the importance of that artificial invention is grounded in the assumption that the soap opera works because the spectator knows that it is a fabricated imaginary: not only do most spectators have little opportunity to live and conduct themselves in the fashion of social subjects portrayed by the soap opera, but only an outrageous naïveté would allow the spectator to believe that the social stratum invoked in the soap opera does, in fact, live in such a fashion. The fabricated imaginary of the soap opera is enormously seductive, which accounts, of course, for its popularity, but the spectator is not asked to subscribe to the sociological validity of the lived human experience it models beyond the most trivial of superficial traces: no ruling class could sustain itself if it were to engage in the pattern of self-destructive behavior that characterizes the majority of Televisa products. As Pablo Helguera says in his introductory note to Ruiz's dossier:

[A] peculiarity of the Latin American televised melodrama, and the artificial setting it constructs, is the indirect relationship it establishes with reality: the outside world is there, but only in an abstract way, simplified by the forces of good and evil, which only operate within the confines of the fairy tale. [. . . One] of the characteristics of the telenovela is that it deals [according to Tomás López-Pumarejo] "more with consequences than with actions, and more with the family circle than with the public world." (no pag.)[8]

Thus, the artificiality of the setting of the soap operas becomes a significant feature of Ruiz's photography. In the case of the Cortés image, the bed on which he is placed is set against a large picture window whose blinds are drawn to reveal the urban cityscape (probably, according to Helguera, the upscale Polanco commercial and residential neighborhood near the Parque Chapultepec). This view is itself the result of a large photographic image mounted as part of the picture window and is, of course, part of the overall set construction, meant to tie in with the presumed sophisticated nature of the bedroom in which the individual being portrayed finds himself. That is, there is a continuity of tone, so to speak, between the backdrop of the city and this private bedroom, meant to be taken as the actual bedroom of a residence that enjoys a panoramic view of one of the most sought-after neighborhoods of Mexico City. Where, however, the naturalized framing of the image is interrupted or displaced is in how Ruiz's camera includes the complex lighting grid mounted above the set as part of the technical details of filming a soap opera. That is, the photo does not bleed, by implication, off into the continuous real world of the subject and his immediate occupied space, but into the cramped quarters of the filming set, where the alleged real world of the social subject being photographed is in reality only one of a series of cubicles in a crowded sound stage, enveloped, in cocoon-like fashion, by the technical apparatus that generates the Televisa artistic product.

The constructed and artificial nature of the television set finds its echo in the equally constructed and artificial nature of the "real" social sub-ject captured by Ruiz's photographic still, a synecdoche (as film stills are meant to be) of the enacted living the film production, which the still evokes, is meant to be. That is, Cortés here enacts a fabricated masculinity that is meant to resonate with the heterosexist imaginary that is presum-ably dominant in Mexican society: the buffed body, the bedroom look his fixed gaze sustains (which would be louche if it were not contained by his self-aware advantage as a pretty boy), the casual way in which his right hand rests on his crotch, drawing attention to and aiding in concealing what would, optimally, be displayed in order to confirm, definitively, his prized masculinity. While we do not know what role he might be respon-sible for enacting in a specific soap opera script, sexual seduction would be central to it.

However, there is much that is problematical about Cortés's pose here as an embodiment of the ur-script of Mexican masculinity, beginning with the fact that a legitimately heterosexual body would have the time or the willingness to pose for the camera: a proper heterosexual masculin-ity must be on display and must be repeatedly reenacted in an overde-termined fashion in order to confirm its compliance with the codes in effect. But it cannot be the object of the privileged gaze of the camera, because that which should be displayed cannot be put on display. This is confirmed by the legendary reaction of the macho toward anyone whose look dwells a second too long on his body. Threatened by the implication of the no matter how transitorily sustained gaze, the macho will angrily demand, "¿Qué me ves?" (What are you looking at?; literally, what do you see in me?). The sort of beefcake photo Ruiz accomplishes here, with the apparent complicity of the subject, suggests a transgression of Mexican heterosexist masculinity that is simply unacceptable within the sociosex-ual conventions of the so-called real public world. Cortés may perhaps not be represented here as someone's boy toy (conventionally, a female someone, but now more possibly a male someone's, thanks to the wid-ening circle of queer enactments in the Mexican soap opera). But he is unquestionably not the Pedro Armendáriz model of the macho.[9]

By contrast, Fernando Colunga, from the series Mañana es para siem-pre (Tomorrow is forever), enacts a pose of irreproachable masculinity on what appears to be an office set. In this case, the intrusion of the techni-cal apparatus of the set is minimal, occurring only in the form of a spot that can be partially seen on the top border of the image. One might even take it as a ceiling fixture in the room the set is meant to represent. The fact that the décor of the room is muted and tasteful, as opposed to the nouveau riche garishness of some of the other settings, particularly the domestic ones, enhances the sobriety of Colunga's pose. This pose is that of, one might say, the fully uniformed businessman: gray suit, discreet shirt and tie, and well-maintained black shoes. The man looks seriously and confidently into the camera, his hands arranged in a common Latin male stance, the right one hanging loosely at his side, and the left one holding the edge of the suit jacket, the thumb jutting up. Although Colunga stands straight, the slight separation of his legs and angle of his stance keep the image from being military in nature. There are none of the audacious display of the body such as we have in the case of Cortés's; none of the sexual suggestiveness of his pose, including the placement of his left hand; none of the ground zero erotic nature of the bedroom. Of course, any space may be appropriate for suggested or actual erotic engagement, and there is no accounting for how any pose of the body, clothed or unclothed, may be judged to be erotic. But the universe of the soap opera has its rather conservative conventions regarding what may be considered erotic, and the paneroticism of the proposition that anything can be used as an erotic fetish, unless we have evidence to the contrary, cannot be presumed to apply. Colunga is unquestionably a handsome man, and he must unquestionably be quite successful in his romantic endeavors; the blurb accompanying the photograph describes him as a dreamer. It also describes him as adoring his mother, which, in an array of Mexican social virtues, ranks high as a distinguishing feature of the proper man: Momism is not considered a failing in Mexican society, nor can it be interpreted as one of the features of a homosexual stereotype.[10]

Colunga, therefore, performs Mexican heterosexist masculinity with ease and confidence, and one would expect that his actions, as he moves in the world of the soap in which he plays, would never suggest any deviance from the steadfast norm. He may not evoke as much the Mexican alpha macho as, say, Alexis Ayala from *Amarte es mi pecado* (Loving you is my sin), or his costar Rogelio Guerra in *Mañana es para siempre*, but he must affect a reasonable simulacrum of it, as all men must in order to survive and navigate the overdetermined heterosexual masculinity of the Mexican soap opera.

Adrián Martiñón's image suggests quite the contrary. Like Cortés, he is photographed as a student at the Televisa Acting School and is not identified with a specific soap opera production. His pose is that of the rebellious naughty boy, which ambiguously serves both to confirm one facet of heterosexuality while at the same time standing in defiant contrast to it. The photograph depends very much for its effectiveness on the vivid contrast between the colors of his clothes and hair and the colors of the spotless kitchen (only a sliver of the top central portion of the setting reveals that it is a television set). But what is outrageous is the double circumstance of his being in the kitchen in the first place and his posing on top of the work counter.

Since this is a shot related to Martiñón's training as an actor and not to a specific soap opera, there is no possibility of recovering a larger narrative context for why and how he happens to be in the kitchen at this moment of shooting. But in the overall terms of the imagined Mexican world of the soap opera, there could be no legitimate reason for a young man to have invaded, so to speak, the separate space of the staff of the residence and to have chosen to place his body in the space normally reserved for routine culinary activities. With his left hand supported by the divide of the double sink and his defiant gaze, it is as though he were challenging perhaps one of the kitchen staff—that is, engaging in the pattern of seduction whereby the men of a household, even in modern Mexican society, customarily feel that the female staff is at their sexual beck and call, as it continues to be reputed that young Mexican men in households such as this have their sexual initiation thanks to willing or unwilling maids and cooks. Other images in Ruiz's dossier capture the stereotypical innocent sexuality of these women who may be preyed on by men of all ages in the household (e.g., Adanely Núñez from *Mañana es para siempre*), which stands in sharp contrast to the intense, exuberant sexuality of the privileged women of the house, such as Susana González in *La que no podia amar* [She who could not love]).

In this sense, then, Martiñón is being both transgressive and compliant in terms of the conventional codes of sexuality operant here. While he is hardly performing the sober masculinity of the mature men I have mentioned, and may even, indeed, be resentful of it in some sort of vaguely or murkily evoked Oedipal way, the fact that he strikes a possessive pose in the female space of the kitchen constitutes an assertion of heterosexual dominance. I underscore possessive pose here, because another micronarrative configuration might be the "sissy" boy who hangs out in the female space of the kitchen as a consequence of his inept assimilation to what passes for proper masculine behavior (one would assume he would be quickly shooed away, if not by the mother, by the kitchen staff fully aware of how they must be complicitous with the codes of masculinity and femininity).[11] Moreover, were the broadly transparent narrative formulas of the soap opera insinuating an improper sexual role identification on the part of Martiñón, he would be portrayed as hanging out in the masculine space of the gardeners, the chauffeurs, or the security guards (the latter, to be sure, engaging in an ultra-overdetermined masculinity).[12] Speculation in such matters as I am engaging in here is made possible by the systematically enforced transparency of soap opera plots and the absolute commitment to no type of ambiguity.[13] Even though there may be a divided enactment of masculinity in this pose on Martiñón's part— a virtual act of gender-marked possession of female space, while yet a substantial deviation from the norm of sober masculinity—there is no question of ambiguous sexual deviancy, for the naughty-boy pose needs only with experience to be fully contained within the sober macho, trans- formed into roguish impudence, as in the case of Alexis Ayala or Sebas- tián Óscar Rulli, from *Un gancho al corazón*.[14]

In the case of Rulli, it is as though we were witnessing the transition from Martiñón to Rogelio Guerra. Rulli strikes a thorough macho pose, and, although it is not completed with a tie, he wears a conventional busi- ness suit and corresponding shoes. His "modern" haircut and his light facial stubble suggest very much the sexual rogue. Within the codes of soap opera masculinity, Martiñón is not yet sexually desirable as far as the experienced women of his universe are concerned, which is why he must hit on the female staff (or, in the same vein, young women socially inferior to him). Rulli, while he may not possess the commanding power- ful sexuality of an alpha macho like Guerra, is useful for a sexual dalliance and is perhaps a bit more erotically interesting than still unpupated Cor- tés, which is another reason why he is potentially more homoerotically alluring than he is a model of the masculinity of a man's man.

Ruiz's photographs, taken in high resolution with high color satura- tion, have very much the quality of production stills for a high-budget television production line. But published in the respected Aperture list, they have an artistic value that derives to a great extent from the produc- tion line to which they correspond. No one would make the claim that Televisa's soap opera line constitutes great narrative filmmaking. It never rises above technically highly skilled mass production television that is, in the end, a vehicle for the lifestyle capitalized on by the products it sells: the products do not exist to promote the soap opera, but rather, unsurpris- ingly, the soap opera exists to sell efficiently and effectively the products.

What is of interest here is how the soap opera continues to exist to sustain what is, at least in its realm, an unquestioned and unquestionable narrative of compulsory heterosexuality. One would not want to assert that Televisa itself is committed to maintain traditional heterosexism in Mexico. If it does through these programs, it is only because they continue to sell efficiently the products they sponsor/are sponsored by. In this way, then, the so-called factory of dreams is driven by two overdetermined sets of conventions that reinforce each other reciprocally in the programming product at issue. First of all, there is the overarching convention of heterosexist love that has been entrenched in the Mexican imaginary throughout the twentieth century and may be directly attributed to the official culture that follows the Revolution of 1910, with its ample share of slogans like "Haz patria, ten hijos" mentioned above.[15] Second, soap opera narratives, because of the conditions of their consumption, traffic in an exceedingly transparent, unambiguous set of conventions regarding heterosexual love, and these two sets of conventions (the more general one perhaps more observed in the breach than as one unanimously sustained by the citizenry) work in tandem to reinforce each other. Some Mexican soap operas have taken up unconventionally heterosexist issues (see Geirola), and the large segments of contestational culture in Mexico such as novels, theater, and narrative filmmaking have made heavy investments in the interpretation of the queer. Yet the Televisa soap operas studied by Ruiz remain virtually fustian in their defense of the codes of masculinity,[16] reinforced by a female sexuality that, by being anything but Marian, exists to allow machos to whet their masculinity and to confirm it in the public display of prime-time broadcasting (Helguera speaks of "certain infallible formulas" [no pag.]).

Ruiz's images do focus on male stars. Indeed, the overall sense of the Televisa soap operas he captures with his images is that of men and women in extensive social congress, with the implication (definitely reinforced by the heightened rhetoric of the titles of the soap operas) of the extensive sexual congress off-camera. But I have focused on the performance of masculinity because, in the end, it is the men who count: they are the heads of households, they are the power brokers, and they are masters of their realms. The women portrayed by Ruiz exist, in the plots of the narratives in question, to confirm the sexuality of the men, not vice versa, no matter how aggressive or predatory some of the women may be: in the end it is not their sexuality that is confirmed, but the performance quality of the men involved.[17] In the end, the dream factory (re)produces macho dominance, and it is for this reason that the quality of the male performance of these popular narratives of heterosexual love is worth examining.

HELEN ZOUT'S *DESAPARICIONES*
Shooting Death

◆ ◆ ◆

Helen Zout's lens is unforgiving. This is how life was during the disap-
pearances. This was society in Argentina, making people disappear, or
merely allowing it to happen. There is no demagoguery in her images.
This is just the way it was. No poetry, no dreams. Black and white. Na-
ked terror in faces finally bereft of all hope.

—Osvaldo Bayer, "An Account of Argentine Death"

One of the historic uses of photography has been the documentation of death, beginning with yellow journalism's publication of
so-called "crime scenes" and including photography as an instrument of forensic investigation: in addition to the bibliography of professional autopsy photography, one can recall the significant work of Weegee
(pseud. Arthur Fellig), who often made it to New York crime scenes with
his camera ahead of the police and published iconic books of images of
death and mayhem. Also of importance has been the use of photography,
from its earliest beginnings, in medical research. John Harley Warner
and James M. Edmonson's *Dissection: Photographs of a Rite of Passage
in American Medicine* is a candid-camera tour of anatomical medicine
in practice—almost 150 photographs of the process of dissection in the
second half of the nineteenth century and early twentieth century, when
there was still the persuasive belief that cadavers belonged to medicine
and not to living heirs. This, in turn, is the principle that sustains the core
collection of the Museo Forense de la Morgue Judicial de Buenos Aires,
which began in the mid-1920s as the first of its kind in Latin America

(of special note is the display, in formaldehyde, of "penes tatuados del hampa" [tattooed penises of the underworld]).

Helen Zout (born in 1957 in Carcarañá, in the province of Santa Fe) has used her photography as a contemporary intervention in the forensics of death, with specific reference to the disappeared persons of the putative Dirty War against subversion that was crucial for the neofascist military dictatorship that assumed power in Argentina in March 1976, with disappearance arguably lasting through the period of tyranny, up to the return to democracy in 1983, and even, perhaps, beyond it.[1] The process of capture, detention, interrogation, and liquidation of individuals accused, directly or indirectly, of subversion, while there is considerable dispute over documented numbers, has left many unresolved issues in Argentine society, one of which is the recovery of remains through the location of sites of disposal and the forensic analysis of remains. DNA testing, along with previously established methods, has been extensively utilized, and the Argentine case has been one of the testing laboratories for forensic anthropology. Official photography—that is, the record of judicial agencies and scientific support components—is an integral part of a process that is far from achieving any sort of social or legal closure. The work of other photographers from the realms of documentary journalism, archival efforts, and creative artwork, therefore, constitutes a supplement to the central forensic undertaking. As such, where the latter must necessarily be circumscribed by precisely defined conventions of evidence and accountability, supplemental work such as I have described may move along a continuum in which the highly affective components of the construction of images, of which photography is unquestionably among the most compelling, can exercise strategies and degrees of rhetoric that would be inadmissible in what we defend as the office of professional photography.

Zout has received support for her photography from the John Simon Guggenheim Foundation (2002). Her images, which have been widely exhibited in Argentina and abroad, focus on social questions and mental health issues, with special emphasis on immigrants and children; in the latter case, she has been particularly concerned with children affected by AIDS.

Desapariciones (2009), Zout's first published dossier, is a collection of photographs that correspond to inquiries into the disappearance of persons during neofascist tyranny in Argentina, including both the remains of victims of the repression and the sites of their extermination and burial. The images of *Desapariciones* have been the basis of several photographic expositions of Zout's work, most recently a single-artist show in the Fotogalería of the Teatro Municipal General San Martín in Buenos

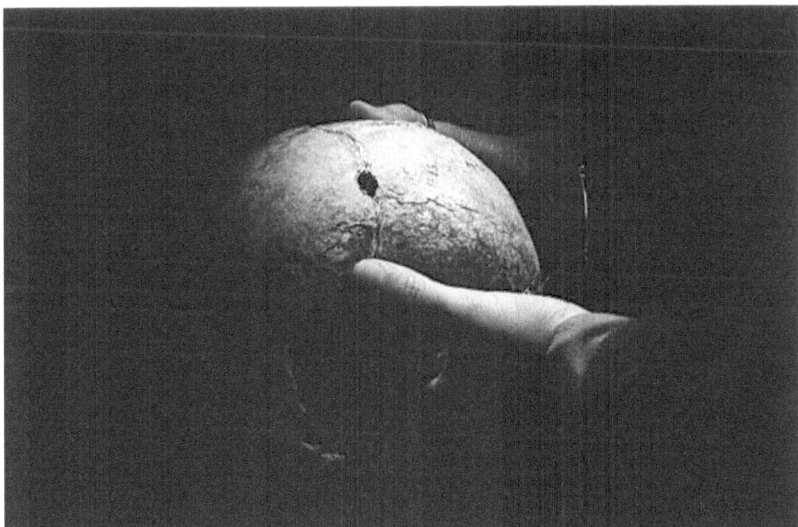

Figure 12.1. Helen Zout, *Cráneo con orificio de bala, morgue judicial, La Plata* (Skull with a bullet hole, police morgue, La Plata). Used with permission of Helen Zout.

Aires (March 2011), a venue created by Sara Facio, the dean of Argentine photography, and one of the most prominent public spaces for the exhibition of photographic work in the country.

Zout's work enters into a dialogue with the work of a large array of Argentine photographers who have concerned themselves, in accord with an unwavering sociohistorical commitment, with an inquiry into the consequences of tyranny. These photographers, whose work I examined in detail in my *Urban Photography in Argentina: Nine Artists of the Post-Dictatorship Era* (2007), deal with a daily dynamic that, in one way or another, continues to be affected by that tyranny. Thus, Zout's documentary photography is related to the work of such important names as Adriana Lestido, Eduardo Gil, Marcelo Brodsky, Gabriel Valansi, Marcos López, and Gabriel Díaz, all of whom have pushed the limits of photography to frame, in a particularly eloquent and impactful manner, current Argentine sociohistorical questions. This chapter will examine the way the discursive rhetoric of Zout's photographic images interprets parameters of state terrorism against social subjects during the neofascist tyranny.

The manner in which Zout's material underscores its supplemental relationship to official forensic photography is evident from the very first image in *Desapariciones*. Indeed, one is immediately struck by a fundamental ambiguity as to whether the photograph is the sort of spontaneous picture opportunity one attributes to photojournalism or whether it is a deliberately contrived, staged tableau that signifies through highly charged insinuation and allusion rather than in the manner of a transparent semiotics of representation. It is profitable to compare this composition, its image of an individual and the elements of an autopsy leaping out of the frame toward the viewer, with what might be the circumstantial shot of an individual engaged in conducting an autopsy, oblivious of the camera that happens to catch him deeply engrossed in his work. The historian Osvaldo Bayer, in his commentary on the photographs, insists that Zout's intent here is to capture the face of the "uniform monster-torturer"

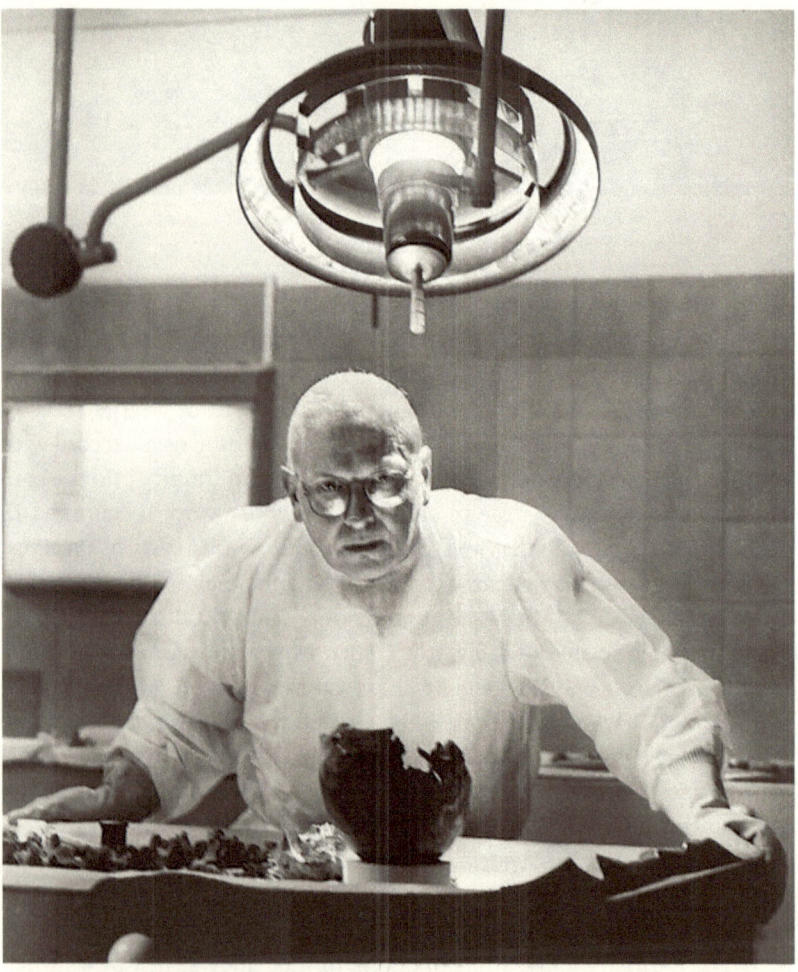

Figure 12.2. Helen Zout, *Exhumación e identificación de restos óseos, morgue judicial, La Plata* (Exhumation and identification of bone remains, police morgue, La Plata). Used with permission of Helen Zout.

(57), and there is ample reason to agree with him. Although Bayer does not engage in any gender-inflected commentary, there is the clear relationship between the woman's camera and the masculine gaze of whom we can agree to call "the doctor." He is a hulking, commanding presence, with his bald head (which some might see as a fetish icon of authority) and his piercing eyes behind severely authoritarian glasses. He grips the autopsy table in a gesture of dominant control, and his privilege is emphasized by his medical smock and his protective gloves. His figure divides an upper and lower plane of the photograph. The upper plane is that of the sophisticated instrument of illumination that enables "the doctor" to proceed with a full visual command of the object of his study. Although the protruding handle of the lamp is a necessary component of its maneuverability, one can be excused for seeing, if not its phallic allusiveness, its similarity to the barrel of a gun or a death ray aimed squarely at the victim or at the victim's remains.

The lower plane of the image constitutes one of the many forms of skeletal remains found in the mass grave sites of the disappeared, often in the fragmented state evidenced in this photograph. (This fragmented skull contrasts with that of a later image, in which a skull is held in the hands of "the doctor" to reveal the sort of death-dealing perforation that would have been produced by a bullet.) However, what is most notable about this image, particularly as the introit to Zout's dossier, is a fundamental ambiguity surrounding the way in which there is a major interchangeability at work here. On the one hand, we have the image, staged or somehow recovered, of a medical professional engaged in the torture and deconstruction of a human body: I mean specifically to evoke here Elaine Scarry's crucial observation that torture produces a destructuring of mind and body. At the same time, there is an overlap between the Dr. Mengele impersonation of Zout's image and the work of the forensic investigator, whose task is to somehow "undo" the deconstruction of torture and murder so as to recover the original identity of the individual—or part of the individual—under examination. The forensic agent, as much as his lethal prefiguration, holds the "universe" of a human being in his hands, and Zout's photographs are as much a trace of the practice of disappearance as they are of the restoration of appearance.

It might be appropriate to allude here to some of the received intellectual opinions regarding photography and the way it is inevitably linked to death, from the profound melancholy Roland Barthes attaches to photography as always recording that which has been—that is, that which is now dead and gone, especially with reference to lived human lives: photography is always aorist, never durative, for Barthes. Concomitantly, Susan Sontag, always so preoccupied with the bad faith of bourgeois art, saw photography as legitimating a viewing of the suffering of others, whose distance from any actual photograph of them may render irrelevant any imperative of authenticity, in favor of the greater importance of the sanitized impact: Zout's doctor may be staring the viewer down, either as the torturer himself or as, alternatively, the accusing face of the forensic specialist angered at the grim task he is called upon to perform (in fact, Zout's own identification for this image states that it is from the La Plata Judicial Morgue). But in either case, he is contained by the frame of the photograph, restrained from ever actually being able to interact with the viewer, who in a blink can dismiss this image and the whole exhibition.

However, Zout counters, with other images, the whole matter of the feigned immediacy of reality that renders photography—at least in the photojournalistic tradition—so problematical. If a trope of ambiguous prefiguration underlies the two images I have discussed to this point, there is a series of other images where a presumed "incompetence" or "incompleteness" of the photographic act underscores the stepping away from, and thus supplemental stance toward, documentary photographic work.

In the case of the photograph of Nilda Eloy, identified as a survivor of the Arana clandestine prison camp in La Plata (the capital of Buenos Aires Province), there are three compositional elements that coalesce to create a disturbing image that defies conventional photographic portraiture. Conventional photographic portraiture is, nevertheless, suggested in the dominant element of the image, Eloy's stunningly beautiful face and the impressive sweep of her hair. Her features are bold and assured, her gaze is steady and commanding, and her mouth is relaxed and yet firm: here is a commanding presence, one of feminine authority derived, we can be assured, from her imprisonment and probable torture, based in turn upon her sociopolitical activism. As a bust, Eloy's image demands a place of privilege in any pantheon of noble survivors of tyranny. And if Zout had chosen to make of her image just Eloy's bust, it would be a conventional, if nevertheless impressive, example of photographic portraiture.

What disrupts the convention, however, is the inclusion, in the lower two-thirds of the photograph, of Eloy's body and the distribution of her hair. It is not that there is something "wrong" or even "unaesthetic" about the inclusion of Eloy's lumpy, matronly body, accentuated by some sort of colorless, formless shift, but rather that it interacts starkly with the beauty of her face. Now, I don't mean to imply, in a rank sexist fashion, that a lumpy, matronly body is not beautiful, but only that it is not part of

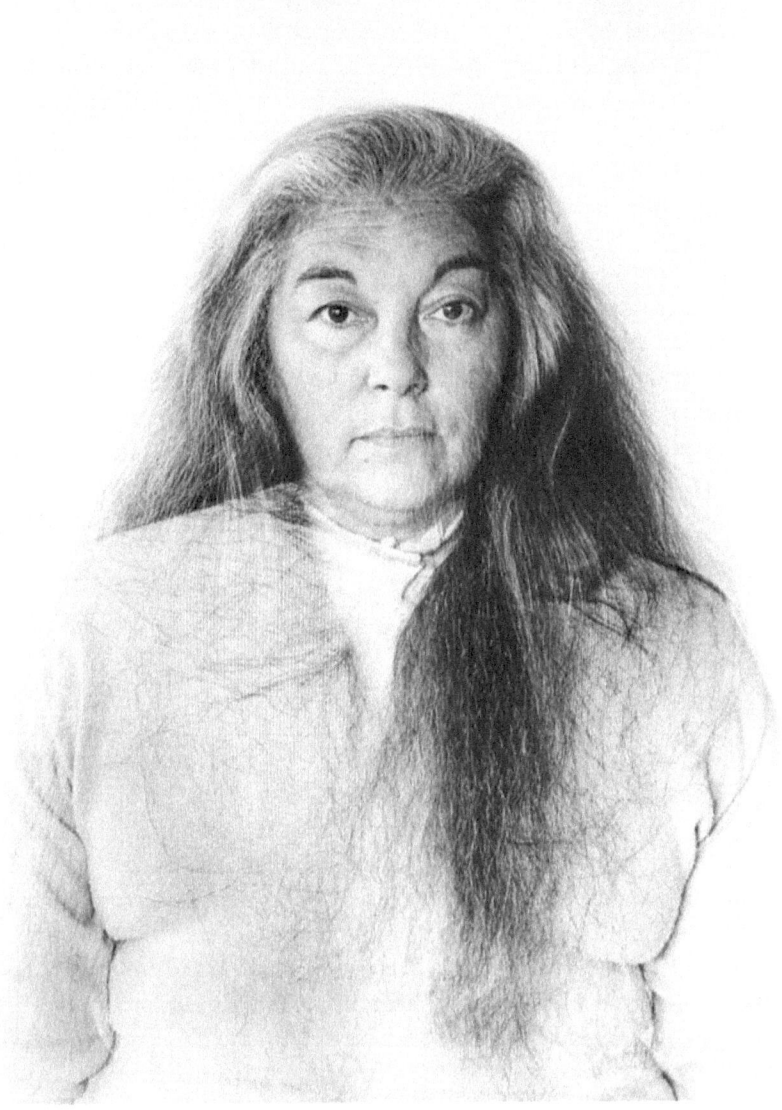

Figure 12.3. Helen Zout, *Nilda Eloy, sobreviviente del centro clandestino Arana, La Plata* (Nilda Eloy, survivor of the Arana Clandestine Center, La Plata). Used with permission of Helen Zout.

conventional photographic portraiture of the twentieth century. The contrast between the two principles—a convention of beautiful/noble faces versus the accurate rendition of real female bodies—is what makes this photograph distinctive, moving it from the realm of interesting human faces to that of dramatically lived-in bodies. This semantic positioning is underscored by the third element, that of Eloy's hair. Where, in the case of her face, her hair is distributed as a lush framing to her stunning facial features, as our gaze moves down to her anti-beauty-principle body, it trails off in disarray. On the right side of the image, the hair is full although disorderly when contrasted with the apparently well-brushed roots that frame Eloy's face. On the left side, the hair is partially combed back over the right shoulder, but, upon close examination, like the filaments of a spider's web, it laces over the woman's body and down to her waist. This suggestion of an additional body covering that results from the comparative disorder of her hair is disturbing because it recalls the disordering, the disruption of the body, as part of the process of disappearance undertaken by the apparatus of repression. While Eloy is a survivor of that process rather than inert remains on the forensic examining table, Zout's image nevertheless captures the way in which she has been an object of that process, something from which she will never fully recover: her body will, in sum, never be "fully composed" again, an ideal composition such as what conventional photographic portraiture would propose to offer.

Another form of corporal disruption is found in the image of Adelina Alaye, the mother of Carlos Esteban Alaye, who was disappeared in 1977. In this case, the most immediate object of bodily destruction was Carlos Esteban, who we can suppose experienced the full arc of the process, from detention to murder and disposal in an unmarked mass grave. As has often been pointed out, the direct victim of repression is not the only one profoundly affected by it. There is a theatrics of disappearance, as captured in part by Zout in the image of a child's drawing of an assault on a woman in a home invasion by members of a so-called Grupo de Tareas, and such as we have recounted in Luis Puenzo's film *Historia oficial* (Official story) or as we see directly portrayed in Marco Bechis's *Garage Olimpo* (Olimpo garage). Both the theatrics and the consequences of disappearance are translative, in the sense that they spread out from the direct victim to family, friends, neighbors, and bystanders, few of whom can remain untouched by the violence of the act of detention, knowing ultimately to one degree or another what the arc of the process put in motion will be.[2] It goes without saying that the mothers of the disappeared are among the most immediately impacted, which is why the Madres as various action groups and as a comprehensive icon have played such an eloquent role in the Argentine imaginary relating to the recent history of tyranny. In this case, Zout's decision to portray Alaye in a blurry fashion functions as an X-ray, so to speak, of her own bodily disruption in the face of her son's disappearance.

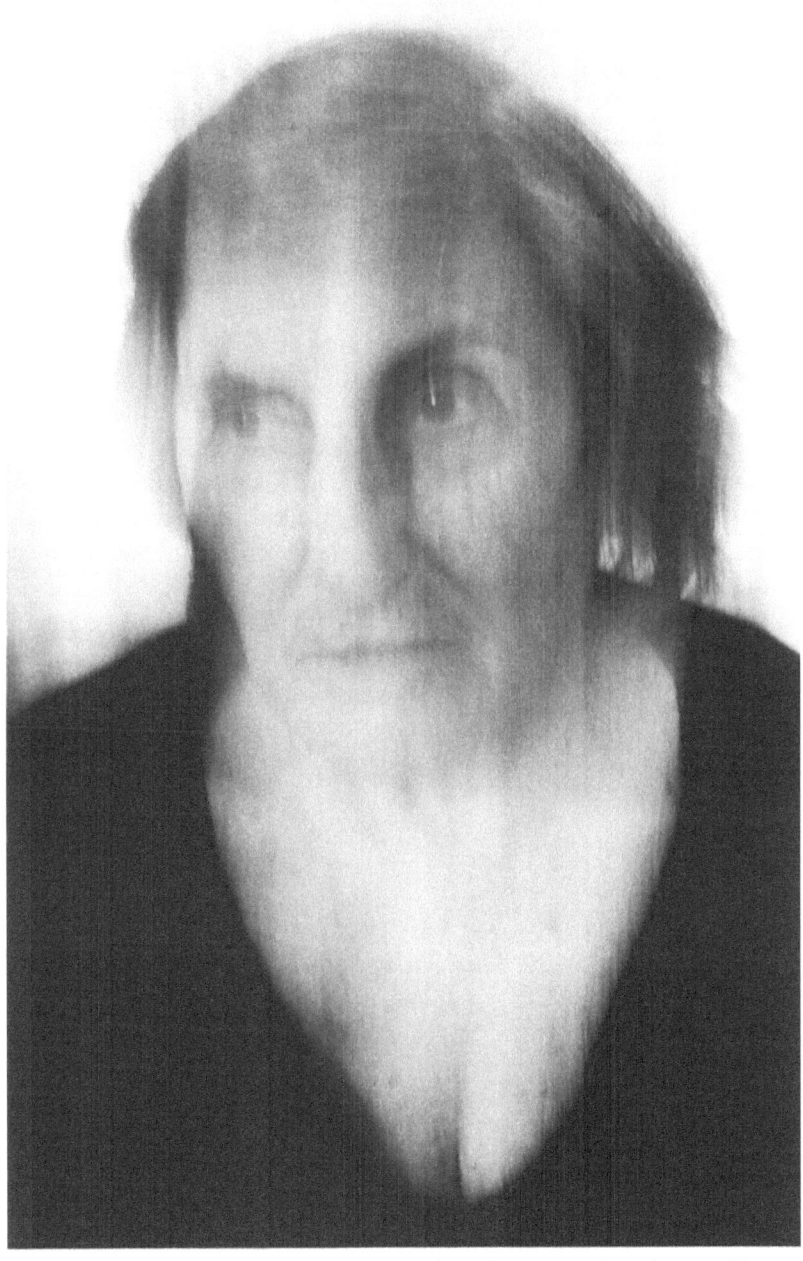

Figure 12.4. Helen Zout, *Adelina Alaye, madre de Carlos Esteban Alaye, desaparecido en 1977* (Adelina Alaye, mother of Carlos Esteban Alaye, disappeared in 1977). Used with permission of Helen Zout.

Historically, photography is grounded in the promise of reproductive fidelity and clarity. Emerging against the backdrop of movements in painting like impressionism and expressionism, photography proffered what painting had at that point realized it could not do: capture reality in perfectly proportional terms. That photography cannot, after all, do any such thing is part of the eventual theorizing about the nature of the art, but an integral part of the origins of photography is the attempt to achieve the highest precision of image possible, and thus any museum of photography will include the apparatuses of literal restraint that were necessary to immobilize the body to prevent blurring. Zout's photograph—and here again I wish to underscore the principle of supplement that characterizes her work—deliberately introduces blurring as a technical principle to be achieved for purposes of transmitting the disruption brought by the shock of the son's disappearance.

Zout makes use of the technique of image blurring in various other photographs representing the sites of clandestine centers and mass burial graves. The principle of supplement is particularly evident in these photographs, because one can compare them to standard examples of photojournalism, which would have as their goal the capturing of the exact detail of the landscape and the survivors and forensic investigators combing it, the former for signs of recognition, the latter for utilizable evidence. Such details are lost—repressed—by Zout's camera in a double process

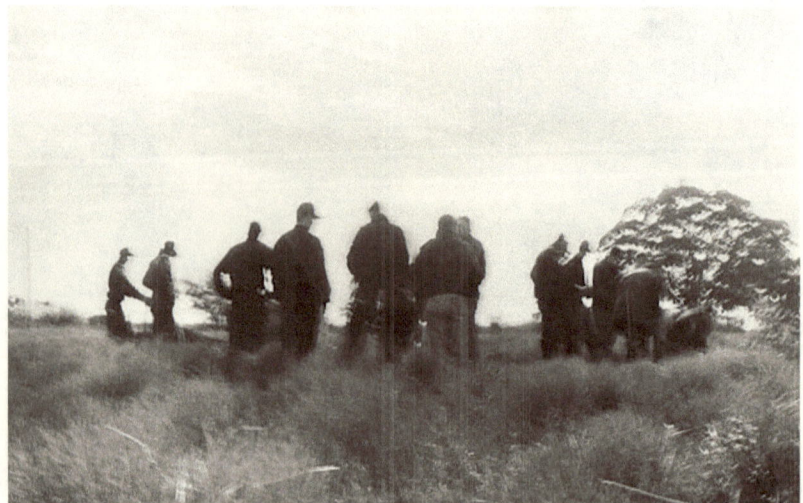

Figure 12.5. Helen Zout, *Búsqueda de restos óseos de desaparecidos, Parque Pereyra Iraola, provincia de Buenos Aires, 2003* (Search for bone remains of disappeared persons, Pereyra Iraola Park, Province of Buenos Aires, 2003). Used with permission of Helen Zout.

that captures the psychological disruptiveness of such sites for those who experience them and the questionable ability of these people to exact an unmediated truth of historical event from them. By contrast to attempts by survivors (as well as agents of repression who have turned state's witnesses) to describe what these sites looked like while they functioned (e.g., "I remember that over there is where the *parrilla* [metal grillwork on which victims were tied down] was"), Zout's images underscore trenchantly the impossibility of rendering precise details: the process of corporal disappearance leaves as its lasting trace the disappearance of precise historical realities.

Several of the photographs constitute something like a suite dealing with the disappearance of prisoners, especially those who were dumped, drugged, into the waters of the Río de la Plata to drown.[3] Many of their bodies eventually floated ashore, with the effect of the tides of the river bringing them to the *balneario* (beach club) area of the Costanera Norte near the Ciudad Universitaria. This area was subsequently developed as the Parque de la Memoria, dedicated to the disappeared and featuring the wall with the names of those whose disappearance was categorically determined (some ten thousand) and including monumental artwork and documentary displays. This suite consists of five photographs, in order: the interior of one of the planes used for the so-called flights of death to dump the bodies (a detail featured in the aforementioned Bechis film);

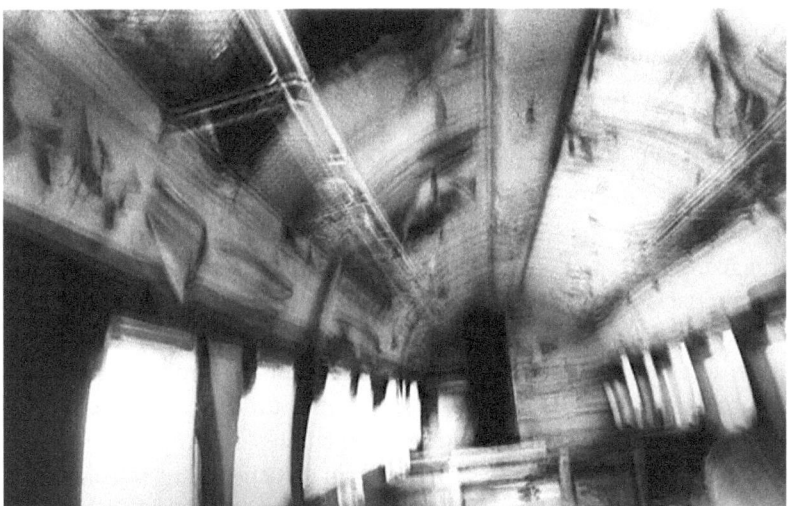

Figure 12.6. Helen Zout, *Interior de un avión usado en los "vuelos de la muerte," Museo Aeronáutico de Morón* (Interior of a plane used in the "death flights," Flight Museum, Morón). Used with permission of Helen Zout.

one of the sites along the Río de la Plata where at least one body was found in 1976; an archival photo from the Dirección de Inteligencia de la Policía de la Provincia de Buenos Aires showing what one assumes to be a hooded police agent pointing a gun; the (water damaged?) photo from the dossier of one of the agents of repression; and the burned-out frame of a Ford Falcon, the vehicle of choice for the agents of repression, in which two identified bodies were found.

The photograph of the interior of one of the planes of the flights of death is especially eloquent. It is photographed as though it were a tunnel of terror in an amusement park, making use of Zout's trademark stylistic device of the blurred image, with the Barthean punctum (central organizing point) of the photograph being the black passageway that, while it may be the access to the cockpit, might also be the access to the back of the plane from which the drugged bodies of the prisoners were dumped (stripped, in the vulturous practice of the guards, of all clothes and personal effects of value).

The photographer's gaze is cast over the arched interior of the plane, inventorying its details in the manner of any prisoner who might have been at least semiconscious and to a degree aware of her surroundings: the blurring of the image in this case also specifically correlates with the drugged state in which a partially conscious prisoner might have been able to perceive her surroundings. As one can see, the interior of the plane is nothing more than a flying coffin. While there are some benches, the majority of the prisoners would have been scattered around the floor, most likely (especially recalling the images in *Garage Olimpo*) heaped on top of each other for the short flight from the detention center to the middle of the river. The dilapidated condition of the interior of the aircraft adds to the quality of oppressive claustrophobia the viewer might experience, and it takes little imagination to suspect that the visual aspect of the interior would have been matched by the inevitable consequences of transporting drugged, semiconscious bodies likely in poor physical condition from torture and lack of medical care. At least there would be the lingering smell of unwashed and untreated bodies, accompanied by bodily fluids (sweat, urine, feces, vomit) produced by the drugs administered to render them semiconscious and perhaps the movement of the aircraft. Although the photograph displays a space empty of human presence, the viewer's effort to supplement that vacancy with the human presence of the prisoners and any accompanying merciless military personnel cannot be anything but profoundly unpleasant.

Zout's work, then, implies a particular ethics of photographic inscrip-

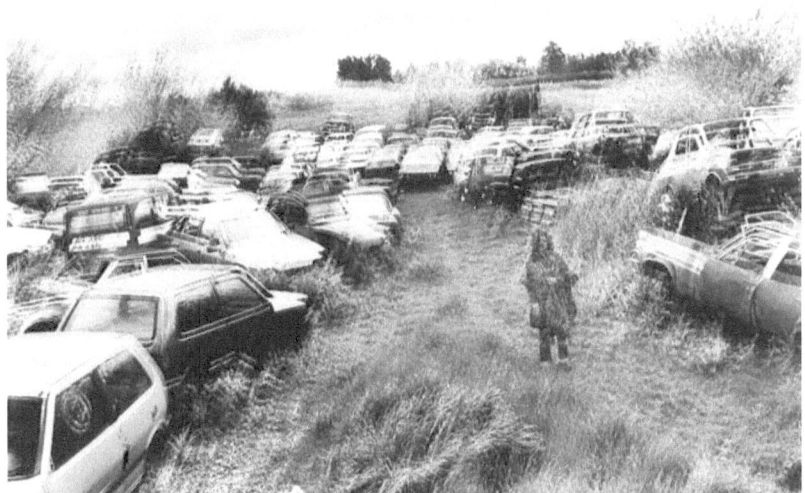

Figure 12.7. Helen Zout, *Cristina Gioglio, sobreviviente del centro clandestino Arana* (Cristina Gioglio, survivor of the Arana Clandestine Center). Used with permission of Helen Zout.

tion. Although there is the implicit proposition that photojournalism and other forms of photography driven by criteria of transparent realism are of limited value, what is directly manifest in the visual protocols of *Desapariciones* is that photography cannot bring about the reappearance of what history has destroyed. There can be no entertaining juxtaposition between "before" and "after" images, whether for individual social subjects or for lived sites—concentration centers, torture chambers, burial grounds, transport vessels, or watery graves. As a consequence, the goal of photographic production must legitimate itself on some other grounds of signification. These grounds are most interestingly pursued by Zout in those images in which the emotional repercussions of tyranny are seen through an imaging of the deconstruction of feelings and consciousness in the process of experiencing tyranny personally. By choosing not to use the camera as an instrument of forensic research, but rather as an affective supplement to that research, Zout intervenes in the still ongoing discussion in Argentina over disappeared persons with a uniquely eloquent photographic language. While it cannot reconstruct that which has been lost, it can undertake to piece together the contexts and the actors of the process of human devastation. Zout's photography is a language that speaks to what continues to be a profoundly dislocated Argentine society, one that is still struggling to refocus itself, so to speak, despite all the government commissions, cultural practice, and sociopolitical and legal discourse. In this regard, I would close with Zout's image of Cristina Gioglio, a survivor of the Arana detention center, wandering, as Bayer points out in his commentary (57), in a graveyard of consumerism—the daily life of capitalism that is what Argentines have been left with by their history. That dump now occupies what was once a site of torture and death.

Yet one of the remarkable features of contemporary Argentine social history has been, in contrast to that of other countries in the Southern Cone that experienced similar tyranny, the way in which a sustained level of commentary about the past of human devastation has been maintained. The record of consciousness of human rights violations and, concomitantly, the remedy of a viable public human rights discourse remain strong in Argentina, and the publication of *Desapariciones* is yet one more entry in the bibliography of cultural production that continues to accompany that public discourse.

DOCUMENTARY PHOTOGRAPHY
AS GENDER TESTIMONY
Daniel Hernández-Salazar's *So That All Shall Know*

◆ ◆ ◆

I want to close this study by shifting the emphasis away from the Argentina-Mexico axis that has prevailed throughout. The considerable amount of gender-marked photography in Latin America has made it impossible for an overarching examination of the pertinent production from all countries, especially in view of the major goal of examining selected texts in some detail. However, the human-rights-oriented photography of Daniel Hernández-Salazar, involving a crisis of masculinity as the consequence of the countrywide repression in Guatemala during the violence of the 1980s, places his work in a directly complementary relationship to that of Helen Zout. Moreover, Hernández-Salazar's photography complements also the significant concern over discussing fully the restoration of human rights in Guatemala, resulting in 1999 in the publication of the ten volumes of the report of the Comisión para el Esclarecimiento Histórico (Commission for Historical Clarification, *Guatemala: memoria del silencio*), an extract of which was published in English in 2012. Hernández-Salazar's photography dates basically from the early 1990s, before the December 1996 Peace Accords that began the shift in

Guatemala from state-sponsored violence to the recognition of human rights abuses and the establishment of the Comisión and the articulation of a commitment to end those abuses and to bring to light their history.

Many of the images in *So That All Shall Know / Para que todos sepan* (2007) deal with women and their particular vulnerability (and equally that of their children) at the hands of the police, the military, and paramilitary units such as death squads, which in many cases were composed of their own menfolk. The brutalizing training of conscripts from lower socioeconomic classes such that they could turn against their own class, engaging in rape, torture, and murder, one of the more dreadful elements of the violence in Guatemala and elsewhere in Latin America, is a story that has been told in documents like *Memory of Silence*, as well as in the accounts of narrative fiction. Certainly, the most immediate treatment of gendered violence in Guatemala is Rigoberta Menchú's *Me llamo Rigoberta Menchú* (1983; translated into English as *I, Rigoberta Menchú*).[1] There have been some high-stakes controversies over the reliability of Menchú's first-person account, especially in what appears to be the mixing of an autobiographical "I" with a synthetic collective "I," with the experiences of many different social subjects conflated under the rubric of a single narrating first person. But no one has seriously questioned the veracity of the abuses recounted.

Perhaps the most eloquent image depicting the oppression of indigenous women in *So That All Shall Know* involves a ranged confrontation between police, outfitted in military gear, and women and children. This image is identified as *Encuentro de dos mundos, 1492–1992 (Clash of Two Worlds, 1492–1992)*. On July 21, 1991, peasants had gone to Guatemala City from the Cajolá plantation to demand that the plantation be turned over to them. Such a protest/demand was common during the five hundredth anniversary of the conquest of the Americas, and the consciousness remains to this day that in 1992 and in the decades since, the first peoples of the Americas are as landless—and, therefore, impoverished and marginalized—as they were after their lands were expropriated by the Spanish in 1492. Significantly (and one does not know if this is by chance or part of the manipulation of the image), the male policemen, who stand a full head taller than the women, even if one counts the latter's headdresses, are ranged on the right-hand side of the image, which evokes the way in which these men, although they all look like they come from mestizo Guatemala, are the agents of the country's right-wing propertied classes: they are the enforcers of the interests of the owners of the Cajolá plantation, who quite likely pride themselves on how their ances-

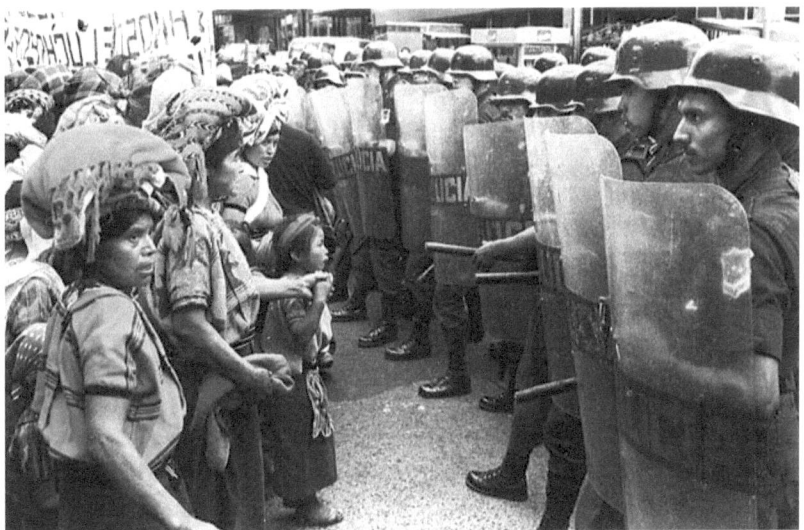

Figure 13.1. Daniel Hernández-Salazar, *Clash of Two Worlds*, 1492–1992.
Used with permission of Daniel Hernández-Salazar.

tors stretch all the way back to the original conquerors of pre-Conquest tribal lands. In terms of the semiotics of the photograph, the menacing policemen occupy close to two-thirds of the frame, stretching from the right-hand side in an arc across the top of the image, quite literally cornering the women. Perhaps one could argue that the stance of the policemen is not really all that menacing, but their tight formation, their gear, their number, and the way in which their very presence overwhelms that of the women cannot help but have an element of menace. Which, to be sure, is what such a police presence is designed to maximize as the first step in the procedure of crowd control.

The women, then, in accord with the facile accusation of the forces of law and order that they are mere pawns of the militant left, are crowded into the lower left-hand side of the image. The color of their traditional garb contrasts vividly with the official blue of the policemen, and it is vital to the reference of the photograph to the opposition between the culture of the Guatemalan first people and the agents of repression of the modern state: the traditional versus the modern, the indigenous tribal display versus the display of the instruments of violence of state-sponsored terrorism.

As Menchú Tum[2] observes in her brief preface to the Hernández-Salazar volume, "Over the years [Hernández-Salazar] has geared his talents to capturing the links between memory and the dignity of victims and survivors of genocide" (x). Far more than a photojournalist,

Hernández-Salazar has sought, not to aestheticize violence, suffering, and death, but to use his camera to provide insights into the intense human experience of the effects of genocide. If on the one hand his photography contributes to the remembrance of the victims, on the other it provides the nonparticipant spectator with highly studied interpretations of the violence in Guatemala. Understandably, this is not an "objective" exercise, and Menchú Tum's prologue quickly establishes the way in which Hernández-Salazar works from the perspective of Guatemalan subalterns and their suffering at the hands of the dynamics of repression, particularly the repression of indigenous societies, that has been an integral fact of Guatemalan history, particularly in its display of gendered social violence in the second half of the twentieth century.

While images relating to the violence against women appear prominently, what stands out in *So That All Shall Know* is the violence against men. These are indigenous or mestizo men who are, in conformance with a widely recognized principle regarding the dynamics of repression,[3] feminized in the way in which they are as equally the subjects of violence as women and, indeed, suffer pretty much the same measure of rape (although often effected through nonbodily instruments), torture, and murder as women (against whom rape may typically be carried out with the penis of the aggressor, although not always: billy clubs have pride of place as the first nonpenile resource). Men may also suffer various forms of torture designed for the anatomy of their genitalia, as well as castration.

The photographer's work as it is collected in this volume falls into several categories.

The first is that of a more journalistic nature, in the sense that it captures a particular moment in the ongoing process of social violence. These images are in both color and black-and-white, and they focus on the chief advocates of the indigenous peoples during the violence on April 26, 1998. The project resulted in the publication that same year of a four-volume treatise, *Guatemala, nunca más* (issued in English as *Guatemala, Never Again!*). The image of an angel appears on the cover of the published volumes. The image is the basis of a separate project by Hernández-Salazar, to which I will return in a moment.

The second group of photos is the dossier "Eros + Thanatos," which deals with the assassination of individuals during the violence. In the case of these images, the photographer moves away from the journalistic idiom of the photographs described above to engage in complex photocompositions, both in terms of the staging of subjects and the execution of large photographic canvases consisting of individual photographs mounted together. There is, for example, the opening image, *Eros*, in which the individual is displayed in his full physical detail, prior to the series of photographs that represent his assassination, dismemberment, and decomposition. The fact that it is not the same individual in the entire sequence is irrelevant, since this is not a documentary representation, but a densely artistic one; the canvas also includes the same image of the angel of the posters used in the march protesting the murder of Monsignor Gerardi. This image, *Para que todos sepan*, is the overarching icon of Hernández-Salazar's photography as represented in the University of Texas Press book. The angel is as much the resurrected human subject of the violence in accord with the promise of religion so present as one dimension of the movement of protest and reclamation (hence the importance of Gerardi, a religious leader) as he is public crier who articulates the demands for justice and revindication.

The image of *Eros* is eloquent. It shows a sturdy, handsome young man, clasping a globe, which one assumes to represent the earth, as though announcing with virile pride that he is in command of his world. Certainly, this is the abiding promise of masculinism, in its assertion of male authority and superiority and the legitimacy of a man (particularly one who adheres properly, so to speak, to the prevailing norms of heterosexist

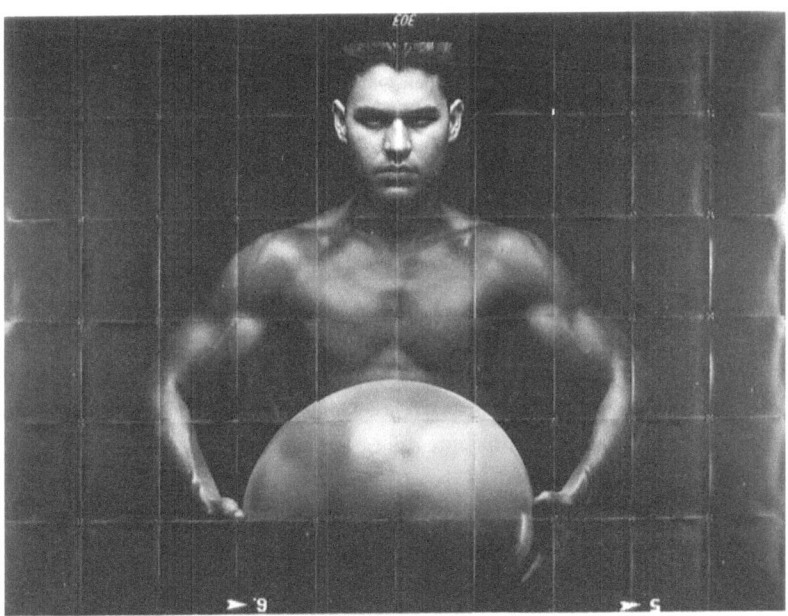

Figure 13.2. Daniel Hernández-Salazar, *Eros*.
Used with permission of Daniel Hernández-Salazar.

masculinism) being in control of his world. If the masculinist promise is a chimera in the real world, and even more so wherever feminism has exercised its influence, it is doubly so in the context of state-sponsored terrorism, where men on the wrong side of the power differential are subject to a universalizing violence that does not respect sexist privileges. The privileged male body will be as humiliated and broken as that of any other social subject in the face of such terrorism.[4]

However, if the male body in *Eros* in an immediate sense represents the healthy male body prior to its being subjected to the violence of state-sponsored terrorism, it is also suggestively a queer body in the way it is here displayed in an erotic fashion (hence, the title) that is inadmissible within the codes of heterosexism, where, with few exceptions, the display of the male body raises uncomfortable questions of the acceptable performance of masculinity. The perfect physique of this body is matched by a face (and hairdo) that verge on a so-called pretty-boy imaginary, and from some points of view his mouth could be called particularly sensuous. To be sure, Hernández-Salazar is likely invoking Eros in its primary sense of the force of life and not necessarily in its secondary reference to sexuality or homoeroticism. This is the body fully endowed with life—Guatemalan manhood as a masculine ideal—before the assault of state-sponsored violence (which we see in the immediately following images).

This image, which will strike many viewers as sexist, especially if taken as a proposal about an ideal Guatemalan manhood, is, therefore, double-edged. On the one hand, it affirms an ideal of human strength, of the physical integrity, the body, of the nation, that will be mutilated by the violence that Hernández-Salazar's photographs (here, photographic montages) reference. On the other hand, if it is legitimate to read a certain measure of queering of the male body represented here, it points toward a strong and healthy homoeroticism that will also be mutilated by the so-called "feminization" of the male body that, in the high sexism of state terrorism, equates the male body of the ideological Other with the female body that is, from the perspective of that high sexism, irreflexively going to be mutilated and destroyed as part of the assault on the individuals who give life but are ideologized to be the enemies of the state and, therefore, necessarily to be disposed of. It is part of the draconian dimensions of such thinking that the equalization of the male and female body in this process of violence, whether or not the male bodies belong to heterosexual or queer social subjects, accomplishes a leveling of sexism—and yet via the application of a more dreadful sexism—that was not prevalent in Guatemalan society before the violence and is not prevalent today.

I used the pronoun "he" above with reference to Hernández-Salazar's angel,[5] although it is customarily affirmed that angels have no sexual identity. Yet Hernández-Salazar's images of a male individual who moves from fully being in the world through torture, death, decay, and redemption are highly erotic and, I would insist, homoerotic in nature. The sexuality of the individual, despite the evocation of Christ's passion, is forthrightly masculine, with the sort of unstinting display of the details of masculinity as to echo customary gay male beefcake. An example of this might be *Cristo de mis pasiones* (Christ of my passions), in which what is an image of a fully offered reclining man is superimposed on the frame of a wooden cross. Equally typical homoerotic poses are involved in *El camino del dolor* (The path of pain) and *Ascensión* (Ascension), in which the nude body is posed in conjunction with railroad ties, perhaps instruments of the system of state that crush his humanity. In addition to complying with an idealizing masculine physique, the languor of the models here contrasts with the aggressive stance of figures of police authority in the journalistic sequence.

These Christological images evoke the prevailing Catholic beliefs of Guatemala, which often overlay indigenous beliefs and are in conflict also with Protestantism and other varieties of Christianity, and in so doing they connect the persecution of the young male body at the hands of state-sponsored terrorism with the agony of Christ, who was, in a proleptic sense, a victim of state-sponsored terrorism himself. But what is so powerful about these images is the way they are so heavily eroticized: if some wish to view the body of Christ in agony as homoerotic in some way (as well as the bodies of Christian martyrs undergoing torment, such as, first among equals, that of Saint Sebastian), their gaze must contend with the customary loincloth. The absence of a loincloth in Hernández-Salazar's sequence foregrounds sexuality in these images of denunciation and repudiation as much as do the mutilation and rape that are integral to dynamics of repression: the annihilation of men, particularly the young men most directly involved in reproduction, is as much a part of the genocide of first-nation peoples as that of women.[6]

Although I have not stressed so far Hernández-Salazar's nonnatural photographic procedures (part of what Weinstein calls his postmodernity), images like *El camino del dolor* are a good opportunity to do so. Consisting of fifteen selenium-toned fiber-based paper sheets joined together in a pattern in which the joints between them are evident, the result is a large twenty-by-twenty-four-inch panel attached (appropriately, given its Christological dimensions) to the wall by nails. Although the panel is meant to constitute one unified image, that of the male body extended over railroad

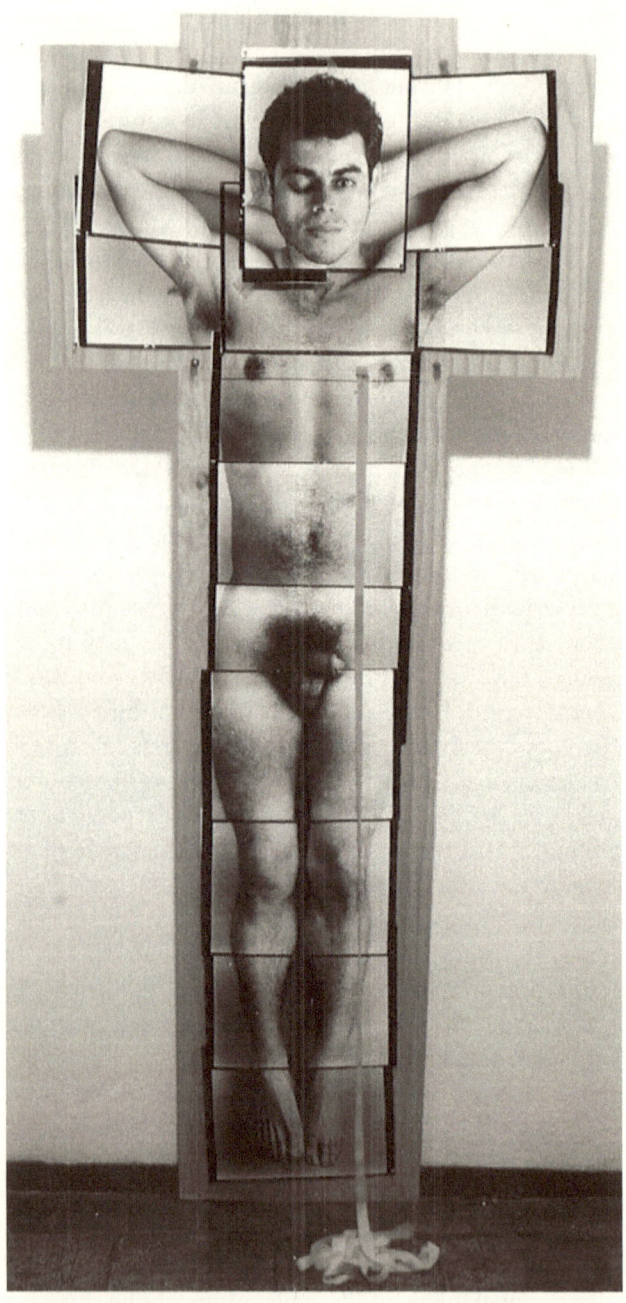

Figure 13.3. Daniel Hernández-Salazar, *Cristo de mis pasiones* (Christ of my passions). Used with permission of Daniel Hernández-Salazar.

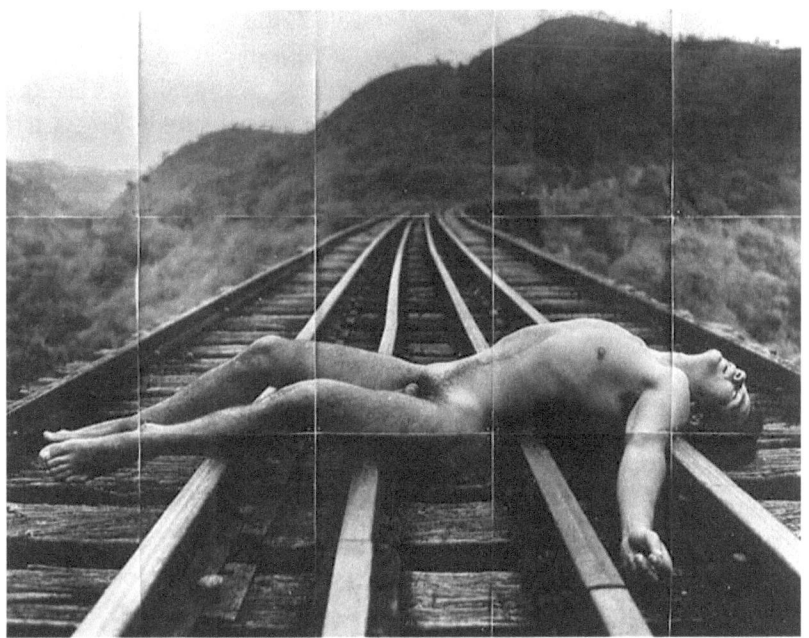

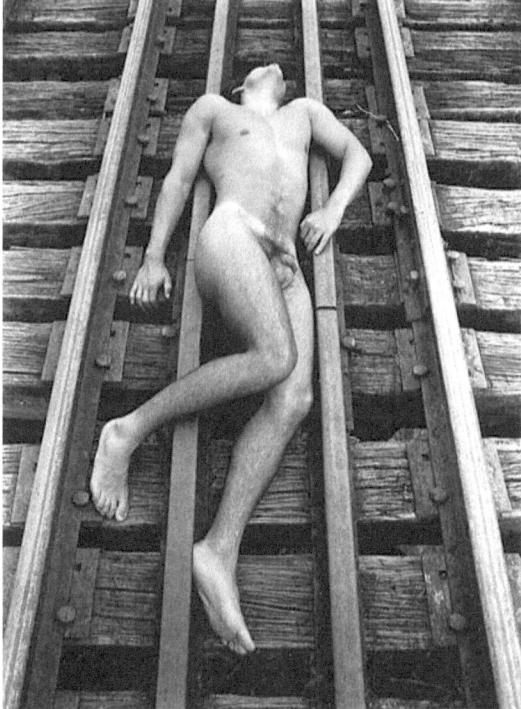

Figure 13.4. Daniel Hernández-Salazar, *El camino del dolor* (The path of pain). Used with permission of Daniel Hernández-Salazar.

Figure 13.5. Daniel Hernández-Salazar, *Ascensión* (Ascension). Used with permission of Daniel Hernández-Salazar.

ties in the same position as though crucified, the slight misfit between the fifteen sheets disrupts the pretense of an unmediated documentary image. This disruption is in turn reinforced by the way the image is so evidently posed, as it is not a verisimilar re-creation of any known practice of the agents of death subjecting their victims to being crushed to death by oncoming trains. Were this the case, one would expect the victim to be nailed (or bound) to the tracks as Christ was nailed to the cross.

The eschewal of recognizably documentary images (like the confrontation between protestors and police in fig. 13.1) makes the image that much more haunting as an evocation of terrorist persecution. The fact that the young man here strikes a pose of (homo)erotic languor makes the photograph all the more alluring, since, if it were not for the context of the photobook as a whole, it might not immediately be read as having to do with the violence of state-sponsored terrorism. To be sure, close examination might lead one to view the body as deceased: is its partially open mouth part of the slackness of an early moment of death rather than the result of the languorous position that makes it difficult to keep the mouth closed?[7] All of this is part of the photographer's disruption of the strict conventions of journalistic naturalism or authenticity, as in the case of the discontinuous montage of images of the male body in the sixteen sheets that make up the following image, *Premonition*. I believe this is the same model as in *El camino del dolor*, and the discontinuous montage certainly can be viewed as foretelling (hence the title) the dismemberment of the body at the hands of the agents of death.

The final set of photographs takes up the image of the proclaiming angel of *Para que todos sepan* (see fig. 13.6). In this case, Hernández-Salazar provides a documentation of the dozens of public sites, within Guatemala and internationally, where the image of the angel has been displayed as an immense poster on buildings and other edifices; in the case of Guatemala, some of them are those of the state, whose actions have been those of repression and murder. Both because of its size and because of the transgressive nature of the angel, what Hernández-Salazar's photographic sequence in this case captures is the transformation of public space—which is recorded in part by the inclusion of individuals reacting to the image—in conformance with what the angel represents: the clamor for justice and revindication. This image of an angel is transgressive because it is a manifestly sexualized male. Although his genitals are not in evidence, the rest of his body is anatomically accurate in a fashion not customarily considered angelic. Moreover, it is the nonwhite body of an indigenous man, whose hair is hardly the flowing locks of conventional iconography, no

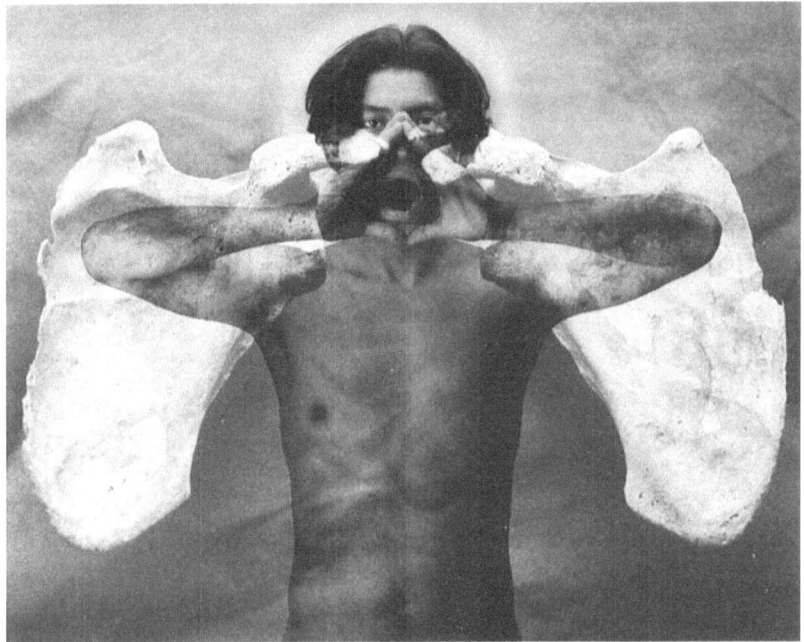

Figure 13.6. Daniel Hernández-Salazar, *Para que todos sepan* (So that all shall know).
Used with permission of Daniel Hernández-Salazar.

more than the gesture of proclaiming, hands cupped around his mouth (which allows the display of his fully tufted axilla), is conventionally angelic. Finally, his wings are shoulder blades, such as those of the skeletons found in the mass burial sites of the victims of state-sponsored terrorism.

This is a rich and complex photographic record, and the photographs are mostly complex montages, although more conventional documentary photography also appears. Hernández-Salazar goes beyond just the recording of the public traces of violence in Guatemala (an honorable goal in itself) to create images that provide a narrative of the assault on the human body and its destruction. But like his angel of redemption, Hernández-Salazar demonstrates how human life can never be totally exterminated. His photographic art is not a transcendence offered to pay the toll of the acts of extermination, but rather the record of how the attempts at extermination will be told and retold in the preservation of human memory and the dignity of the individual.

– ◆ –

NOTES

◆ ◆ ◆

1. At the same time, my research interest on the cultural production related to the city of São Paulo has led me to the history of Brazilian photography, which quite rightly touts the fact that Emperor Dom Pedro II was one of the country's first major photographers and, therefore, an important stimulus to that art. My *São Paulo: Perspectives on the City and Cultural Production* (2011) includes three chapters (out of ten) focused on photographers of the city, two of them women, and both of them foreign-born: Hildegard Rosenthal and Madalena Schwartz (the third is the founding anthropologist Claude Lévi-Strauss, also, of course, foreign-born).

2. See the wealth of information on the subject in Sara Sefchovich's *¿Son mejores las mujeres?* (2011), which is perhaps the most comprehensive overview of feminist issues in Mexico, including the realm of cultural production.

3. *Urban Photography in Argentina* includes the work of the following women: Adriana Lestido, Gabriela Liffschitz, and Gabriela Messina, three of the nine photographers represented.

4. The bulk of these essays has been published elsewhere. Since the majority of the mainline academic journals in Hispanic Studies do not publish articles on photography, these essays have appeared in lesser-known journals, including online ones. Some of them were published originally in Spanish in social science journals in Spain and Mexico. I have not included here essays on gender-marked photography that have appeared in my own monographs on larger cultural topics or in volumes edited by others, with the exception of

the essay on Argentine women in crisis in the photography of Silvina Frydlewsky, and this only because the version here is substantially different from the one included in the book edited by Cynthia Schmidt-Cruz. The essays on Mexican soap opera, on Sanguinetti, and on Helen Zout's human rights photography are published here for the first time. The great Brazilian photographer Madalena Schwartz is examined in my essay "Madalena Schwartz: A Jewish Brazilian Photographer," and it is also included (as indicated above, along with an essay on Hildegard Rosenthal) in my book *São Paulo: Perspectives on the City and Cultural Production* (2011). In the case of those essays originally published elsewhere, I have noted their source in the initial endnote to each chapter.

5. With the exception of Schwartz, whose work dates from the mid-twentieth century.

6. A third foreign-born photographer needs to be mentioned here, the French Giselle Freund, also of Jewish origins. Her official photography of Evita Perón is part of the iconographic record relating to the most important woman in Argentine sociopolitical history.

7. For a different take on men's bodies as display text, see my essay "Toreros de moda: la fotografía de Ruven Afanador." Afanador is Colombian.

CHAPTER 1: DREAMING IN FEMININE

Originally published as Foster, "Dreaming in Feminine: Grete Stern's Photomontages and the Parody of Psychoanalysis," *Ciberletras* 10 (2003).

1. Stern herself acknowledges that it was "un momento en que los conceptos de ideas psicoanalíticas penetraban en todas las capas de la sociedad, y dicha página [en la revista *Idilio*] fue recibida con agrado por el público lector, mayormente femenino" (*Sueños* 51).

2. Between 1948 and 1950, Grete Stern published in the magazine *Idilio* approximately 150 photomontages of the series devoted to dreams. Today, only 45 photographic negatives exist of that work (and only one copy) that the author turned over to the editorial office of the magazine.

3. Following the publication of the original version of these comments, K. M. Sibbald published her excellent analysis of Stern's work, with an emphasis also on a feminist revision of masculinist culture. However, while their perspective constitutes a duplication, our actual analyses are different. Sibbald performs the important task of describing the hold psychoanalysis already had in Argentina. However, she analyzes different images and, more important, is only briefly interested in the rhetorical analysis of Stern's photomontages.

4. In Varo's painting, the woman is carrying the Freud-like head of the psychoanalyst upside down by some strands of his beard; she is wrapped in a cape that includes a fallen mask, as though now she could show her real face to the world.

5. Stern's photomontages, in any case, were done well before there was much research on women's erotic needs, such as inaugurated in the United States by Shere Hite, whose *Hite Report* has been widely translated into Spanish, mostly in Spain, where, to judge from the number of editions, it was a best seller in the post-Franco era. Hite's report, however, is not itself free from the restrictions of the era in which it was assembled, as there is no reference to oral and anal sex, or to B&D and S&M.

6. I will base myself on the full-page photomontages that are identified as belonging to the "Colección de la artista" and the "Colección Jorge Helft," setting aside the reproductions taken from surviving issues of *Idilio* and reproduced (with much less quality) in groups of four per page. I do this because I am taking the chance of assuming that those images in the

photographer's personal possession and in the formal Jorge Helft collection represent the ones Stern was most interested in preserving. Moreover, I would suggest that a comparison between the two groups demonstrates the far greater artistic merit of those that survived independently of the pages of *Idilio*.

7. The French scholar Sarah Kofman begins her analysis of Freud and women with this statement: "Didn't Freud himself predict it? Feminists would take to the warpath against his text, which, on the subject of women, would be seen as rife with masculine prejudice" (11). See also Slipp; Gallop. It is important to note that there is a 1982 Spanish translation of Kofman's work. For an overview in Spanish of the relationship between women and psychoanalysis, see Meier.

8. Germani was mostly known for his work in sociology and served as founding director of the Instituto de Sociología at the Universidad de Buenos Aires, but he also published the volume *Estudios de psicología*, contemporaneous with his work with Stern; he also wrote a preface for the Spanish translation of Erich Fromm's *The Fear of Freedom* (also published as *Escape from Freedom*). See the long interview by Alberto Noé with Juan Carlos Marín on Germani's place in Argentine social sciences. What clearly emerges from this interview is Germani's authoritarianism; moreover, the interview is transparently masculinist in nature.

CHAPTER 2: ANNEMARIE HEINRICH

First published as the article "Annemarie Heinrich: Photography, Women's Bodies, and Semiotic Excess," by David William Foster, in *Studies in Latin American Popular Culture* 25 (2006): 253–270. Copyright © 2006 by the University of Texas Press. All rights reserved.

1. Neyer provides a chronology of Freund's career, and places her in Argentina between 1946 and 1952. She published her images of Evita in numerous U.S. and foreign magazines; perhaps the most viewed were those in the dossier she published in *Life* to accompany an article by Robert Neville. Her most famous images are to be found in Freund, *Itinéraires* 76–79, and in Freund, *Gisèle Freud: Photographer* 188.

2. This photograph, of a very young Evita in a swimsuit, cheesecake pose, may be seen in Heinrich, *Un cuerpo* 18.

3. It is interesting to note that, while Dujovne Ortiz mentions Heinrich on several occasions (the English translation has a useful index), she never mentions Freund's work.

4. Silvia Pellarolo has published an excellent study on the "melodramatic seductions" of Evita's body, and argues for the recovery of the performing body beyond the façade of the propaganda, publicity, and political images of her that sustain the congealed images of special interests and their myths about her.

5. An excellent dossier of photographic icons of Evita as a public face of the Peronista government is to be found in *Evita: imágenes de una pasión*, which includes 220 images. Unfortunately, there is no registry of attribution.

6. The concept of "semiotic excess" I am using here is also akin, in more grammatical terms, to redundancy and overdetermination (see Greimas and Courtés 258–259). Bell uses the term "overload," while Fiske directly uses the word "excess" with reference to the singer Madonna's personae and performances.

7. Cabrera's study on the famed director Hugo del Carril does not address the issue; see 119–124 for an enthusiastic endorsement of the quality of the film.

8. Perón had supported successfully early in his government the mandatory teaching of

Catholic doctrine in the Argentine public schools, despite the long-standing lay tradition of the latter in a country that counted several hundred thousand Jews. Regarding Perón and the Catholic Church, see Kennedy 204–214; McGeagh 65–100.

9. It is the Church's refusal to collaborate in the ecclesiastical process of canonization that brings about a split between Perón and the Church, which grows, for other reasons, into full opposition during the remaining years of his regime.

10. I have not been able to attribute this image of Crawford, but it may be found on the open-access page of the entry for her at the International Movie Database (imdb.com).

11. See the display of such bodies in the swim team scene with Jane Russell in Howard Hawkes's 1953 *Gentlemen Prefer Blondes*, in which Russell's imposingly athletic body echoes that of the male models who ignore her.

12. I am not here subscribing to the facile belief that fashion is only about selling sex, just that sexualizing women through fashion is one way of selling women's clothes. For an overview of feminist research on fashion, see Mackie.

13. The lack of interest, even on the part of the photographers who worked for Eva Duarte's lover-protector, Emilio Kartulowicz, stands in contrast to the magnificent photographs that Annemarie Heinrich took during that period in mid-1939. This carelessness cannot, therefore, be explained only on the basis of the insignificance of the model but as a consequence of the mediocrity of the photographer.

14. I will not dwell on the Thamar image here, because it is not included in *Un cuerpo*, but the reader may easily find it on the Internet, where it is included in an obituary on the occasion of Heinrich's death (http://www.zonezero.com/magazine/obituaries/annmarie/).

CHAPTER 3: WOMAN, PROSTITUTION, AND MODERNITY
IN FIN-DE-SIÈCLE MEXICO

Originally published as Foster, "Mujer, prostitución y modernidad en el México finisecular," *Magazine modernista: revista digital* 13 (2009).

1. The best study on the sporting life of the period, in addition to numerous essays by Carlos Monsiváis, is the book by Sergio González Rodríguez. For parallel cases in Buenos Aires, the veritable center of Latin American prostitution at the time, see the pertinent sections of Bergero's study.

2. This dossier is a new and expanded edition of the one that Vargas published with the title *La casa de cita: Mexican Photography from the Belle Epoque* (London: Quartet Books, 1986).

3. French includes a reference to *Casa de citas* in the documentation on prostitution as "something of a boom field" during the period of the presidency of Porfirio Díaz (1876–1911) (258n24).

4. "In the end, this human paradise, so celebrated by Greek eloquence, is the Valley of Tempe, in whose meadows we can believe unending spring was born, such that no other is in any measure like it" (my translation).

5. Nevertheless, Tenenbaum (24n48) underscores how light is used in the photographs of *La casa de citas* so as to make the models employed appear to be lighter in skin color than would otherwise have been the case.

CHAPTER 4: BUENOS AIRES AND WOMEN IN CRISIS

An earlier and shorter version of this essay appeared as Foster, "Sociohistorical, Gender, and Genre Contexts," in *Crisis in Buenos Aires*, ed. Cynthia Schmidt-Cruz (Newark, DE: Juan de la Cuesta, 2007).

1. Porteño = someone from the port city of Buenos Aires.
2. Another intertextual reference can be seen in the evocation of the Argentine café as a school for social life in Argentina, as in the tango lyrics by Enrique Santos Discépolo and Mariano Mores on the recording *Cafetín de Buenos Aires*. Like Scalabrini Ortiz's contemporary essay, these lyrics are also relentlessly masculinist, leading one to wonder what a feminist version of this text might look like.
3. *Corralito* was the informal name for the economic measures taken in Argentina at the end of 2001 by neoliberal Minister of Economy Domingo Cavallo in order to stop a bank run; some of these measures were fully in force for three years. The *corralito* almost completely froze bank accounts (people were allowed to withdraw only $250 weekly from their accounts) for over a year or so and forbade withdrawals from U.S.-dollar-denominated accounts.

CHAPTER 5: GIRLS WILL BE GIRLS

First published as the article "Review Essay: Daniela Rossell, *Ricas y Famosas*," by David William Foster, in *Studies in Latin American Popular Culture* 22 (2003): 217–222. Copyright © 2003 by the University of Texas Press. All rights reserved. I have been unable to obtain use permission for the photographs of Daniela Rossell, who has no personal website. The images may, however, be found at numerous sites on the Internet.

1. "The following images depict actual settings. The photographic subjects are representing themselves. Any resemblance with real events is not coincidental."
2. In a colophon, Rossell states: "This book is dedicated to the people that appear in it. I want to thank each and every one of them for opening the doors of their homes and workplaces and for having the strong character needed to be photographed next to their personal belongings. . . . This project, which was concluded in 2001 [it was begun in 1994], had the sole mission of documenting the objects that this particular group of people decided to bring into their homes, the personal environment they inhabit and the style they choose to identify with." This English version is preceded by the same text in Spanish. It is interesting to note that it is followed by a list of about two dozen acknowledgments, of, one assumes, the women and their husbands who allowed the photographs to be taken. Gallo's superb examination of the social contexts of this photography in *New Tendencies* uses as a title the very ethically laden term "Voyeurism."
3. My translation of this passage follows:

What is radical about Rossell's images is not only how they open for us the doors to houses protected by guards, walls, and electric gates, the function that social columns and the gossip magazines fulfill without upsetting anyone. More than showing us "how the privileged live," Ricas y famosas references how they would like to live—not how they are, but how they would like to be.
Rossell's photographs repeatedly stage a multitude of fantasies that have been acquired

in a disorderly fashion in antique stores, department stores, safaris, trips, and an endless string of supermarkets. What Rossell has documented is the desperate effort of a class to create for itself "an other space" that is different from the collage of rural misery, barbarous industrialization, and paraplegic urbanism that the rest of us inhabit.

Trudy Balch's translation of the entire note appears in "Daniela Rossell" (332). "Daniela Rossell" also contains Medina's further elaboration of his review, "The Stage and the Stereotype" (311–327).

4. In the original public presentation of the book on August 28, 2002, Rossell had a stand-in for her read a statement that included the following assertion: "As an artist, I defend and have the right to the ambiguity with which I present this work, and I do not need to provide explanations about my moral positions related to it" (English translation by Trudy Balch, included [331] in "Daniela Rossell").

5. Rubén Gallo, in his introductory note to a selection of Rossell's photographs included in his *The Mexico City Reader*, observes: "In contrast to the exuberance of their surroundings, however, most of these women appear to be lacking something. They are not arrogant or haughty, snobbish or even wholly self-assured. On the contrary, it seems that they are suffering from an intense *horror vacua* [sic], as if trying to fill an internal void through this compulsive accumulation of objects" (115).

6. The Indian director Mira Nair's 1996 film *Kama Sutra: A Tale of Love* shows the women of the harem learning the techniques of the famed erotic manual by practicing with each other.

CHAPTER 6: PEDRO MEYER

Originally published as Foster, "Pedro Meyer: construir masculinidades, construir fotografías," *Sociotam: revista internacional de ciencias sociales y humanidades* 20.1 (2010): 39–58. Translated by Solymar Torres-García.

1. Although it pre-dates his digital work examined here, Meyer (1985) expresses his ethos as a photographer and his commitment to ethically recording sociohistorical reality in "¿Para quién y para qué se fotografía?"

2. Snow examines, in detail, Meyer's digital processes.

3. This study is based on four main sources on masculinities and masculinisms: the general theories of Judith Butler (*Gender Trouble; Bodies That Matter; Undoing Gender*); Marta Lamas's compilation of essays; the well-known work of Guillermo Núñez Noriega in Mexico (*Sexo entre varones; Masculinidad e intimidad*); and the special edition of the journal *Desacatos* entitled *Masculinidades diversas* (Ponce 2004).

4. It is obvious that Meyer does not exclusively photograph Mexican images. However, for the purposes of this article, I limit myself to his extensive work in Mexico. For his international work, refer to *The Real and the True*. See also Kaplan.

5. All the photographs in *Truths and Fictions* appear with two dates: the first alludes to the original photo, while the second refers to the digital elaboration of the montage, according to what is stated on page 5 of *Truths and Fictions*. That explains the subtitle of the dossier, "un periplo de la fotografía documental a la digital" ("A Journey from Documentary to Digital Photography"). Refer to Meyer (2006).

6. It is important to note the role that accusations of sodomy among the indigenous

played. On one hand, the conquistadors were incapable of understanding gender structures and the sexuality that they encountered among the indigenous. However, of more importance is acknowledging how this lack of understanding facilitated the "feminization" of indigenous men: since they were all "women," it was justifiable, as a stringent principle of sexist masculinity, to subdue them with violence.

7. That does, in fact, exist in innumerable societies. For another Latin American photographic project that deals with the intersection between gender and violence, see *So That All Shall Know: Photographs / Para que todos sepan: fotografía* by the Guatemalan Daniel Hernández-Salazar, examined in chapter 13 of this volume.

8. Like the nursery rhyme says, "We must trick the sheriff in order to save the princess."

9. Fulfilling his pedagogical impulses, Meyer provides a detailed analysis of the making of the photo (Meyer, *Truths* 117). Said analysis has the following subtitle: "The Representation of Dreams."

10. The Mexican writer Anita Brenner analyzes, although through the lens of a Jewish intellectual, this fissure in Mexico between the popular-folkloric and the official in relation to the idols behind the altars. Frank Graziano (*Cultures of Devotion*) studies a wide range of folkloric saints in Mexico, complementing the analysis done by the Mexican chronicler Carlos Monsiváis ("Protagonista: el Niño Fidencio"), who through the optic of his Protestant formation comments on the phenomenon of Niño Fidencio. Castillo and Rodríguez have each written an important study about the projections of the Virgin of Guadalupe that do not fit comfortably within the official versions; Rodríguez does so with an emphasis on Mexican American women. The unofficial attributions of miracles to the Virgin of Guadalupe seem to proliferate, to a higher degree, among Mexican Americans: see Kristy Nabhan-Warren's study.

11. For an excellent study of Meyer's photography in terms of another topic not totally unrelated to masculinity, see Kaplan's chapter dedicated to him in his book about photography and U.S. ethnic cultures.

CHAPTER 7: DISCOVERING THE MALE BODY

A shorter version of this commentary appeared as a review note in *Chasqui: revista de literatura latinoamericana* 39.1 (2010): 202–203.

1. Even Leonardo, a provincial taxiboy, while possessing a more urban body, is a far cry from the models available in upscale "escort" services in Buenos Aires.

CHAPTER 8: QUEERING GENDER IN GRACIELA ITURBIDE'S *JUCHITÁN DE LAS MUJERES*

Originally published as Foster, "Género y fotografía en *Juchitán de las mujeres*, de Graciela Iturbide." *Ámbitos: revista de estudios de ciencias sociales y humanidades* 2.11 (2004): 63–69. My translation.

1. Nevertheless, various researchers are inclined to rein in the idealization of the Juchitecan women, including the American anthropologist Howard Campbell (*Mexican Memoir* 63–64) and his wife Obdulia Ruiz Campbell, who is herself Juchitecan. Ruiz Campbell was a consultant for the documentary *Blossoms of Fire* (see note 13).

2. The images of the original 1989 edition have no captions, and I have taken the captions I use from Iturbide's photographic retrospective, *Images of the Spirit*, from which I have taken the images that appear in this chapter. I draw on this edition precisely because of the difficulty in accessing the 1989 edition of *Juchitán de las mujeres*, which has been long out of print. For the same reason, the comments by Poniatowska that I have just transcribed and that appear in *Juchitán de las mujeres* are referenced here on the basis of her own subsequent volume, *Luz y luna, las lunitas*, which includes some of Iturbide's images of Juchitecan women taken from the 1989 book they published together. For another dossier of images on the women of Juchitán, some of which are very much like Iturbide's, see Doniz.

3. Another index of her importance is that she is also known among Mexicans as La Virgen de América, the overarching figure of the Virgin Mary for all of Latin America, despite the existence of each country's own national version of the Holy Mother.

4. *Let Us Now Praise Famous Men: Three Tenant Families*, by James Agee and Walker Evans, is one of the most famous American photobooks. Although the images of North American (Southern) peasants who lived in abject poverty during the Great Depression include women and their daughters, the title of the dossier (in addition to its aggressive irony) makes the presence of women disappear: "men" in this sort of context in English never means the existence of "women" by either extension or inclusion.

5. I am working off the principles of the queer, particularly with reference to cultural production, that I elaborate in Spanish in my *Producción cultural e identidades homoeróticas*. See also Mira Nouselles.

6. Not to mention the violence. One will recall that Joan of Arc's greatest sin, for which she was burned at the stake, was cross-dressing as a man, and only a papal authorization allowed Catalina Erauso, La Monja Alférez, to do so with impunity in the seventeenth century.

7. Where, in Eve Kosofsky Sedgwick's terms, a close relationship of solidarity between men serves to confirm patriarchal law and the exclusion of women from both the material and the symbolic spheres of power.

8. One recalls the famous anecdote in Luis Buñuel's autobiography of how he asked Pedro Armendáriz, one of the paradigmatic machos of Mexican film, to wear a short-sleeve shirt in one of his films. Armendáriz immediately vetoed the idea by saying that only *maricones* (fairies) wore short-sleeve shirts.

9. It should be evident that I am basing myself, in a very general way, on the array of theorization regarding the construction of gender, and the reiterated conjugation of the signs of that construction, that we associate with the line of thinking promulgated by Judith Butler. In the Zapotecan language spoken in Juchitán, *muxés* is the word for those men whom Bennholdt-Thomsen speaks of as the "third sex," neither masculine nor feminine. See also Müller (269–278).

10. See Foster, *Queer Issues* 22–32. Ripstein bases himself on the novel (1966) of the same name by the Chilean José Donoso (see Foster, *Gay and Lesbian Themes* 87–93).

11. Primary characteristics are genital; secondary characteristics are other physical features of the body directly related to the primary ones, such as the relative hairiness of the man or the deepness of his voice versus the soft skin of women and their bodily curves.

12. It is important to remember that in Mexico men can have names normally associated with the feminine gender in Spanish, as long as they evoke the Catholic religion: Guadalupe, Trinidad, Rosario (and María as a second name) are, at least popularly, permissible for men in Spanish, but not Magnolia.

13. Concerning the feminine homosocialism of the women of Juchitán, see the study by Müller, as well as the global-scope study by Bennholdt-Thomsen in which it is included. The documentary by Maureen Gosling and Ellen Osborne, *Blossoms of Fire* (2001; distrib-

uted in Spanish as *Ramo de fuego*), underscores the feminine homosociality of Juchitán and includes interviews with men and women regarding homoerotic relations and, in the case of men, transvestism.

CHAPTER 9: GUILLE AND BELINDA

1. Sanguinetti was born in New York in 1968. However, she lived in Buenos Aires between 1970 and 2003, during which time she took the images for this dossier. Her formation in Argentina and her photographic work in that country, therefore, make it legitimate to consider her an Argentine photographer for the purposes of this chapter. For reasons beyond my control, it has not been possible to include Sanguinetti's images here. The reader may consult them at her website: http://alessandrasanguinetti.com/index.php/project/the-adventures-of-guille-and-belinda/.

2. Cristoff, in her introduction to the dossier, which provides information about the identity and world of Guille and Belinda, speaks of the *pacto* (pact) between the two women, without venturing to identify it in any sexual sense.

3. The masculinism of the heartland is evident in a central photograph, an assembly in the middle of a field of an array of rural types. In the foreground stands a young Belinda: she could almost be taken for a young man, except for her clothes, which would not be worn by a young rural boy. She stares off blankly as if totally disassociated or alienated from this all-male environment (*La jineteada* [Horsemanship]). Sanguinetti photographed the two women over an approximately five-year period (1999–2004), during which we see them mature from girls into young women. *La jineteada* is from 1999.

4. Foster, *Urban Photography in Argentina*, has as its underlying premise that photography has been essentially an urban cultural genre in Argentina. I first saw the Guille and Belinda photographs in a show at the Ruth Benzacar Galería de Arte in Buenos Aires in 2010. Ruth Benzacar is one of the most prestigious galleries in Buenos Aires. The photographs have also been displayed in major galleries internationally; see the listing in *Las aventuras* (60–61).

5. Argentina was the first country in Latin America to validate on a national scale same-sex marriages, which it did in July 2010.

6. I reference this urban anchor in "Más allá de la visibilidad gay."

7. One of the most significant films in recent Argentina is Albertina Carri's *La rabia* (2008), which deconstructs multiple narremes of the idyllic Argentine heartland (Tompkins).

8. This photograph alludes to Sir John Everett Millais's 1852 painting *Ophelia*.

9. See Zimmerman's book on the subject of lesbian liquidity.

10. I duly note that when *sueño* means "sleep," it almost always occurs in the singular only, but a poetic text is not confined to everyday usages of language.

11. In another image, *La soñadora* (The dreamer), Belinda is lying alone on her side in a meadow.

12. This is, then, a "June wedding," since December in Argentina is the equivalent of June in the Northern Hemisphere.

13. See my examination of this photobook in "Género y fotografía."

CHAPTER 10: HOMOSOCIALISM ◀▶ HOMOEROTICISM
IN THE PHOTOGRAPHY OF MARCOS LÓPEZ

Originally published as Foster, "Homosocialism ◀▶ Homoeroticism in the Photography of Marcos López," *Dissidences* 1 (30 Aug. 2005).

1. Also identified as *Asado en Mendiolaza*.

2. The fact that Argentines may no longer so easily assemble to affirm their identity through the ritual of the *asado*—beef has become too expensive for the twice-daily consumption it once had, or even the once-a-week-on-the-weekend blowout of more recent times—lends an aura of nostalgia to *Asado criollo*. If, on the one hand, it is a clever framing of the importance of the barbecue for Argentines, it is, on the other, a reminder that such rituals are no longer so easily observed. Like a religious persecution of the celebration of the Mass, the consequences of neoliberalism and globalization constitute something like the persecution of the celebration of the *asado*.

3. "South" here unquestionably refers to López's Southern Hemisphere origins, but, in the context of his parodies of social and cultural icons, at least in English it evokes the phrase "to go south" = "become inferior in quality or substance." Thus, the "south of realism" = "the trivialization of realism."

4. It is not completely clear why this should be so. In one sense, perhaps it is because homosociality relies on a hierarchy of power that is disrupted and restructured in the throes of passion (even when passion involves a fictive, theatrical show of power, as in S/M, B/D, etc.). Perhaps it is because most versions of masculine heterosexism are grounded on the belief that sex always involves a domination and submission that would both counter the sociofinancial domination and submission of patriarchal society and produce irresolvably conflicting structurings of it: a man cannot be both the active master in a sociofinancial arrangement and the passive slave in an erotic one. Since women are, in patriarchal heterosexuality, always passive, the "feminization" of one of the men in the homoerotic coupling is radically destabilizing. The fact that such a narrative may not be true of all, many, or any homoerotic relationships is a problem of the imaginary of patriarchal heterosexuality, not of verisimilar functioning of those relationships. On another level, homoeroticism may involve the threat of a "truer" democracy of human relationships than is possible in patriarchal heterosexuality. This is the Whitmanesque principle, although it is certainly at work in the feminist rejection—as in, for example, ecofeminism—of the deceits, regarding democracy and social equality, of the patriarchy and its economics of capitalism. On the other hand, the so-called male homosexuality of ancient Greece (best synthesized by Halperin) is founded on a tight system of male homosociality, whereby the two are not incompatible.

Carrillo discusses "nonsexual homosociality" in the context of homosexual identities in Mexico (358–362).

5. Hence, the Mexican narrative of the two men who wake up in bed together, and one says to the other that he was so drunk last night that he can't remember what happened (a version of this appears in Alfonso Cuarón's 2001 film *Y tu mamá también*), or the American war movie motif of soldiers dying in each other's arms. See the Argentine variant on this motif in José Hernández's *Martín Fierro* (Geirola) or the Brazilian one in Bruno Barreto's 1981 film *O beijo no asfalto* (Foster, *Gender and Society* 129–138).

6. Military discipline—and certainly that of other quasi-militaristic organizations like religious orders—may require the weak homoeroticism of homosocialism; see the American motif of "two Marines and a six-pack" and the phenomenon of "barracks buddies." The homoerotic pornography of strong homoeroticism is built around such real-life circum-

stances. The Argentine sociologist Néstor Perlongher insisted on homoerotic—not just homosocial—bonding as a factor in the network of survival among the São Paulo male hustlers he studied.

7. Homosociality among women, as one might expect, works completely differently. While one form of it may be promoted to keep the women entertained—the practice of women assembling in the drawing room for coffee after a meal, while the men remain at table for a cigar and an after-dinner drink—strong female-female bonding is frowned upon as virtually the top of the slippery slope of men-hating and lesbianism. On the other hand, female homosociality is often viewed as an important strategic component, "sisterhood," of women united against male oppression (see the entry "Homosociality" in Kowaleski Wallace). Queer sociality would, therefore, have its own dimensions of solidarity, visibility, resistance, and social revindication: "happy together" (see "Homosocialismo" in Mira Nouselles's encyclopedia in Spanish of queer culture).

8. The importance of meat in Argentine culture and its relationship to violence, homosociality, and homosexual rape were understood as early as the 1830s by Esteban Echeverría, whose short story "El matadero" is a founding text of Argentine fiction (probably written in the late 1830s, but not published until 1871). Echeverría describes the violence surrounding the utilization of beef-eating as a political tool by the Rosas dictatorship, the male homosociality of spaces like the slaughterhouse and the relationship of its denizens to the violent politics of Rosas, and the use of homosexual rape, depicted specifically in Echeverría's story but present elsewhere in the period, through the use of the corncob (the *mazorca*) as an instrument of terror by the enforcers of the regime known as La Mazorca. In the relationship between the enforcers and their victim, there is a displaced homosexuality (a bull's pizzle is used in Echeverría's story), and, in their interpretation of the victim as "rapable," there is the understanding of his body as open to feminization or as already feminized—that is, as a male body available for sex at the hands of another (displaced) male body. For the relevance of "El matadero" to the history of homosexuality in Argentina, see Bazán (82–84); Piglia speaks of the violence in Echeverría's story (8–10), and his comments are accompanied by Enrique Breccia's intense graphic representation (10–18). Not all readers would agree that the bull's pizzle is used to penetrate the unfortunate *unitario*, since explicit reference is limited to whipping his bared buttocks. However, such same-sex discipline is customarily understood as a form of homoeroticism that may or may not involve subsequent penetration; Bazán clearly understands that rape is involved (82).

9. Serge Bramly, one of Da Vinci's major biographers, includes a discussion of the latter's homosexuality, and Freud's comments on the subject are famous.

10. One of the two major sequences of Paul Leduc's 1986 film *Frida, naturaleza viva* involves her nurse; one of the final memorable scenes of the film is the same nurse accompanying Frida, who is on a stretcher, into Mexico City's Palacio de Bellas Artes for her first major exhibition. The nurse is holding aloft a serum bottle.

11. In Peter Medak's 1981 film *Zorro, the Gay Blade*, George Hamilton gives a queer twist to the twin motif, when we discover that the supermacho Zorro has a gay twin, known as Bunny Wigglesworth.

12. Historically, gynecology has involved men manipulating women's bodies, and the profession has always attempted to dispel the specter of medical rape in any of its stages by draping the woman so that her body is hidden, by having a female aide present, and by averring that the woman's body is no more than a medical specimen. Yet a large number of women prefer today female gynecologists (although this does not address the lesbian potential); female proctologists with male patients, meanwhile, remain an essentially nonexistent species.

13. Of many possible cultural references, one can think immediately of the doctor/patient relationship in Peter Glenville's 1961 film *Summer and Smoke*, based on the drama of the same name by the gay Tennessee Williams; there is very much of the gay parable about this work in both of its versions, despite the principal actors being a man and a woman. However, the fact that in the film the doctor is played by the gay British actor Laurence Harvey and his patient by Geraldine Page, who played women-who-might-really-be-gay-men in a number of plays and movies (in 1962, she also starred in the film version of Williams's *Sweet Bird of Youth*), cannot be overlooked: in a still-closeted Hollywood (and Broadway) such formulations were as close as one got to the circumstances of actual gay lives.

14. At least one major American gay play is built around the bathhouse, Terrence McNally's *The Ritz* (1975); it is well known that gay-friendly Bette Midler got her start performing in gay men's bathhouses. The homosocial space of the bathhouse appears in the Mexican Jaime Humberto Hermosillo's 1979 film *María de mi corazón* (script by Gabriel García Márquez), and the bathhouse as homoerotic space appears in another Mexican film, Jorge Fons's 1995 *El Callejón de los Milagros*.

15. One of the most significant analyses of homoeroticism within macho hypermasculinity for Latin America is Núñez Noriega's study *Sexo entre varones*, devoted to northwestern Mexico.

16. The Marlboro Man ads have, for years, sold an image of hypermasculinity, undisturbed by the feminine or the effeminate. However, the death from AIDS of Tom McBride, one of the models for these ads, is a real-world reminder of the homoeroticism always already present in the hypermasculine.

17. Other "penile" compositions authored by López include *En el jardín botánico*, where a parody of a Fidel Castro–Che Guevara army-fatigued macho brandishes a plastic pistol that is somewhat flesh-colored rather than gun-metal gray. (Alberto Korda's famous photograph of the stern Che Guevara is parodied in *La Habana*, where the lean revolutionary icon is juxtaposed to a fleshy [Argentine?] tourist wearing a tank top whose color and design evoke the Cuban flag.) The way in which Cuba was, throughout the 1990s until the Argentine economic bust of late 2001, a gay Mecca for Argentine tourists is ironic, given Guevara's notorious homophobia. Walter Salles in his 2004 film *The Motorcycle Diaries* plays up Guevara's heterosexual persona by using the Mexican heartthrob Gael García Bernal to play the Argentine; see, on the other hand, the revision of the Korda image in the Che Gay poster from the early 1970s (reproduced in Kunzle 95; Kunzle claims that it is probably British in origin). Castellote, in his excellent commentary on López's work, refers specifically to the parody of Che Guevara ("Perdonen el resentimiento" 13–14).

See also *Antena*, where a rosy-pink French tickler arises in the foreground against the backdrop of the cactuses of the Argentine desert: the cylindrical botanical features of the natural landscape are disrupted by the (probably imported) sex toys of urban life.

18. English does register "merman," although the concept belongs more to the realm of circus sideshow hoaxes than to a centuries-old poetic tradition.

19. A motif that, according to Conner et al. (306), has a lesbian dimension; certainly, the siren that calls men to their death at sea is not a very comforting heterosexual formulation.

20. The photographic and filmic record of which is examined by Waugh.

CHAPTER 11: PERFORMING MASCULINE HETEROSEXUALITY IN STEFAN RUIZ'S
PHOTOGRAPHY OF MEXICAN SOAP OPERAS

Since Stefan Ruiz's agents insist that his images be reproduced in full color, we were unable to use them in this book. However, the reader is directed to Ruiz's website for the photo-book discussed in this chapter: http://www.stefanruiz.com/work/books/factory-of-dreams/.

1. I am using "soap opera" here as a convenient translation for *telenovela*, although the researcher Teresa Páramo Ricoy details accurately the substantial differences between the American paradigm and the Mexican product.

2. Useful studies on the media in Mexico and Televisa are by Raúl Trejo Delarbe and Efraín Pérez Espino, and in the collection *Televisa: quinto poder*. Sam Quiñones provides an interesting personal essay assessing Televisa's soap operas.

3. One of the best studies on compulsory heterosexism in Mexico is Robert McKee Irwin's work, along with just about anything Carlos Monsiváis wrote.

4. None of this realm includes the separation from machismo represented by emotional-ism, such as in the study by Magdalena Guerrero Martínez of men's tears, or the alternative masculinities examined by Graciela Iturbide and Pedro Meyer in their photography (see chapters 8 and 6, respectively, in this volume).

5. An extensive bibliography exists for the English-language reader; for the Spanish-language reader, the best source is the writing of the Spanish philosopher Beatriz Preciado. See also Foster, *Producción cultural*.

6. This narrative schema is driven by the facile and essentially erroneous belief that, from the point of view of identity and erotic acts, nonmasculine men are "homosexual" and masculine men are "heterosexual." The recent debate in Mexico over the thoughtless homophobic comments by an Olympic silver medal winner, the diver Iván García, brought a swift response from the writer José Ramón Zúñiga to the effect that "Los gays también somos hombres" (We gays are also men). This exchange demonstrates the degree to which, in some sectors, the Mexican imaginary can understand that performed heterosexuality has no direct correlation with identity and erotic practices. See Zúñiga, "El clavadista Iván García se disculpa."

7. In the case of lesbian desire, one must take into account the considerably divergent history of women in Mexican society, which means that in addition to a dynamic similar to machismo driven by the overdetermination of the feminine as performed between women, there is as well the assimilation to the model of male machismo (De Lauretis's "lure of the dyke") as a reduplication of what really counts for power in Mexican society, the performance of male domination.

8. One can contrast the melodramatic world of the soap opera with the banality of gaudy wealth and luxury as portrayed by Daniela Rossell in her controversial photographic dossier, *Ricas y famosas* (2002), which evoked outrage on the part of her subjects when they understood the implications of the way in which the dossier portrayed them. See chapter 5 on Rossell's photobook.

Helguera provides an incorrect documentation for López Palmarejo's comment. See correct citation in López Palmarejo 6–7.

9. Armendáriz, whose enactment of heterosexist Mexican masculinity is something of the ultimate paradigm in Mexican culture, might be described as the John Wayne of the Golden Age of Mexican filmmaking.

10. See the essay on Mexican mothers ("Madrecita santa") by one of Mexico's most important feminist scholars, Marta Lamas. See also the texts in Santiago and Davidow, some of which refer to Mexican and Mexican American mothers.

11. One is tempted to see some insinuation of the sissy in Ricardo Abarca, from *Un gancho al corazón* (A blow to the heart), a pretty boy who has also invaded the space of the kitchen, but this time with a measured respect. There is also a sharp contrast between his clothes and the kitchen's décor.

12. See the conventional rough trade image as embodied by Fabián Robles from *La que no podía amar*. He is described as Rogelio [Guerra]'s right-hand man who toys with the affections of a woman.

13. This is what makes possible the efficient use of queer innovations in the Mexican soap opera, such as the ones Gustavo Geirola examines. I have not been able to discover any of these in Ruiz's photographs (the only same-sex pairing that occurs involves two prim young maids posing in the sort of living room it is their duty to maintain). But were they to occur, they would be effected by the most blatant form of stereotyping, not as the consequence of any latent homophobia in the production system, but only because the practice of narrative here demands absolute transparency of intention, meaning, and consequence. Queer in the sense of complicated patterns in the disruption of heterosexism could not be possible in the soap opera because of the way in which it would violate the criterion of absolute transparency.

14. There is, however, always the possibility of viewing Martiñón as enacting—parodying?—the pose of the aggressive tigress. I am grateful to Magdalena Maiz for this suggestion.

15. During the bloodbath between 1910 and 1920, Mexico lost (calculated conservatively) over a million of its citizens, something between 7 and 8 percent of its total population. Moreover, in the first large migration northward, tens of thousands of Mexicans fled across what was a very porous border to the United States. As a consequence, it is no exaggeration to speak of demographic panic on the part of the Mexican ruling establishment, particularly with its commitment to take up again, with renewed intensity, the project of modernity interrupted by the 1910 civil war (and which in part provoked it).

16. Indeed, one might say, of the Porfirian, pre–Revolution of 1910 Mexican pseudobourgeoisie. The reference here is to the regime of the so-called perpetual president, Porfirio Díaz (1876–1911). Páramo Ricoy details the traditional, conservative values featured in the Mexican soap opera (203).

17. See the essay by Ramírez Salgado on the sexist images of women in the Mexican soap operas.

CHAPTER 12: HELEN ZOUT'S *DESAPARICIONES*

A version of this essay also appears in the proceedings of a human rights conference held at the University of Minnesota in November 2011, *Layers of Memory and the Discourse of Human Rights: Artistic and Testimonial Practices in Latin America and the Iberian Peninsula*, ed. Ana Focinito, *Hispanic Issues Online* 14 (Spring 2014).

1. Formally, the forensic investigation of remains from the Dirty War has been, since 1984, in the hands of the Equipo Argentino de Antropología Forense, with the important founding contributions of Dr. Clyde C. Snow. Analyses of the work of the Equipo are those of Salado Puerto and Fondebrider; and Portalet. Salado Puerto and Fondebrider provide the following historical context for the work of the Equipo:

En diciembre de 1983 un nuevo presidente civil fue elegido democráticamente y, ante el clamor de gran parte de la sociedad, se impulsaron una serie de medidas que permitieran saber qué había sucedido con las miles de personas desaparecidas y quiénes eran los responsables de tales hechos. La necesidad de investigar lo sucedido se convirtió en una demanda fundamental de los familiares de las víctimas y de amplios sectores de la sociedad.

A través de una "comisión de la verdad" (Comisión Nacional sobre la Desaparición de Personas, CONADEP) y de la actuación de la Justicia, el estado argentino intentó dar una respuesta a los familiares de las víctimas y juzgar a los responsables de los hechos.

Es en este contexto post dictadura donde la necesidad de exhumar e identificar cuerpos que se hallaban enterrados en cementerios, se torna una necesidad apremiante para los jueces a cargo de las investigaciones.

Los cuerpos periciales, dependientes del poder judicial y de las fuerzas de seguridad—policías—, presentaban una serie de factores que los hacían no aptos para la tarea:

a) o contaban con la confianza de los familiares de las víctimas, ya que habían sido parte del sistema oficial durante la dictadura y en varios casos cómplices de ella.

b) no tenían la capacidad técnica ni la experiencia para exhumar cuerpos que ya se hallaban esqueletizados ni para analizar restos óseos.

Prueba de esta impericia es que, durante el periodo 1983–84, estos especialistas forenses participaron en cientos de exhumaciones realizadas de manera incorrecta con palas mecánicas o por sepultureros, destruyendo o mezclando restos, perdiendo piezas óseas y realizando análisis deficientes que no dieron resultados. (214)

2. Salado Puerto and Fondebrider comment as follows on the anguish of family members regarding disappeared loved ones:

Angustia, temor e incertidumbre de gran cantidad de familias y víctimas. La desaparición es un proceso que se perpetúa en el tiempo. No saber si su familiar está vivo o muerto, la falta de cuerpo, la no respuesta del Estado, son todos procesos que afectan no sólo a los familiares directos de la víctima sino también a amplios sectores de la comunidad. [. . .]

Además el sistema judicial no investiga sus casos y por años viven en una especie de limbo de incertidumbre. Incluso en países donde las familias saben que sus seres queridos han sido posiblemente asesinados, aún se aferran a la posibilidad de que puedan volver con vida. Hasta que los cuerpos son encontrados o su muerte es confirmada no puede haber ritos funerarios ni fin de la búsqueda. Por lo tanto en cada caso hay dolor, angustia, miedo y una vida familiar y social profundamente perturbada, junto con una necesidad de recuperar los restos y poder darles un entierro adecuado, y cerrar—al menos parcialmente—la impotencia que produce la ausencia de respuestas. (219–220)

3. Portalet notes that a large number of detainees were dumped into the Río de la Plata:

Sin embargo, antes de reconstruir los pasos que sigue el EAAF para elaborar su propio archivo, es necesario realizar un conjunto de aclaraciones previas que den cuenta del accionar represivo durante la última dictadura militar para hacer más claro cuál es el "camino" de información que deben recorrer los investigadores. Como se desprende del Nunca Más [the report of the official Comisión Nacional sobre la Desaparición de Personas] y de otras investigaciones posteriores, los principales mecanismos que utilizaron las fuerzas represivas para deshacerse de los cuerpos fue el lanzamiento de los cuerpos al mar, la incineración, el entierro en fosas comunes de cementerios y el entierro en fosas individuales en cementerios.

CHAPTER 13: DOCUMENTARY PHOTOGRAPHY AS GENDER TESTIMONY

Expanded from a brief review originally published in *Chasqui: revista de literatura latinoamericana* 38.1 (2009): 191–192.

1. This is the title of the original Cuban Casa de las Américas edition. Subsequent editions in Spanish bear the title *Me llamo Rigoberta Menchú y así me nació la conciencia.*

2. Menchú has now added Tum, her mother's maiden name, as part of her full name in specific acknowledgment of the particular persecutions of indigenous women during the violence in Guatemala and throughout Latin America.

3. "Dynamics of violence" is the phrase that is used in *Guatemala, Never Again!* (see the chapter "The Intelligence behind the Violence")

4. Throughout this discussion, my comments about the male body and the question of its legitimate display within heteronormativity are inspired by Bordo's influential work on these subjects.

5. This angel is part of what Weinstein, in his characterization of the postmodern aspects of Hernández-Salazar's photography, calls the "angel polyptych," which is entitled *Esclarecimiento* (Clarification) in direct reference to the official truth commission (Weinstein 43). One of the panels from the polyptych is reproduced as an independent panel titled *Para que todos sepan.*

6. *Guatemala, Never Again!* devotes an entire chapter to the assault on women. Touching on the overall matter of genocide, another chapter, devoted to violence against children, is eloquently titled "Destroying the Seed."

7. The title *El camino del dolor* might well refer to the process of torture, mutilation, and death of victims in pursuit of the alleged antisubversive, but in reality genocidal, goals of the Guatemalan dictatorship. But, given the homoerotic resonance of some of these images, it may also, in a conjunctive way, refer to the pain, at the hands of homophobic agents of death, of the path for any of these men of nonheteronormative conformity.

– ◆ –

WORKS CITED

◆ ◆ ◆

Actis, Munú, et al. *Ese infierno: conversaciones con cinco mujeres sobrevivientes de la ESMA.* Buenos Aires: Editorial Sudamericana, 2001.

Afanador, Ruven. *Torero.* Thawil/Zurich; New York: Edition Stemmle, 2001.

Agee, James, and Walker Evans. *Let Us Now Praise Famous Men: Three Tenant Families.* Boston: Houghton Mifflin, 1960.

Amor prohibido. Dir. Luis César Amadori. Argentina. Argentina Sono Film, 1958. 99 min. DVD.

Amores perros. Dir. Alejandro González Iñárritu. Mexico. Altavista Films, 2000. 154 min. DVD.

Archetti, Eduardo P. *Masculinidades: fútbol, tango y polo en la Argentina.* Buenos Aires: Editorial Antropofagia, 2003.

Balbuena, Bernardo de. 1604. *La grandeza mexicana y fragmentos del Siglo de Oro y El Bernardo.* Intro. Francisco Monterde. 3rd ed. México: Universidad Nacional Autónoma de México, 1963.

Barreda, Fabiana. *La ciudad subterránea.* Buenos Aires: Magna Publicidad, 1998.

Barthes, Roland. *Camera Lucida: Reflections on Photography.* Trans. Richard Howard. New York: Hill and Wang, 1981.

Bayer, Osvaldo. "An Account of Argentine Death." In Helen Zout, *Desapariciones.* Buenos Aires: Dilan Editores, 2009. 57–59.

Bazán, Osvaldo. *Historia de la homosexualidad en la Argentina: de la conquista de América al siglo XXI.* Buenos Aires: Marea Editorial, 2004.

Bécquer Casaballe, Amado. "Grete Stern (1904–1999)." *Fotomundo* 382 (1999): 24–27.

O beijo no asfalto. Dir. Bruno Barreto. Brazil. Embrafilme; Filmes do Equador; Luiz Carlos Barreto Produções Cinematográficas, 1981. 90 min. DVD.

Bell, David F. "Introduction: Overload." *SubStance* 33.3 (2004): 3–5.

Bennholdt-Thomsen, Veronika, ed. *Juchitán, la ciudad de las mujeres.* Oaxaca: Instituto Oaxaqueño de las Culturas; Fondo Estatal para la Cultura y las Artes, 1997. Orig. pub. in German as *Juchitán Stadt der Frauen.* Berlin: Rowohlt, 1994.

———. "Los muxés, el tercer sexo." *Juchitán, la ciudad de las mujeres.* Ed. Veronika Bennholdt-Thomsen. Oaxaca: Instituto Oaxaqueño de las Culturas; Fondo Estatal para la Cultura y las Artes, 1997. 279–305.

Bergero, Adriana J. *Intersecting Tango: Cultural Geographies of Buenos Aires, 1900–1930.* Pittsburgh: U of Pittsburgh P, 2008.

Bergero, Adriana, and Fernando Reati, eds. *Memoria colectiva y políticas de olvido: Argentina y Uruguay, 1970–1990.* Rosario: Beatriz Viterbo Editora, 1997.

Bordo, Susan. *The Male Body: A New Look at Men in Public and in Private.* New York: Farrar, Straus and Giroux, 1999.

Bousquet, Jean Pierre. *Las locas de la Plaza de Mayo.* Trans. Jacques Despres. Buenos Aires: El Cid Editor, 1983. Orig. pub. in French as *Les Folles de la Place de Mai.* Paris: Stock, 1982.

Bramly, Serge. *Leonardo: The Artist and the Man.* London: Penguin Books, 1994.

Brenner, Anita. *Ídolos tras los altares.* México: Editorial Domés, 1983.

Brodsky, Marcelo. *Buena memoria: un ensayo fotográfico / Good Memory: A Photographic Essay.* With texts by Martín Caparrós, José Pablo Feinmann, and Juan Gelman. Buenos Aires: La Marca Editora, 1997.

———. *Memory Works.* Salamanca: Universidad de Salamanca; Valladolid: Universidad de Valladolid, 2003.

———. *Nexo, un ensayo fotográfico de Marcelo Brodsky. A Photographic Essay.* Buenos Aires: La Marca Editora; Centro Cultural Recoleta, 2001.

Brodsky, Marcelo, et al. *Memory under Construction / Memoria en construcción: el debate sobre la ESMA.* Buenos Aires: La Marca Editora, 2005.

Brooksbank Jones, Anny. "A Scandalous Family Album." *Visual Culture in Spain and Mexico.* Manchester: Manchester UP, 2007. 62–82.

Brown, Dan. *The Da Vinci Code.* New York: Anchor Books, 2003.

Butler, Judith. *Bodies That Matter: On the Discursive Limits of "Sex."* New York: Psychology, 1993.

———. *Gender Trouble: Feminism and the Subversion of Identity.* 1990. New York: Routledge, 1999.

———. *Undoing Gender.* New York: Routledge, 2004.

Cabrera, Gustavo. *Hugo del Carril, un hombre de nuestro cine.* Buenos Aires: Ediciones Culturales Argentinas, 1989.

El Callejón de los Milagros. Dir. Jorge Fons. Mexico. Alameda Films; Consejo Nacional para la Cultura y las Artes (CONACULTA); Instituto Mexicano de Cinematografía (IMCINE), 1995. 140 min. DVD.

Campbell, Howard. *Mexican Memoir: A Personal Account of Anthropology and Radical Politics in Oaxaca.* Westport: Bergin & Garvey, 2001.

Campbell, Howard, et al. *Zapotec Struggles: Histories, Politics, and Representations from Juchitán, Oaxaca.* Washington, DC: Smithsonian Institution P, 1993.

Camps, Martín. Rev. of Daniela Rossell, *Ricas y famosas. Chasqui: revista de literatura latinoamericana* 32.2 (2003): 168–171.

Carretero, Andrés M. *Chicos de la calle.* Buenos Aires: Corregidor, 1996.

Carrillo, Héctor. "Neither *Machos* nor *Maricones*: Masculinity and Emerging Male Homosexual Identities in Mexico." *Changing Men and Masculinities in Latin America*. Ed. Matthew C. Gutman. Durham: Duke UP, 2003. 351–369.

Castellote, Alejandro, ed. *Mapas abiertos: fotografía latinoamericana 1991–2002*. With texts by Alejandro Castellanos, Rubens Fernández Junior, Juan Antonio Molina, and Iván de la Nuez. Barcelona: Lunwerg Editores, 2003.

———. "Perdonen el resentimiento." *Marcos López* by Marcos López. México: KBK Arte Contemporáneo, 2004. 5–8, 11, 13–14. Also as "Sorry about the Resentment," 21–22, 25, 26–27, 31–32.

Castillo, Ana. *Goddess of the Americas: Writings about the Virgin of Guadalupe*. New York: Riverhead Books, 1997.

Cirlot, J. E. *A Dictionary of Symbols*. Trans. Jack Sage. New York: Philosophical Library, 1962.

Connell, R. W. *Masculinities*. Berkeley: U of California P, 1995.

Connor, Randy P., David Hatfield Sparks, and Mariya Sparks. *Cassell's Encyclopedia of Queer Myth, Symbol, and Spirit: Gay, Lesbian, Bisexual, and Transgender Love*. London: Cassell, 1997.

Coria, Clara. "Grupos de reflexión, dependencia económica y salud mental de las mujeres." *Estudios sobre la subjetividad femenina: mujeres y salud mental*. Ed. Mabel Burin. Buenos Aires: Grupo Editor Latinoamericano, 1987. 261–291.

Cristoff, María Sonia. "Un tiempo palpable." *Las aventuras de Guille y Belinda y el enigmático significado de sus sueños* by Alessandra Sanguinetti. Buenos Aires: Dilan Editores, 2007. 5–7. Translated into English as "A Tangible Time," 63–65.

D'Amico, Alicia, Sara Facio, and Julio Cortázar. *Humanario*. Buenos Aires: La Azotea Editorial Fotográfica de América Latina, 1976.

"Daniela Rossell." *Witness to Her Art: Art and Writings*. Ed. Rhea Anastas and Michael Brenson. Annandale-on-Hudson: Center for Curatorial Studies, Bard College, 2006. 283–332.

Danzón. Dir. María Novaro. Mexico. Fondo de Fomento a la Calidad Cinematográfica; Gobierno del Estado de Veracruz; and Instituto Mexicano de Cinematografía (IMCINE), 1991. 120 min. DVD.

Dead Ringer. Dir. Paul Henreid. United States. Warner Bros., 1964. 115 min. DVD.

Dead Ringers. Dir. David Cronenberg. Canada and United States. Morgan Creek Productions, 1988. 116 min. DVD.

De Lauretis, Teresa. *The Practice of Love: Lesbian Sexuality and Perverse Desire*. Bloomington: Indiana UP, 1994.

Díaz, Gabriel. *Muertes menores: Minor Deaths*. Buenos Aires: n.p., n.d.

Dijkstra, Bram. *Idols of Perversity: Fantasies of Feminine Evil in Fin-de-Siècle Culture*. New York: Oxford UP, 1986.

Doniz, Rafael. *H. Ayuntamiento Popular de Juchitán: fotografías*. Prologue by Carlos Monsiváis. Juchitán: H. Ayuntamiento Popular de Juchitán, 1983.

Dreizik, Pablo M., ed. *La memoria de las cenizas*. Buenos Aires: Dirección Nacional de Patrimonio; Museos y Artes, 2001.

Duffy, Margaret. "Body of Evidence: Studying Women and Advertising." *Gender and Utopia in Advertising: A Critical Reader*. Ed. Luigi Manca and Alessandra Manca. Lisle: Procopian P, 1994. 5–30.

Duhalde, Eduardo Luis. *El estado terrorista argentino*. 1st ed. Barcelona: Argos Vergara, 1983.

Dujovne Ortiz, Alicia. *Eva Perón: la biografía*. Trans. Alicia Dujovne Ortiz. Buenos Aires: Aguilar, 1995. Orig. pub. in French as *Eva Perón: madone des sans-chemise*. Paris: B. Grasset, 1995. Also issued in English as *Eva Perón*. Trans. Shawn Fields. New York: St. Martin's P, 1995.

Eltit, Diamela, and Paz Errázuriz. *El infarto del alma*. Ed. Francisco Zegers. Santiago: F. Zegers, 1999.

Erauso, Catalina. *Historia de la monja alférez doña Catalina de Erauso: con la última y tercera relación en que se hace historia de los últimos años y muerte de este personaje, escrita por ella misma*. Pamplona: Editorial Gómez, 1959.

Evans, Jessica. "Photography." *Feminist Visual Culture*. Ed. Fiona Carson and Claire Pajaczkowska. Edinburgh: Edinburgh UP, 2000. 105–120.

Evita: imágenes de una pasión. México: Grupo Editorial Zeta, 1987.

Facio, Sara. "Adriana Lestido." *Leyendo fotos*. Buenos Aires: La Azotea Editorial Fotográfica de América Latina, 2002. 87–91.

———. "La búsqueda de la belleza / The Search for Beauty." *El espectáculo en la Argentina 1930–1970*. Ed. Annemarie Heinrich. Buenos Aires: La Azotea Editorial Fotográfica de América Latina, 1987. 4–14.

———. "De la dictadura a la democracia: la memoria cuestionada." *Leyendo fotos*. Buenos Aires: La Azotea Editorial Fotográfica de América Latina, 2002. 39–51.

———. *Fotografía argentina actual*. Buenos Aires: La Azotea Editorial Fotográfica de América Latina, 1981.

———. *Fotografía argentina dos*. Buenos Aires: La Azotea Editorial Fotográfica de América Latina, 1996.

———. "La fotografía. Género: femenino." *Leyendo fotos*. Buenos Aires: La Azotea Editorial Fotográfica de América Latina, 2002. 195–201.

Farred, Grant. "Crying for Argentina: The Branding and Unbranding of Area Studies." *Nepantla: Views from the South* 4.1 (2003): 121–132.

Feitlowitz, Marguerite. *A Lexicon of Terror: Argentina and the Legacies of Torture*. New York: Oxford UP, 1998.

Fellig, Arthur (pseud. Weegee). *Weegee's New York. Photographs: 1935–1960*. 1982, 1996. Munich: Schimer Art Books, 2000.

Fiske, John. *Reading the Popular*. Boston: Unwin Hyman, 1989.

Foster, David W. *El ambiente nuestro: Chicano/Latino Homoerotic Writing*. Tempe: Bilingual P/Editorial Bilingüe, 2006.

———. "Annemarie Heinrich: Photography, Women's Bodies, and Semiotic Excess." *Studies in Latin American Popular Culture* 25 (2006): 253–270.

———. *Buenos Aires: Perspectives on the City and Cultural Production*. Gainesville: UP of Florida, 1998.

———. *Contemporary Argentine Filmmaking*. Columbia: U of Missouri P, 1992.

———. "Defying the Masculinist Gaze: Gabriela Liffschitz's *Recursos humanos*." *Chasqui* 32.1 (2003): 10–24. Also in Foster, *Urban Photography in Argentina: Nine Artists of the Post-Dictatorship Era*. Jefferson: McFarland Publishing, 2007. 185–203.

———. "Dreaming in Feminine: Grete Stern's Photomontages and the Parody of Psychoanalysis." *Ciberletras* 10 (2003): n. pag. Web. 16 Oct. 2012. <http://www.lehman.cuny.edu/ciberletras/v10/foster.htm>.

———. *Ensayos sobre culturas homoeróticas latinoamericanas*. Ciudad Juárez: Universidad Nacional Autónoma de Ciudad Juárez, 2009.

———. "Gabriel Valansi: Neoliberal Nights in Buenos Aires." *Significação: revista brasileira de semiótica* 18 (2002): 89–113. Rpt. in *Fisura: revista de literatura y arte* 1.3 (2003): 27–33.

———. *Gay and Lesbian Themes in Latin American Writing*. Austin: U of Texas P, 1991.

———. *Gender and Society in Contemporary Brazilian Cinema*. Austin: U of Texas P, 1999.

———. "Género y fotografía en *Juchitán de las mujeres*, de Graciela Iturbide." *Ámbitos: revista de estudios de ciencias sociales y humanidades* 2.11 (2004): 63–69.

———. "Homosocialism ◄► Homoeroticism in the Photography of Marcos López." *Dis-*

sidences 1 (30 Aug. 2005): n. pag. Web. 17 Aug. 2013. <http://www.dissidences.org/Marcos Lopez.html>.

———. "El kitsch argentino: la fotografía de Marcos López." *Guaraguao: revista de cultura latinoamericana* 8.18 (2004): 79–101. Also as "Argentine Kitsch: The Photography of Marcos López." In Foster, *Urban Photography in Argentina: Nine Artists of the Post-Dictatorship Era.* Jefferson: McFarland Publishing, 2007. 136–168.

———. "Madalena Schwartz: A Jewish Brazilian Photographer." In David William Foster, *São Paulo: Perspectives on the City and Cultural Production.* Gainesville: UP of Florida, 2011. 98–111. Also in *Latin American Jewish Cultural Production.* Ed. David William Foster. Nashville: Vanderbilt UP, 2009. 198–212.

———. "Más allá de la visibilidad gay en Buenos Aires." *Las ciudades latinoamericanas en el nuevo [des]orden mundial.* Ed. Patricio Navia and Marc Zimmerman. México, DF: Siglo XXI Editores, 2004. 125–132.

———. "Mujer, prostitución y modernidad en el México finisecular." *Magazine modernista: revista digital* 13 (Noviembre 2009): n. pag. Web. 9 Aug. 2013. <http://magazinemodernista.com/?p=2795>.

———. "Pedro Meyer: construir masculinidades, construir fotografías." *Sociotam: revista internacional de ciencias sociales y humanidades* 20.1 (2010): 39–58.

———. *Producción cultural e identidades homoeróticas: teoría y aplicaciones.* San José: Editorial de la Universidad de Costa Rica, 1999.

———. *Queer Issues in Contemporary Latin American Cinema.* Austin: U of Texas P, 2003.

———, ed. *The Redemocratization of Argentine Culture, 1983 and Beyond: An International Research Symposium at Arizona State University.* 16–17 Feb. 1987. Tempe: Center for Latin American Studies, Arizona State University, 1989.

———. "Review Essay: Daniela Rossell, *Ricas y Famosas.*" *Studies in Latin American Popular Culture* 22 (2003): 217–222.

———. Rev. of *Desnudos sudamericanos. Chasqui* 39.1 (2010): 202–203.

———. Rev. of *Madres e hijas* by Adriana Lestido. *Chasqui: revista de literatura latinoamericana* 33.1 (2004): 165–167.

———. Rev. of *So That All Shall Know; Photographs by Daniel Hernández-Salazar/Para que todos lo sepan; fotografías de Daniel Hernández-Salazar. Chasqui* 38.1 (2009): 191–192.

———. *São Paulo: Perspectives on the City and Cultural Production.* Gainesville: UP of Florida, 2011.

———. "Sara Facio as Urban Photographer." *Buenos Aires: Perspectives on the City and Cultural Production.* Gainesville: UP of Florida, 1998. 170–194.

———. *Sexual Textualities: Essays on Queer/ing Latin American Writing.* Austin: U of Texas P, 1997.

———. "Sociohistorical, Gender, and Genre Contexts." *Crisis in Buenos Aires: Women Bearing Witness* by Cynthia Schmidt-Cruz. Newark, DE: Juan de la Cuesta, 2007. 29–45.

———. "Toreros de moda: la fotografía de Ruven Afanador." *Revista de estudios colombianos* 29 (2006): 6–11. Web. 16 Oct. 2012. <http://www.colombianistas.org/Portals/0/Revista /REC-29/4.REC_29_DavidFoster.pdf>.

———. *Urban Photography in Argentina: Nine Artists of the Post-Dictatorship Era.* Jefferson, NC: McFarland, 2007.

———. "Women's Society in Prison: Adriana Lestido's *Mujeres presas.*" *Journal of Latin American Urban Studies* 6 (2004): 1–18.

French, William E. "Imagining and the Cultural History of Nineteenth-Century Mexico." *Hispanic American Historical Review* 79.2 (May 1999): 249–267.

Freund, Gisèle. *Fotografien 1932–1977.* Köln: Rheinland-Verlag; Bonn: In Kommission bei R. Habelt, 1977.

———. *Gisèle Freund: Photographer.* Trans. John Shepley. New York: Harry N. Abrahams Publishers, 1985.

———. *Itinéraires: Catalogue de l'œuvre photographique Gisèle Freund.* Paris: Editions du Centre Pompidou, 1991.

Frida, naturaleza viva. Dir. Paul Leduc. Mexico. Clasa Films Mundiales, 1986. 108 min. DVD.

Gallo, Rubén, ed. *The Mexico City Reader.* Trans. Lorna Scott Fox and Rubén Gallo. Madison: U of Wisconsin P, 2004.

———. *New Tendencies in Mexican Art: The 1990s.* New York: Palgrave Macmillan, 2004.

Gallop, Jane. *Thinking through the Body.* New York: Columbia UP, 1988.

Gamboa, Federico. *Santa.* 1903. Ed. Javier Ortiz. Madrid: Cátedra, 2002.

Garage Olimpo. Dir. Marcos Bechis. Italy. Classic etc., 1999. 98 min. DVD.

Geirola, Gustavo. "Eroticism and Homoeroticism in *Martín Fierro.*" *Bodies and Biases: Sexuality in Hispanic Cultures and Literatures.* Ed. David William Foster and Roberto Reis. Minneapolis: U of Minnesota P, 1996. 316–332.

———. *Zona de riesgo: lesbianas, gays y sida en las telenovelas: negociaciones culturales de la representación melodramática y televisiva en tiempos de globalización.* Saarbrücken: Editorial Académica Española, 2012.

Gentlemen Prefer Blondes. Dir. Howard Hawkes. United States. Twentieth Century-Fox Film Corporation, 1953. 91 min. DVD.

Germani, Gino. *Estudios de psicología.* México: Instituto de Investigaciones Sociales, Universidad Nacional, 1956.

Gil, Eduardo. *(argentina).* Buenos Aires: Ediciones Cuarto 14, 2002.

González, Horacio. "Mármol, imagen y martirio / Marble, Image and Martyrdom." *Memory Works* by Marcelo Brodsky. Salamanca: Universidad de Salamanca; Valladolid: Universidad de Valladolid, 2003. 13–17.

González, Valeria. "Las fotografías de Marcos López en el contexto del arte argentino de los noventa / The Photography of Marcos López in the Context of Marcos López." *Subrealismo criollo (fotografías color 1993–2003)* by Marcos López. Salamanca: Ediciones Universidad de Salamanca, 2003. 23–29.

González, Valeria, and Marcos López. *Al sur del sur: 8 fotógrafos argentinos.* Madrid: Casa de América, 2001.

González Rodrígues, Sergio. *Los bajos fondos.* México: Cal y Arena, 1990.

Graziano, Frank. *Cultures of Devotion: Folk Saints in Spanish America.* Oxford: Oxford UP, 2007.

———. *Divine Violence: Spectacle, Psychosexuality, & Radical Christianity in the Argentine "Dirty War."* Boulder: Westview P, 1992.

Greimas, A. J., and J. Courtés. *Semiotics and Language: An Analytical Dictionary.* Trans. Larry Crist et al. Bloomington: Indiana UP, 1982.

Guagnini, Nicolás. "Entrevista / Interview." *Memory Works* by Marcelo Brodsky. Salamanca: Universidad de Salamanca; Valladolid: Universidad de Valladolid, 2003. 117–123.

Guatemala: memoria del silencio. Guatemala: Comisión para el Esclarecimiento Histórico, 1999.

Guatemala, Never Again! REHMI, Recovery of Historical Memory Project: The Official Report of the Human Rights Office, Archdiocese of Guatemala. Maryknoll: Orbis Books; London: CIIR, in association with the Latin American Bureau, 1999. A selection from the four-volume *Guatemala, nunca más: proyecto interdiocesano de Recuperación de la Memoria Histórica.* Guatemala: ODHAG, 1998.

Guerrero Martínez, Magdalena. "Los espacios masculinos del llanto." MA thesis Universidad de las Américas, 2006.

Gutiérrez, Fernando. *Treinta mil.* Buenos Aires: La Marca Editora, 1997.

Gutman, Matthew G., ed. *Changing Men and Masculinities in Latin America.* Durham: Duke UP, 2003.

Halperin, David M. *One Hundred Years of Homosexuality and Other Essays on Greek Love.* New York: Routledge, 1990.

Heinrich, Annemarie. *Un cuerpo, una luz, un reflejo.* Ed. Juan Travnik. Buenos Aires: Ediciones Larivière, 2004.

———. *El espectáculo en la Argentina 1930–1970.* Buenos Aires: La Azotea Editorial Fotográfica de América Latina, 1987.

Helguera, Pablo. "The Factory of Dreams: The Mexican Telenovela as Portrayed by Stefan Ruiz." *The Factory of Dreams* by Stefan Ruiz. New York: Aperture, 2012. n. pag.

Hernández-Salazar, Daniel. *So That All Shall Know: Photographs / Para que todos sepan: fotografías.* Ed. Oscar Iván Maldonado. Austin: U of Texas P, 2007.

Historia oficial. Dir. Luis Puenzo. Argentina. Historias Cinematográficas Compañías, 1985. 122 min. DVD.

Hite, Shere. *The Hite Report: A Nationwide Study of Female Sexuality.* 1976. New York: Dell Books, 1981.

Huyssen, Andreas. "Memory Sites in an Expanded Field: The Memory Park in Buenos Aires." *Present Pasts: Urban Palimpsests and the Politics of Memory.* Stanford: Stanford UP, 2003. 94–109. Rpt. as "El arte mnemónico de Marcelo Brodsky / The Mnemonic Art of Marcelo Brodsky" in *Memory Works* by Marcelo Brodsky. Salamanca: Universidad de Salamanca; Valladolid: Universidad de Valladolid, 2003. 7–11.

Invernizzi, Hernán, and Judith Gociol. *Un golpe a los libros: represión a la cultura durante la última dictadura militar.* Buenos Aires: EUDEBA, 2002. See also the exhibit catalog *Un golpe a los libros 1976–1983.* Buenos Aires: Dirección General del Libro; Secretaría de Cultura; Gobierno de Buenos Aires, 2002.

Irwin, Robert McKee. *Mexican Masculinities.* Minneapolis: U of Minnesota P, 2003.

Iturbide, Graciela. *Images of the Spirit: Photographs.* Preface by Roberto Tejada. Epilogue by Alfredo López Austin. New York: Aperture, 1996.

———. *Juchitán de las mujeres.* Text by Elena Poniatowska. Ed. Pablo Ortiz Monasterio. Mexico City: Ediciones Toledo, 1989.

Jelin, Elizabeth, and Pablo Vila. *Podría ser yo: los sectores populares urbanos en imagen y palabra.* Photography by Alicia D'Amico. Buenos Aires: Centro de Estudios de Estado y Sociedad; Ediciones de la Flor, 1987.

Kama Sutra: A Tale of Love. Dir. Mira Nair. United Kingdom, United States, and India. Channel Four Films; Mirabai Films, 1996. 117 min. DVD.

Kaplan, Louis. "Digital Chicanos: Pedro Meyer, Truths and Fictions, and Border Theory." *American Exposures: Photography and Community in the Twentieth Century.* Minneapolis: U of Minnesota P, 2005. 155–171.

Kennedy, John J. *Catholicism, Nationalism, and Democracy in Argentina.* Notre Dame: U of Notre Dame P, 1958.

Kofman, Sarah. *The Enigma of Woman: Woman in Freud's Writing.* Trans. Catherine Porter. Ithaca: Cornell UP, 1985.

Köhler, Michael. *Akte: eine Geschichte der erotischen Fotografie.* München: W. Heyne, 1991.

Kowaleski Wallace, Elizabeth, ed. *Encyclopedia of Feminist Literary Theory.* New York: Garland Publishing, 1997.

Kunzle, David. *Che Guevara: Icon, Myth, and Message.* Los Angeles: UCLA Fowler Museum of Cultural History in collaboration with the Center for the Study of Political Graphics, 1997.

Lamas, Marta. *El género: la construcción cultural de la diferencia sexual.* México: Universidad Nacional Autónoma de México; M. A. Porrúa, 1996.

———. "Madrecita santa." *Mitos mexicanos.* Ed. Enrique Florescano. México: Editorial Aguilar, 1995. 173–178.

Leibovitz, Annie. *Women.* Essay by Susan Sontag. New York: Random House, 1999.

Lestido, Adriana. *Madres e hijas.* Buenos Aires: La Azotea Editorial Fotográfica de América Latina, 2003.

———. *Mujeres presas.* Buenos Aires: Impresa Latin Gráfica, 2001.

Liffschitz, Gabriela. *Efectos colaterales.* Buenos Aires: Grupo Editorial Norma, 2003.

———. *Recursos humanos.* Buenos Aires: Filòlibri, 2000.

———. Rev. of *(argentina)* by Eduardo Gil. *Chasqui: revista de literatura latinoamericana* 32.1 (2003): 128–129.

López, Marcos. *Fotografías.* Ed. Sara Facio. Buenos Aires: La Azotea Editorial Fotográfica de América Latina, 1993.

———. *Marcos López.* México: KBK Arte Contemporáneo, 2004.

———. *Pop latino: fotografía y textos.* Buenos Aires: La Marca Editora, 1999.

———. *Sub-realismo criollo (fotografías color 1993–2003).* Salamanca: Ediciones Universidad de Salamanca, 2003.

López Palmarejo, Tomás. "Telenovelas: A Global Product." *Telenovela Institute: Los del este/ Eastenders.* Ed. Pablo Helguera. London: Royal College of Art, 2004. 6–7.

El lugar sin límites. Dir. Arturo Ripstein. Mexico. Conacite Dos, 1978. 110 min. DVD.

Mackie, Erin. "Fashion." *Encyclopedia of Feminist Literary Theory.* Ed. Elizabeth Kowaleski Wallace. New York: Garland Publishing, 1997. 146–148.

Magialardi, Silvia, and A. Bécquer Casaballe, eds. *Buenos Aires: una visión fotográfica.* Buenos Aires: Fotomundo; FM Tango; Ediciones Culturales Argentinas, 1992.

Manrique, Jaime. "Legs." *Eminent Maricones: Arenas, Lorca, Puig, and Me.* Madison: U of Wisconsin P, 1999. 3–38.

Manrupe, Raúl, and María Alejandra Portela. *Un diccionario de films argentinos.* Buenos Aires: Corregidor, 1995.

María de mi corazón. Jaime Humberto Hermosillo. Mexico. Clasa Films Mundiales; Universidad Veracruzana, 1979. 137 min. DVD.

Martínez, Tomás Eloy. *Santa Evita.* Buenos Aires: Planeta, 1995. Issued in English as *Santa Evita.* Trans. Helen Lane. New York: Knopf, 1996.

Mattoso, Glauco. *O calvário dos carecas: história do trote estudantil.* São Paulo: EMW Editores, 1985.

Maturi, Aníbal. *Los chicos de la calle.* Buenos Aires: Editorial Galerna, 1987.

Mavor, Carol. *Pleasures Taken: Performances of Sexuality and Loss in Victorian Photographs.* Durham: Duke UP, 1995.

McGeagh, Robert M. *Relaciones entre el poder político y eclesiástico en la Argentina.* Buenos Aires: Itinerarium, 1987.

McGee Deutsch, Sandra, and Ronald H. Dolkart. *The Argentine Right: Its History and Intellectual Origins, 1910 to the Present.* Washington, DC: Scholarly Resources, 1993.

Medina, Cuauhtémoc. "Mundos privados, ilusiones públicas." *Reforma* (September 11, 2002): 2C. Trans. by Trudy Balch as "Private Worlds, Public Delusions." Included (332) in "Daniela Rossell." *Witness to Her Art: Art and Writings.* Ed. Rhea Anastas and Michael Brenson. Annandale-on-Hudson: Center for Curatorial Studies, Bard College, 2006. 283–332.

———. "The Stage and the Stereotype: Daniela Rossell's *Ricas y famosas.*" Included (311–323) in "Daniela Rossell." *Witness to Her Art: Art and Writings.* Ed. Rhea Anastas and

Michael Brenson. Annandale-on-Hudson: Center for Curatorial Studies, Bard College, 2006. 283–332.

Meier, Irene. "La querella psicoanalítica por las mujeres: el debate sobre la sexualidad femenina." *Revista foros temáticos* 13 (1999): n. pag.

Memory of Silence: The Guatemalan Truth Commission Report. Ed. Daniel Rothenberg. New York: Palgrave Macmillan, 2012. A selection from the ten-volume *Guatemala: memoria del silencio*. Guatemala: Comisión para el Esclarecimiento Histórico, 1999.

Menchú, Rigoberta. *Me llamo Rigoberta Menchú: testimonio*. Ed. Elizabeth Burgos-Debray. La Habana: Casa de las Américas, 1983. Published in English as *I, Rigoberta Menchú: An Indian Woman in Guatemala*. Ed. and introd. Elizabeth Burgos-Debray. Trans. Ann Wright. London: Verso, 1984.

Menchú Tum, Rigoberta. "Foreword: The Vantage Point of Memory / Prólogo: el mirador de la memoria." In Daniel Hernández-Salazar, *So That All Shall Know: Photographs / Para que todos sepan: fotografías*. Ed. Oscar Iván Maldonado. Austin: U of Texas P, 2007. ix–xii.

Mercader, Martha. *Solamente ella*. Buenos Aires: Editorial Bruguera, 1981.

Meyer, Pedro. "¿Para quién y para qué se fotografía?" *Casa de las Américas* 25 (1985): 14–21.

———. *The Real and the True: The Digital Photography of Pedro Meyer*. With texts by Louis Kaplan, Pedro Meyer, Alejandro Castellanos, and Douglas Cruickshank. Berkeley: New Riders, 2006.

———. *Truths and Fictions: A Journey from Documentary to Digital Photography*. New York: Aperture, 1995.

Mira Nouselles, Alberto. *Para entendernos: diccionario de cultura homosexual, gay y lésbica*. Barcelona: Ediciones de la Tempestad, 1999.

Monsiváis, Carlos. "Protagonista: el Niño Fidencio. Todos los caminos llevan al éxtasis." *Los rituales del caos*. México: Ediciones Era, 1995. 97–108.

Monsiváis, Carlos, and Carlos Bonfil. *A través del espejo: el cine mexicano y su público*. México: Ediciones el Milagro; Instituto Mexicano de Cinematografía, 1994.

The Motorcycle Diaries. Dir. Walter Salles. United States, Argentina. FilmFour; Wildwood Enterprises; Tu Vas Voir Productions, 2004. 126 min. DVD.

Müller, Christa. "Amor entre mujeres en una ciudad centrada en la mujer." *Juchitán, la ciudad de las mujeres*. Ed. Veronika Bennholdt-Thomsen. Oaxaca: Instituto Oaxaqueño de las Culturas; Fondo Estatal para la Cultura y las Artes, 1997. 261–278.

Myths, Dreams & Realities: Contemporary Argentine Photography. Exhibit catalog. Houston: Houston Center for Photography; Pan American Cultural Exchange, 1999.

Nabhan-Warren, Kristy. *The Virgin of El Barrio: Marian Apparitions, Catholic Evangelizing, and Mexican American Activism*. New York: New York UP, 2005.

Neumaier, Diane. *Reframing: New American Feminist Photography*. Foreword by Anne Wilkes Tucker. Philadelphia: Temple UP, 1995.

Neville, Robert. "How Evita Helps Run Argentina." *Life* (December 11, 1950): 69–82. Gisèle Freund's photographs occupy pp. 69–73 under the title "Eva Perón: First Look at the Private Life of a Controversial First Lady."

Neyer, Hans Joachim. *Gisèle Freund*. Berlin: Argon Verlag, 1988.

Noé, Alberto. "Entrevista a Juan Carlos Marín." N.d. Web. 24 Oct. 2003.

Nunca más: informe de la Comisión Nacional sobre la Desaparición de Personas. Buenos Aires: EUDEBA, 1984. Rpt. in English as *Nunca más, the Report of the Argentine National Commission on the Disappeared*. Intro. Ronald Dworkin. New York: Farrar, Straus and Giroux; London: Index on Censorship, 1986.

Núñez Noriega, Guillermo. *Masculinidad e intimidad: identidad, sexualidad y sida*. México: M. A. Porrúa; Hermosillo: Programa Universitario de Estudios de Género–El Colegio de Sonora, 2007.

————. *Sexo entre varones: poder y resistencia en el campo sexual*. 1994. México: M. A. Porrúa; and Hermosillo: Coordinación de Humanidades; Instituto de Investigaciones Sociales, Programa Universitario de Estudios de Género–El Colegio de Sonora, 2001.

Pagés Larraya, Fernando, ed. *La bacanal de los niños: antropología del chico de la calle*. Buenos Aires: Seminario de Antropología Psiquiátrica, 1998.

Panera Cuevas, F. Javier. "Marcos López (fotografías en color 1993–2003) / Marcos López (Colour Photography 1993–2003)." *Sub-realismo criollo (fotografías color 1993–2003)* by Marcos López. Salamanca: Ediciones Universidad de Salamanca, 2003. 9–14.

Páramo Ricoy, Teresa. "Globalización, televisión y telenovelas: la experiencia mexicana." *Polis* 1 (2000): 193–222.

Pecado. Dir. Luis César Amadori. Mexico. Cinematográfica Filmex S.A., 1951. 115 min. DVD.

"Pedro Luis Raota." *Raota Fotografía*. José Luís Raota and Pedro Luís Raota. N.d. Web. 27 May 2003. <http://www.raota.com>.

Pellarolo, Sylvia. "The Melodramatic Seductions of Eva Perón." *Corpus Delecti: Performance Art of the Americas*. Ed. Coco Fusco. London: Routledge, 2000. 23–39.

Pérez Espino, Efraín. *Los motivos de Televisa: el proyecto cultural de XEQ Canal 9*. México: Instituto de Investigaciones Sociales–UNAM, 1991.

Perlongher, Néstor. *O negócio do michê: prostituição viril em São Paulo*. São Paulo: Editora Brasiliense, 1987.

Piglia, Ricardo. *La Argentina en pedazos*. Buenos Aires: Ediciones de la Urraca, 1993.

Plotkin, Mariano Ben. *Freud in the Pampas: The Emergence and Development of Psychoanalytic Culture in Argentina*. Stanford: Stanford UP, 2001.

Ponce, Patricia, ed. *Masculinidades diversas*. Spec. issue of *Desacatos: revista de antropología social* 15–16 (2004).

Poniatowska, Elena. "Juchitán de las mujeres." *Luz y luna, las lunitas*. Photography by Graciela Iturbide. México: Ediciones Era, 1994. 77–95.

Portalet, Daniel. "La investigación del archivo del Equipo Argentino de Antropología Forense." N.d. Web. 26 Dec. 2011. <http://www.derhuman.jus.gov.ar/conti/2011/10/mesa_21/portalet_mesa_21.pdf>.

Praz, Mario. *The Romantic Agony*. Cleveland: World Publishing, 1933.

Preciado, Beatriz. *Manifiesto contra-sexual*. Madrid: Opera Prima, 2002.

Priamo, Luis. "Los Sueños de Grete Stern." *Sueños*. Valencia: IVAM Centre Julio González, Generalitat Valencia, Conselleria de Cultura, Educaciò i Ciència, 1995. 21–46.

Prignano, Ángel O. *Crónica de la basura porteña: del fogón al cinturón ecológico*. Buenos Aires: Junta de Estudios Históricos de San José de Flores, 1998.

Prongher, Brian. *The Arena of Masculinity: Sports, Homosexuality, and the Meaning of Sex*. London: GMP Publishers, 1990.

Quiñones, Sam. "Telenovela." *True Tales from Another Mexico: The Lynch Mob, the Popsicle Kings, Chalino, and the Bronx*. Albuquerque: U of New Mexico P, 2001. 53–77.

La rabia. Dir. Albertina Carri. Argentina. Hubert Bals Fund; Instituto Nacional de Cine y Artes Audiovisuales (INCAA); and Matanza Cine, 2008. 85 min. DVD.

Ramírez, Mari Carmen. *Cantos paralelos: la parodia plástica en el arte argentino contemporáneo / Visual Parody in Contemporary Argentinean Art*. Austin: Jack S. Blanton Museum of Art, U of Texas at Austin; Buenos Aires: Fondo Nacional de las Argentinas, 1999.

Ramírez Salgado, Raquel. "Representación de las mujeres en la telenovela mexicana *Los Aparicio: ¿Una mujer entera no necesita media naranja?*" *Revista de investigaciones en ciencias sociales y humanidades* 1.1 (2012): 95–124.

Ramo de fuego. Dir. Maureen Gosling and Ellen Osborne. United States, Mexico. New Yorker Films, 2001. 75 min. DVD.

Raota, Pedro Luis. *Faces of Life.* Buenos Aires: Escuela Superior de Arte Fotográfico, 1983.

Rich, Adrienne. "Compulsory Heterosexuality and Lesbian Existence." *Blood, Bread, and Poetry: Selected Prose, 1979–1985.* New York: W. W. Norton, 1986. 23–75.

Rodríguez, Jeanette. *Our Lady of Guadalupe: Faith and Empowerment among Mexican-American Women.* Austin: U of Texas P, 1994.

Rossell, Daniela. *Ricas y famosas.* Textos de Barry Schwabsy. México: Editorial Océano, 2002.

Royce, Anya Peterson. *Prestigio y afiliación en una comunidad urbana: Juchitán, Oaxaca.* México: Instituto Nacional Indigenista y Secretaría de Educación Pública, 1975.

Ruiz, Stefan. *The Factory of Dreams.* New York: Aperture, 2012.

Ruiz Campbell, Obdulia. "Representations of Isthmus Women: A Zapoteca Woman's Point of View." *Zapotec Struggles: Histories, Politics, and Representations from Juchitán, Oaxaca.* Ed. Howard Campbell et al. Washington, DC: Smithsonian Institution P, 1993. 137–141.

Salado Puerto, Mercedes, and Luis Fondebrider. "El desarrollo de la antropología forense en la Argentina / The Development of the Forensic Anthropology in Argentina." *Cuadernos de estudio de medicina forense* 14.53–54 (2008): 213–221. Web. 26 Dec. 2011. <http://scielo.isciii.es/scielo.php?pid=S1135-76062008000300004&script=sci_arttext>.

Sánchez de Balcero, Inés. *Cultura y marginalidad urbana: estudio antropológico entre los trabajadores de la basura.* Bogotá: Universidad de Bogotá Jorge Tadeo Lozano, 1999.

Sanguinetti, Alessandra. *Las aventuras de Guille y Belinda y el enigmático significado de sus sueños.* Buenos Aires: Dilan Editores, 2007.

———. *On the Sixth Day.* Tucson: Nazareli P, 2005.

Santiago, Esmeralda, and Joie Davidow, eds. *Las mamis: Favorite Latino Authors Remember Their Mothers.* New York: Vintage–Random House, 2000.

Sarlo, Beatriz. *La pasión y la excepción.* Buenos Aires: Siglo Veintiuno Editores Argentina, 2003.

Scalabrini Ortiz, Raúl. *El hombre que está solo y espera.* Buenos Aires: Gleizer, 1931.

Scarry, Elaine. *The Body in Pain: The Making and Unmaking of the World.* New York: Oxford UP, 1985.

Schmidt-Cruz, Cynthia. *Crisis in Buenos Aires: Women Bearing Witness.* Photography by Silvina Frydlewsky. Newark, DE: Juan de la Cuesta, 2007.

Sebreli, Juan José. *La era del fútbol.* Buenos Aires: Editorial Sudamericana, 1998.

———. *Fútbol y masas.* Buenos Aires: Editorial Galerna, 1981.

———. "Historia secreta de los homosexuales en Buenos Aires." *Escritos sobre escritos, ciudades bajo ciudades.* Buenos Aires: Editorial Sudamericana, 1997. 275–370.

Sedgwick, Eve Kosofsky. *Between Men: English Literature and Male Homosocial Desire.* New York: Columbia UP, 1985.

Sefchovich, Sara. *¿Son mejores las mujeres?* México: Paidós; Debate Feminista, 2011.

Señorita extraviada. Dir. Lourdes Portillo. Mexico. Xochitl Productions; Women Make Movies, 2001. 74 min. DVD.

Shua, Ana María. *Cabras, mujeres y mulas: antología del odio/miedo a la mujer en la literatura popular.* Buenos Aires: Editorial Sudamericana, 1998.

Sibbald, K. M. "Through a Glass Darkly: Techniques of Feminist Irony in Grete Stern's *Sueños.*" *Hispanic Journal* 26.1–2 (2005): 243–258.

Slipp, Samuel. *The Freudian Mystique: Freud, Women, and Feminism.* New York: New York UP, 1993.

Snow, K. Mitchell. "Digital Illusions in the Frame of Reality." *Américas* 48.2 (1996): 28–37.

Sontag, Susan. *On Photography.* New York: Farrar, Straus and Giroux, 1990.

Stern, Grete. "Apuntes sobre fotomontaje." *Sueños.* Valencia: IVAM Centre Julio González, Generalitat Valencia, Conselleria de Cultura, Educació i Ciència, 1995. 51–57.

————. *Fotografía en la Argentina, 1937–1981*. Buenos Aires: La Azotea Editorial Fotográfica de América Latina, 1988.

————. *Obra fotográfica en la Argentina*. Buenos Aires: Fondo Nacional de las Artes, 1995.

————. *Sueños*. Valencia: IVAM Centre Julio González, Generalitat Valencia, Conselleria de Cultura, Educació i Ciència, 1995.

Summer and Smoke. Dir. Peter Glenville. United States. Hal Wallis Productions, 1961. 118 min. DVD.

Sweet Bird of Youth. Dir. Richard Brooks. United States. Roxbury Productions Inc.; Metro-Goldwyn-Mayer (MGM), 1962. 120 min. DVD.

Taylor, Julie M. *Eva Perón: The Myths of a Woman*. Chicago: U of Chicago P, 1979.

Tenenbaum, Barbara. *Mexico and the Royal Indian—The Porfiriato and the National Past*. Latin American Studies Center Series, No. 8. College Park: Latin American Studies Center, University of Maryland, 1994.

Todorov, Tzevan. *La conquista de América: el problema del otro*. Trans. from French by Flora Botton Burlá. México: Siglo Veintiuno Editores, 1987.

Tompkins, Cynthia. "Cuestiones metodológicas resultantes del montaje ejemplificadas mediante la representación de procesos psíquicos en *La rabia* (2008) de Albertina Carri." *Estudios sobre las culturas contemporáneas* 36.18 (Dec. 2012): 189–210.

Travnik, Juan. "Una conversación con Alicia y Ricardo Sanguinetti." *Un cuerpo, una luz, un reflejo*. Ed. Annemarie Heinrich. Buenos Aires: Ediciones Larivière, 2004. 28–31.

————. "Un cuerpo, una luz, un reflejo." *Un cuerpo, una luz, un reflejo*. Ed. Annemarie Heinrich. Buenos Aires: Ediciones Larivière, 2004. 11–27.

Trejo Delarbe, Raúl. *La sociedad ausente*. México: Cal y Arena, 1992.

————, ed. *Televisa: el quinto poder*. México: Claves Latinoamericanas, 1985.

El Tren Blanco. Dir. Nahuel García, Sheila Pérez Giménez, and Ramiro García. Argentina. Aquelarre Servicios Cinematográficos, 2004. 80 min. DVD.

UNICEF. *Declaración de los derechos del niño [comentada por Mafalda y sus amiguitos para el UNICEF]*. Bogotá: Editorial Retina, 1977.

Vallejo, Fernando. *Chapolas negras*. Bogotá: Alfaguara, 1995.

Vallejos, Soledad. "Lolas a la vista." N.d. Web. 18 Oct. 2012. <http://www.pagina12.com .ar/2001/suple/Las12/01-01/01-01-12/nota4.htm>.

Vargas, Ava. *La casa de cita: Mexican Photographs from the Belle Epoque*. London: Quartet Books, 1986.

————. *La casa de citas en el barrio galante*. Prólogo de Carlos Monsiváis. México, DF: Grijalbo; Consejo Nacional para la Cultura y las Artes, 1991.

Varo, Remedios. *Remedios Varo 1908–1963*. México: Museo de Arte Moderno, 1994.

Vezzetti, Hugo. *Aventuras de Freud en el país de los argentinos: de José Ingenieros a Enrique Pichón-Rivière*. Buenos Aires: Paidós, 1996.

Warner, John Harley, and James M. Edmonson. *Dissection: Photographs of a Rite of Passage in American Medicine, 1880–1930*. New York: Blast Books, 2009.

Watriss, Wendy, and Lois Parkinson Zamora, eds. *Image and Memory: Photography from Latin America, 1866–1994*. Austin: U of Texas P; published in association with FotoFest, 1998.

Waugh, Thomas. *Hard to Imagine: Gay Male Eroticism in Photography and Film from Their Beginnings to Stonewall*. New York: Columbia UP, 1996.

Weinstein, Michael A. "Daniel Hernández-Salazar, Postmodern Humanist. Daniel Hernández-Salazar, un humanista posmoderno." In Daniel Hernández-Salazar, *So That All Shall Know: Photographs / Para que todos sepan: fotografías*. Ed. Oscar Iván Maldonado. Austin: U of Texas P, 2007. 39–52.

Weitz, Rose. *Rapunzel's Daughters: What Women's Hair Tells Us about Women's Lives*. New York: Farrar, Straus and Giroux, 2004.

Yako, Dani. *Extinción: últimas imágenes del trabajo en la Argentina*. Text by Martín Caparrós. Buenos Aires: Grupo Editorial Norma, 2001.

Y tu mamá también. Dir. Alfonso Cuarón. Mexico. Anhelo Producciones; Bésame Mucho Pictures, 2001. 106 min. DVD.

Zimmerman, Bonnie. *The Safe Sea of Women: Lesbian Fiction 1969–1989*. Boston: Beacon P, 1990.

Zimmermann, Marcos. *Desnudos sudamericanos*. Buenos Aires: Ediciones Larivière, 2009.

Zorro, the Gay Blade. Peter Medak. United States. Melvin Simon Productions, 1981. 93 min. DVD.

Zout, Helen. *Desapariciones*. Buenos Aires: Dilan Editores, 2009.

Zúñiga, José Ramón. "El clavadista Iván García se disculpa por comentarios 'homofóbicos' publicados en Twitter." *NotieSe*. 13 Sept. 2012. Web. 14 Sept. 2012. <http://www.notiese .org/notiese.php?ctn_id=5950>.

– ◆ –

INDEX

◆ ◆ ◆

www.ingramcontent.com/pod-product-compliance
Lightning Source LLC
Chambersburg PA
CBHW030314290526
45785CB00001B/352